I0796067

The Samurai

正成
正行
櫻井宿ニ別ヲ告ル圖

The Samurai

THE HISTORY OF JAPAN'S LEGENDARY WARRIOR CASTE

ROD JOHNSON

Note on the Japanese Language
For all Japanese names I have chosen to keep the Japanese rules for word order, with the surname first, followed by the first name. When a name has to be shortened, the usual approach is only to use the surname, but in the case of some particularly important people, it is common to only use the first name, as in the case of Toyotomi Hideyoshi, whom we call 'Hideyoshi'. In many cases, we shall also do this to avoid the confusion that could occur between members of the same family, for example when talking about the Minamoto.

The names of some emperors begin with the prefix Go-. This means there was a previous emperor with the same name, which is why in some texts it is translated as 'the second', and why we can find Go-Shirakawa written as 'Shirakawa II'. Here we have respected the Japanese form.

The use of the macron has also been maintained. This is a diacritical mark consisting of a horizontal bar over a vowel, as seen in the word *taikō*, which indicates that the vowel should be pronounced with twice its normal length.

SIRIUS
This edition published in 2025 by Sirius Publishing, a division of
Arcturus Publishing Limited,
26/27 Bickels Yard, 151–153 Bermondsey Street,
London SE1 3HA

ISBN: 978-1-3988-5785-8
AD010989UK

Printed in Malaysia

Contents

Introduction

Left: Shōgun Tokugawa Ieyasu chased by Sanada Yukimura in a woodblock print by Nobukazu Watanabe.

Below: An ukiyo-e print of the victorious samurai, Onikojima Yatarō Kazutada, by Utagawa Kuniyoshi, 1854.

Who were the samurai? A fierce band of warriors, killing and fighting for a warlord with fearful swords, striking down all those who failed to show subservience to them? Or coarse and vulgar men, taking whatever they needed from the populace and fighting for personal gain? Then again, perhaps they were fearless heroes, fighting for justice and right under a strict code of honour and respect? None of these descriptions truly represents the samurai. They are idealized images from movies and novels and there is far, far more to their story. They were originally bodyguards and fighters, rising through Japanese society to, in some cases, become rulers over vast areas of the country with their own large armies.

It is in written documents in the Japanese National Archives from the 10th century, in the era known as the Heian period (794–1185), that the word 'samurai' first appears. Before that time such people were called *bushi (mono-no-fu)*, literally a person who carries (a sword in this case). In usage the meaning of the word 'bushi' became 'an armed man, a warrior, a vigilante'. A document from the Heian period lists the professions that existed at the time, and the bushi are found in it along with scholars, doctors, singers, and dancers! But the bushi were originally neither landowners nor even armed peasants: they were professional warriors who were paid for their service. The name 'samurai' comes

Right: These five samurai were among the first and last to be photographed. It was at the end of the 19th century. Each of them carries the two swords, symbols of the warrior class of feudal Japan. The samurai in the centre holds in his right hand a *sai-hai*, a baton of rank and authority as well as a signaling device.

from the Japanese word *saburau*, meaning 'those who served in close proximity to the nobility'.

To understand the samurai and their emergence from the common bushi, it will be necessary to become familiarized with the centuries-old history and culture of this military class. Although the function of the warrior was the basis of the samurai's life, they were also farmers, politicians, writers, lawmakers and enforcers. Eventually, they would become the ruling military force and part of a high-ranking elite that stood above ordinary citizens and soldiers. These samurai played a crucial role in the latter centuries of Japanese history, significantly influencing the nation's cultural and historical development.

FEUDAL JAPANESE SOCIETY & SAMURAI STRUCTURE

Outside of the social structure

Accepted Outer Class

- NOBILITY
  Courtiers and Poets
- RELIGIOUS
  Buddhist monks and Shinto priests

Untouchable Below Class

- BURAKUMIN
  Social Outcasts, Actors, Musicians and Criminals
  Oiran, Courtesans, Geisha and Prostitutes
- ETA Unclean Workers, Butchers, Executioners and Tanners
- AINU
  Ethnic Minority

Structured Hierachy

- EMPEROR
  The figurehead at top of the social structure
- SHŌGUN
  The Military Ruler of Japan
- DAIMYŌ or BUKE
  Feudal Lords and families
- SAMURAI
  The Warrior Class serving the daimyō
- FARMERS & FISHERMEN PEASANTS
  Producers of Food
- CRAFTSMEN & ARTISANS
  Producers of goods and services
- MERCHANTS
  Non-productive movers of goods

The Samurai

Samurai rank determined a samurai's stipend, the area of his residence, style of clothing, work and rules of etiquette

- HATAMOTO
  (bannerman)
  highest rank
- YAKUNIN
  Officer or Guard
- GOKENIN
  retainers
- GOSHI
  Rustic Farmer Warrior
- ASHIGARU
  Foot Soldier
- RŌNIN
  Masterless Samurai

Japanese society in this era was structured into three distinct classes**.** The *uji*, loosely translated as 'clan', were families closely tied to the imperial dynasty through loyalty and intermarriage. These clans formed the ruling elite, significantly influencing cultural development until the 19th century. Below the *uji* were artisans, organized into hereditary communities based on their occupation. These skilled groups included armourers, builders, weavers, potters and temple servants. At the lowest rung of society were merchants, domestic slaves, and the *eta*, individuals engaged in traditionally unclean occupations.

Timeline

550–710
ASUKA PERIOD
710–794
NARA PERIOD
500
550
600
650
700
750
800
850
587
Battle of Shigisan
Late 6th century Buddhism is introduced to Japan
c. 592–628
Prince Shōtoku establishes diplomatic relations with China.
645
The Taika reforms are introduced, beginning the Fujiwara era.
672
Jinshin War
710
Nara becomes the first permanent capital
720
Hayato Rebellion
774
Thirty-Eight Year War
780
Hōki Rebellion
794
The imperial residence moves to Heian-kyō (Kyoto).
801
Sakanoue no Tamuramaro conquers the Emishi
1185–1867 THE SHŌGUNATE
from Heian
1185–1333
KAMAKURA PERIOD
1333–1573
MUROMACHI PERIOD
1200
1250
1300
1350
1400
1450
1500
1185
Battle of Dan-no-Ura
1192
Minamoto Yoritomo is appointed Shōgun and establishes the Kamakura government.
1201
Kennin Rebellion
1219
The Minamoto clan is eliminated by the Hōjō family.
1221
Battle of Uji
1221
Jōkyū War
1247
Miura Rebellion
1274
First attempted Mongol Invasion of Japan
1281
Second attempted Mongol invasion of Japan
1331–33
Genkō War
1333
The Kamakura government falls
1336 Battle of Minatogawa
1338
Ashikaga Takauji establishes the Muromachi government and a second emperor in Kyoto
1359
Battle of Chikugogawa
1467–77
Onin War
1526
Siege of Kamakura
1530
Battle of Ozawahara
1542
Siege of Toda Castle
1542
Portuguese introduce firearms and Christianity to Japan

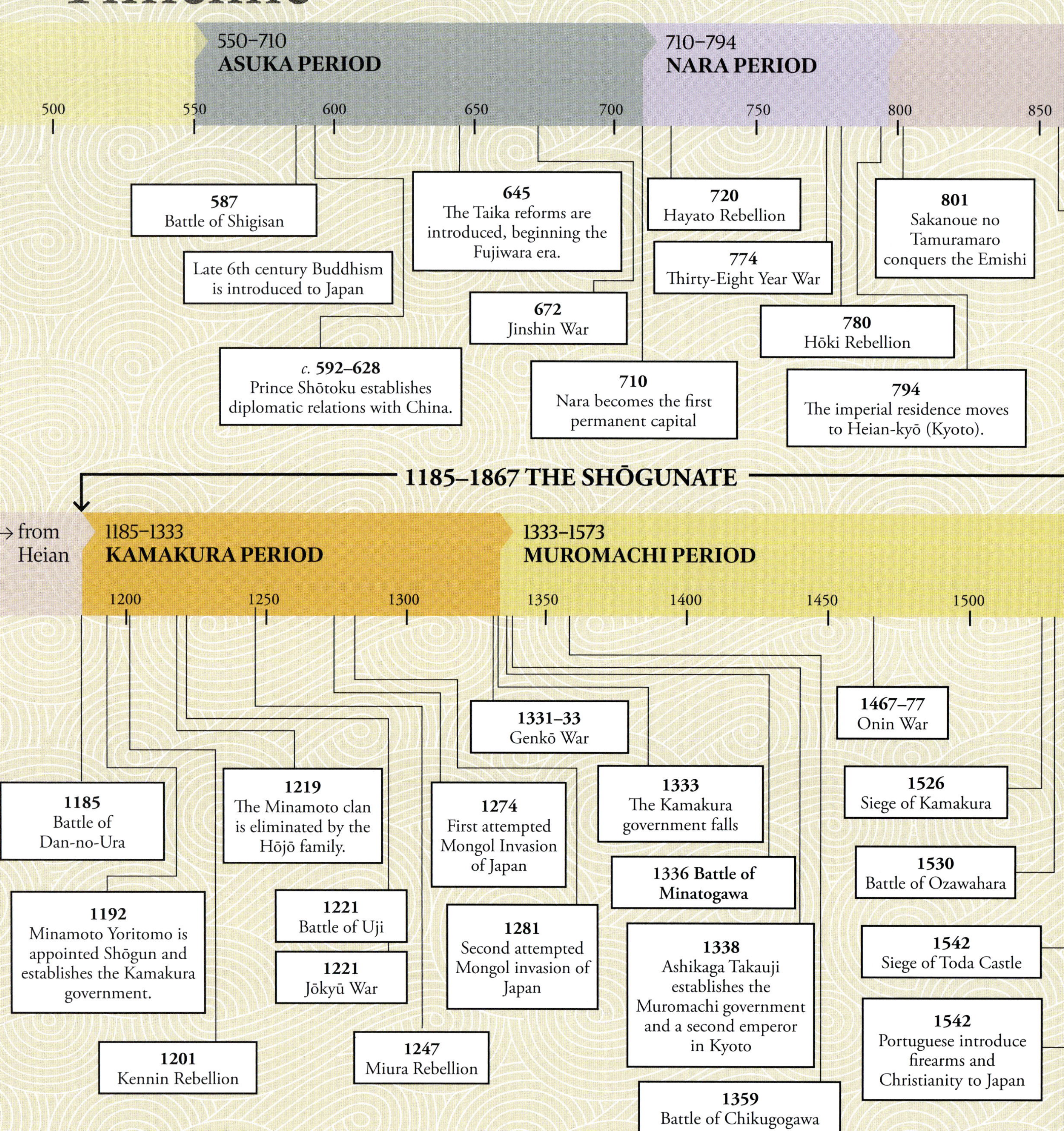

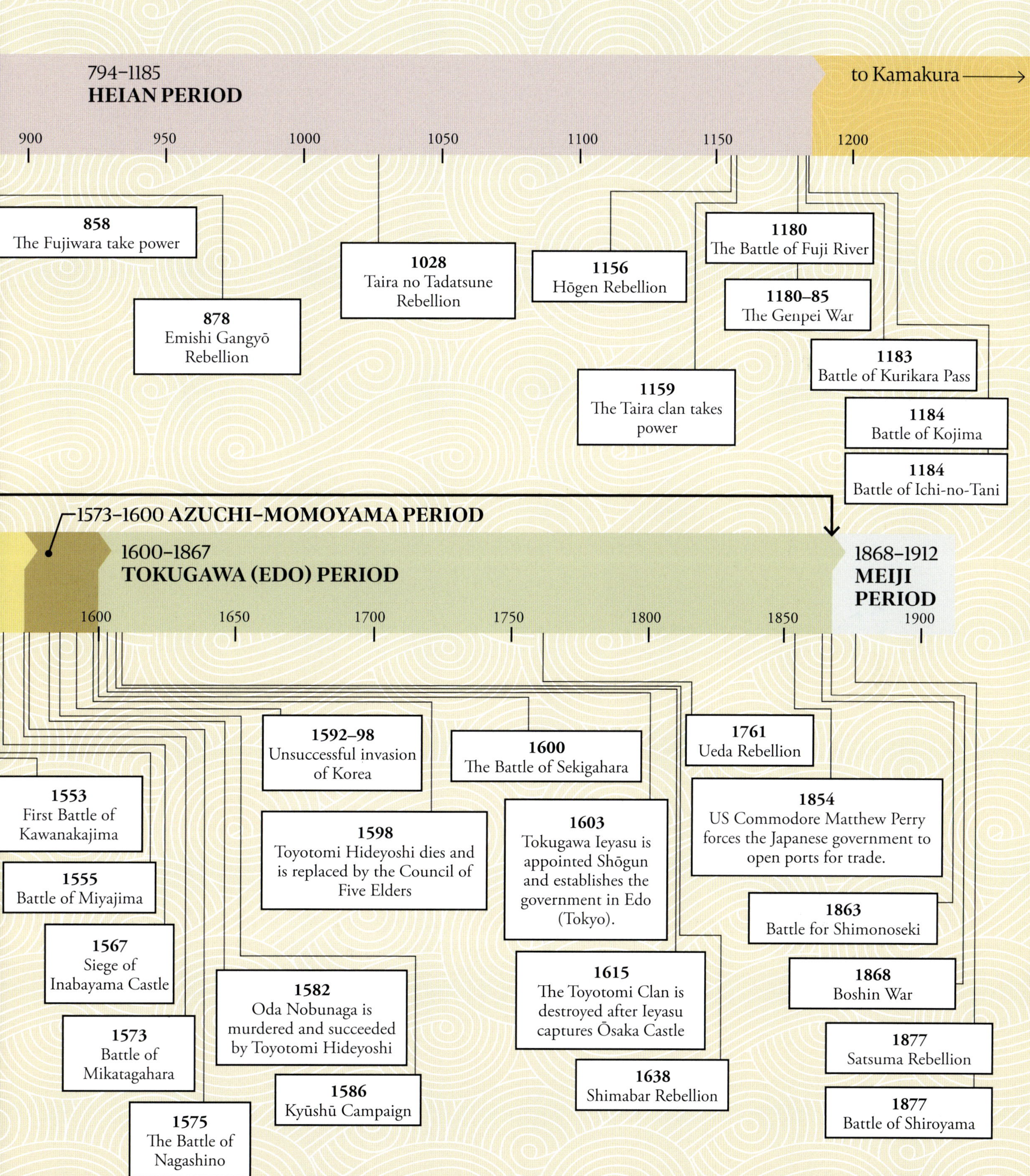
794–1185
HEIAN PERIOD
to Kamakura
900
950
1000
1050
1100
1150
1200
858
The Fujiwara take power
878
Emishi Gangyō Rebellion
1028
Taira no Tadatsune Rebellion
1156
Hōgen Rebellion
1159
The Taira clan takes power
1180
The Battle of Fuji River
1180–85
The Genpei War
1183
Battle of Kurikara Pass
1184
Battle of Kojima
1184
Battle of Ichi-no-Tani
1573–1600 AZUCHI-MOMOYAMA PERIOD
1600–1867
TOKUGAWA (EDO) PERIOD
1868–1912
MEIJI PERIOD
1600
1650
1700
1750
1800
1850
1900
1553
First Battle of Kawanakajima
1555
Battle of Miyajima
1567
Siege of Inabayama Castle
1573
Battle of Mikatagahara
1575
The Battle of Nagashino
1592–98
Unsuccessful invasion of Korea
1598
Toyotomi Hideyoshi dies and is replaced by the Council of Five Elders
1582
Oda Nobunaga is murdered and succeeded by Toyotomi Hideyoshi
1586
Kyūshū Campaign
1600
The Battle of Sekigahara
1603
Tokugawa Ieyasu is appointed Shōgun and establishes the government in Edo (Tokyo).
1615
The Toyotomi Clan is destroyed after Ieyasu captures Ōsaka Castle
1638
Shimabar Rebellion
1761
Ueda Rebellion
1854
US Commodore Matthew Perry forces the Japanese government to open ports for trade.
1863
Battle for Shimonoseki
1868
Boshin War
1877
Satsuma Rebellion
1877
Battle of Shiroyama

CHAPTER 1

The Beginning

In early times, families set up residences and farmed the land or fished the sea. Then, as their estates grew, they took in non-family members as helpers, servants and, if they were particularly successful, defenders when their land came under attack from covetous neighbours and marauding bands of thieves. Then, in the 6th century, the Yamato, one of many tribes who had settled the lands in earlier times, founded a state modelled on the Chinese imperial system, China being the main political influence on Japan in this period. From their power base in central Japan, the Yamato extended their influence across the southern half of the country and established an imperial court under a divine emperor.

Japan is about one and a half times larger than the UK and comprises of four main islands – Hokkaido, Honshu, Shikoku and Kyūshū – and some 7,000 smaller ones. However, in prehistory times Japan was part of the Asian mainland connected to Siberia, Korea, and China by land. Tens of thousands of years ago, Japan was split from the mainland, caused by ocean movement and plate tectonics, and so forming the Japanese archipelago. It was here that the ancestors of the Japanese people, began to live.

About 10,000 years ago, people began making crude pottery, with rope patterns, to store and cook food. This era is known as the Jōmon period. People of this time lived by hunting and gathering nuts and fruits.

Around the 2nd or 3rd century BCE, rice was introduced from the Korea Peninsular, and people's lives became centred on agriculture. Bronze and iron tools came into use and the pottery became plainer and simpler in shape, known as Yayoi pottery.

Places where people lived gradually expanded, they came to be called 'Kuni' (provinces) and were ruled by influential and powerful people. By the 3rd century, these were consolidated into about 30 kuni, made up of mountains, plains, basins, and independent geographic entities. The 'centre of the state' was Yamatai, originally ruled by the priestess and sorceress, Queen Himiko, who symbolized the unity of the Yayoi people.

Left: This haniwa offers a unique opportunity to study the attire and equipment of a late Kofun period warrior. The Kofun period dates to the 4th to 6th centuries and the name derives from the monumental tombs of that era, which were often adorned with ritual clay figures such as this one.

Japan sent envoys to China frequently, importing advanced culture. Among these, ironware and swords made from copper were treasured as possessions of the powerful who ruled the country. From the end of the 3rd century, the Yamato Imperial Court gradually unified Japan, and sent troops to the Korean Peninsula to fight against the Silla and Goguryeo Kingdoms.

At this time, the political system in Japan was centred around the emperor and was organized by powerful clans such as the Mononobe, Taitomo, Nakatomi, and Soga, but as the power of the Soga grew, they fought with other clans. The Soga destroyed the Mononobe who opposed them, and even killed Emperor Sushun (the 32nd emperor). After that, Empress Suiko came to the throne as the emperor. This emperor appointed her nephew, Prince Shōtoku, who was only 19 years old, as regent to rule in

Below: A map of Japan, showing the main islands of the archipelago.

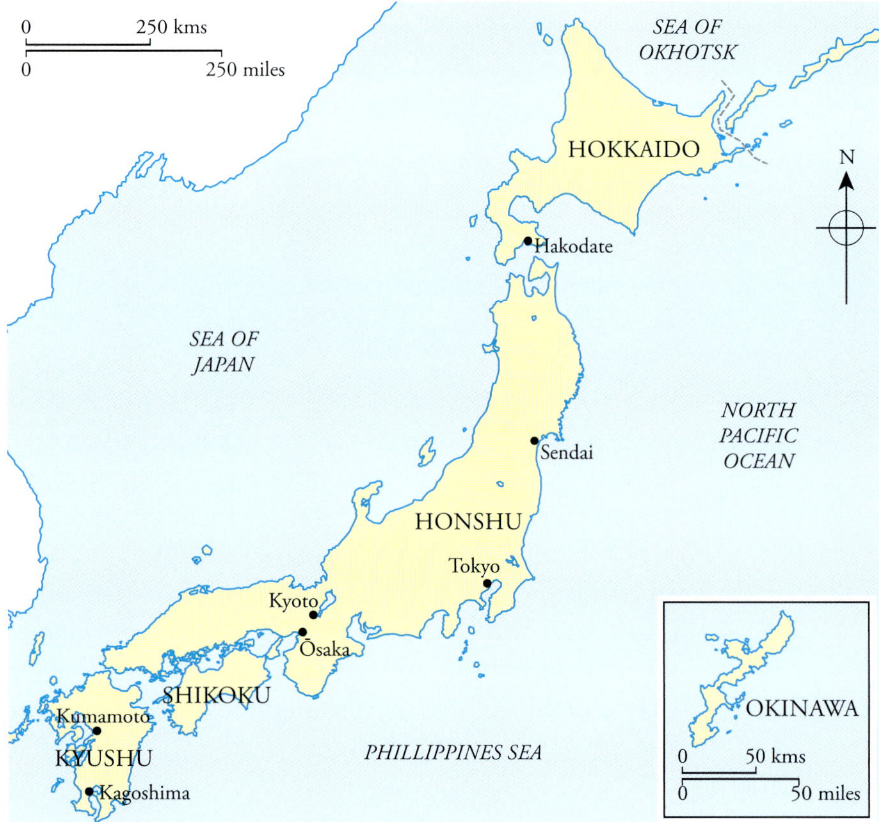

her place, and left political, legal, financial, military and religious aspects to him.

At the end of the 6th century, Prince Shōtoku, opened diplomatic relations with China, adopted the advanced culture of the continent centred on Buddhism, and adopted politics to enhance the status of the emperor. Prince Shōtoku was a devoted follower of Buddhism and tried to base his political affairs on Buddhist teachings. At this time, the capital was located in the Asuka region, so this period is called the Asuka period.

The Soga clan began to gain influence, so in 645, Prince Nakano Ōe, who was to become the 38th emperor and known as Emperor Tenji, destroyed the

Below: Tanko period armour from the 5th century CE.

Above: A 7th–8th century portrait of Prince Shōtoku (centre) with his brother and son.

Soga clan with Fujiwara no Kamatari and others, started a new government taking control of all the land and people. The Imperial Court made it a point to support the emperor.

At the beginning of the 8th century, a law called Taiho Ritsuryo was created to determine the fundamentals of politics, and Japan's first full-fledged capital, Nara, was built. In the capital of Nara, Emperor Shomu, the 45th emperor, believed deeply in Buddhism and conducted politics based on Buddhist teachings. In the east, temples and legends were created, and the capital was greatly revitalized. However, religious monks became involved in politics and lines of power and influence were blurred. As a result, local politics did not go well and the state gradually became chaotic.

In 740, the nobleman Fujiwara Hirotsugu raised an army of over 10,000 men in Kyūshū in rebellion against

Right: The provinces of Yamato are expanding east and west with a push against the Emishi in the east and north. Support to Baekje, South Korea, is failing and the aggressive Silla unified the Korean Peninsula. After the fall of Baekje and Goguryeo, the Tang dynasty established a short-lived military government to administer parts of the Korean Peninsula.

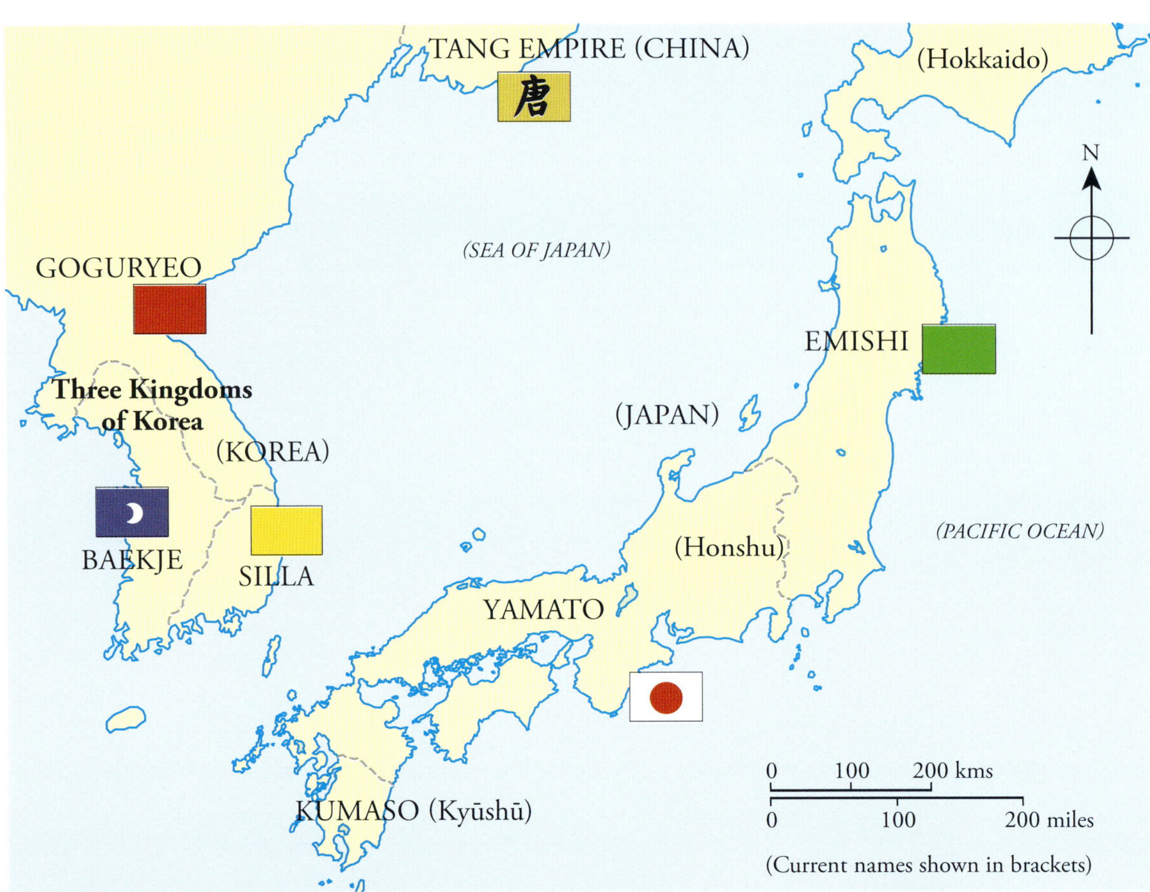

Below: The reconstructed audience hall in Heijo palace in Nara, the first capital of Japan.

Above: An Emishi sword from the 8th century, found on Hokkaido.

the central government in Nara. The government dispatched its own army under Prince Tachibana Moroe, and the two forces met in battle, with Hirotsugu's force defeated and the nobleman himself executed shortly thereafter.

In 749, significant deposits of gold were discovered in the northern regions of the main Japanese island of Honshu. Unfortunately for the Japanese court, this part of Honshu was not under its control, and the inhabitants of that region, known as Emishi, or barbarians, did not recognize the authority of the state. Resisting the encroachment of the Japanese government, the Emishi attacked the military forces sent to subdue them and initially achieved enormous success, capturing and destroying many garrisons and military outposts. But despite these early victories, the war would last for another 38 years. In 794, the government finally decided that a conscripted army was not an effective fighting force against the Emishi and ended the practice of drafting civilians into the military.

In 794, Emperor Kanmu, the 50th emperor, moved the capital to Heian-kyō (modern Kyoto), and reformed the politics. Kyoto would remain the imperial capital for over 1000 years after his death. His reign saw battles against the Emishi (natives to the north), resulting in further expansion and securing of the northern borders of the state.

Private ownership of land had increased and aristocrats in high positions in the imperial court expanded their private land and then owned many estates that were beyond the reach of the state's power. Among the aristocrats, the Fujiwara clan, descendants of Fujiwara no Kamatari, came to dominate politics as regent and *Kanpaku (*chief advisor to the emperor).

In 858, Fujiwara no Shokufusa became the first commoner to become regent and then followed by his adopted son, Fujiwara no Mototsune who became Kanpaku to four successive emperors. In the early 11th century, during the reign of Fujiwara Michinaga, the Fujiwara clan was the most powerful and at its pinnacle with culture and splendour centred around the aristocracy, and the relationship with China. Around this time, the lords (daimyō) who ruled over rural areas as governors, gradually increased power

Opposite: Nara-period upper-class clothing was much simpler than some later styles, taking no more than a few minutes to don, with the clothing itself allowing for freedom of movement. Worn with a straight bladed sword.

Right: Statue of Emperor Kanmu at Tomb of Emperor Kanmu in Kyoto. Emperor Kanmu appointed the first *Sei-i-Tai Shogun* 'Barbarian conquering General', Otomo Otomaro in 794 CE. The shōgun was the military dictator of Japan with near absolute power over territories through the military. Once the Emishi and the Ainu were defeated, the Heian court dropped the shōgun title.

and influence and the growth of managed estates spread throughout the country. Because the court government had no police force, the daimyō employed trained warriors for policing and defence of the lands. These warriors, their armed guards, became known as 'samurai'.

These daimyō/samurai groups managed large areas of profitable rice land in eastern Japan, in the Kantō Region around modern-day Tokyo, so gaining more power. Samurai strength rested on discipline and strong group loyalty to their lord. These warriors started to shape the country through both warfare and their conduct as well trained and organized military.

The 72nd emperor, Emperor Shirakawa, continued to hold real political power and began to govern with skill supported by aristocrats who were dissatisfied with the Fujiwara clan's regent politics. He also gained the support of the daimyō who had been expanding their power. He was the first emperor to apparently retire to a monastery, but in fact continue to exert considerable influence over his successor. This process would become known as 'Cloistered Rule'.

The Fujiwara clan, whose size had greatly increased, and so not able to provide full employment or court position, encouraged offshoot families. The Minamoto and Taira clans so formed were both of the imperial dynasty and were distant relatives. The Minamoto clan was first given the surname 'Minamoto' by Emperor Saga in 814, when he granted it to his seventh son, Minamoto no Makoto. The Taira was another branch of the imperial dynasty, strategically relegated to the nobility by Emperor Kanmu (782–805 CE) to ease succession disputes. These clans with their aristocratic connections were able to create large vassal estates in the country.

After the triumph of the Minamoto in the Genpei War of 1180–85 (see pages 27–29), Minamoto Yoritomo received the title of 'Shōgun' in 1192 to signify his military control over the country. This led to the establishment of Japan's first shōgunate at Kamakura,

Below: Kemari in Heian period by Kin-u. With relative peace, leisure activities developed in the Court. Here nobles are playing a game imported from China where the object is to keep a ball in the air.

Right: The Heian Court – Poetry and pleasures for the aristocrats. The six classical poets, or Rokkasen, from the Heian period – Ariwara no Narihira, Sōjō Henjō, Kisen Hōshi, Omotomo no Kuronushi, Bunya no Yasuhide and Ono no Komachi.

which was to dominate Japan from 1192 to 1333. The Kamakura government was run by a network of daimyō and samurai throughout the country, pledged to keep the peace. Gradually the samurai took the lead in developing the law of the nation and the power of the government in Kyoto became weaker.

This was to be the 'Golden Age of the Samurai'.

From the end of the 12th century until the abolition of the 'Samurai Order' in the 1870s the samurai would control three military governments. These were known as 'shōgunates' or 'bakufu' and were named the Kamakura, Ashikaga and the Tokugawa shōgunates. Shōgunate Japan (1185–1868) was a time of malicious warfare, as different family clans and individuals fought for the power, which ultimately controlled Japan. Japan's rulers had changed from being courtly aristocrats to warriors. The shōguns were the head of the warrior samurai class and supervised vast private estates, placed provinces under military control and created legal posts. Whilst Kyoto remained the Imperial capital, the emperor was little more than a figurehead. As the Shōgunate era came to an end and Japan entered the modern era, the samurai were disbanded only to rule as politicians in a democracy.

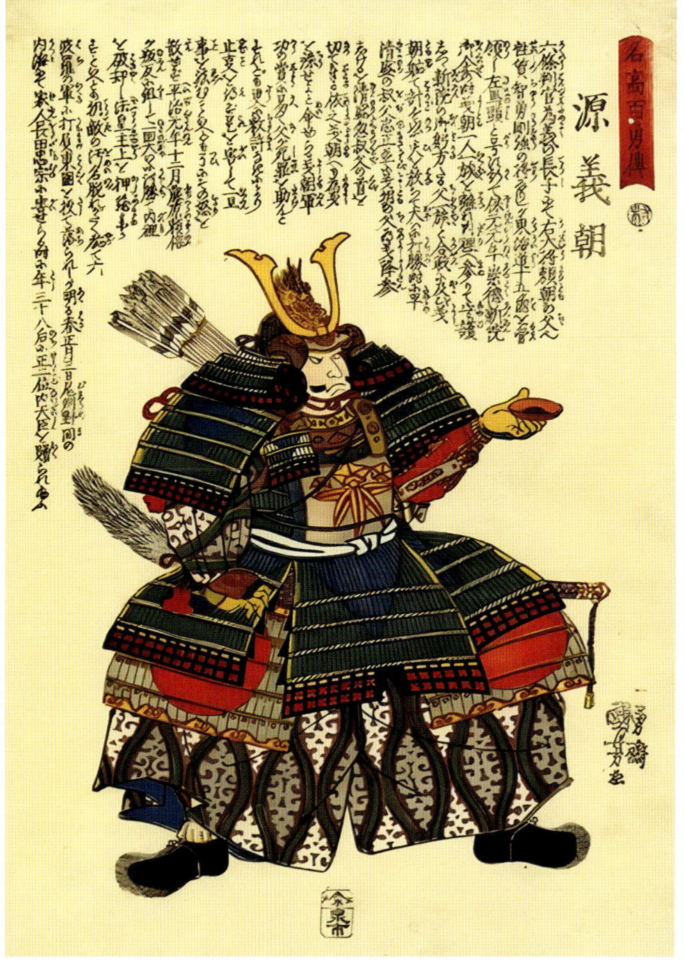

Above: A portrait of Minamoto Yoritomo (1147–1199). The first shōgun of the Kamakura shōgunate and the first ruling shōgun in the history of Japan, he ruled from 1192 until 1199.

The Female Samurai

Before the samurai class existed, in early Japan both men and women mastered some form of martial art and knew how to handle weapons. Some women came to the fore as confident warriors prepared to battle on equal terms against any opponent and stand out for their leadership. They have been described alongside their male samurai counterparts as the onna bugeisha ('women warriors').

The main weapon used by samurai women was the *naginata*. It was a long wooden or metal shaft with a curved single-edged blade on the end. Women were instructed in its use from an early age, especially during the Sengoku period (1477–1573) and the Tokugawa period (1600–1867). In addition to her short sword (*tanto*), Tomoe is said to have carried a *naginata* to finish off her enemies. Many female samurai and *onna bugeisha* mastered the art of archery and riding. Later, the use of firearms became an additional skill. After the introduction of guns to Japan, the era of bow and arrow warfare ended; archery became a form of exercise for the body and mind known as *kyudo*, meaning 'the way of the bow'.

Below: Naginata training, *c.* 1900.

Empress Jingu

The first woman warrior was supposedly the empress Jingu who, after the death of her husband, ruled Japan from 201–269. She was undoubtedly an inspiration for the *onna bugeisha* that were to come. However, it was not until the Kamakura period (1185–1333) that the samurai, and therefore

the *onna bugeisha*, appeared as a differentiated group from the warrior class.

'Samurai' refers to both an individual and his family. The samurai were a social class, not a profession. If you were born into a samurai family, regardless of whether you were male or female, you were of the samurai social class. By the Sengoku period (1477–1573), being a samurai was hereditary, with one or two rare exceptions.

Although many women in samurai families received martial arts training, they rarely fought in battle. With their husbands in combat almost continuously, women from samurai families were expected to help protect their families and homes. The weapon they are most frequently associated with is the *naginata*, a long pole with a blade attached to the end.

Over and above these 'domestic' women warriors, the *onna bugeisha* stood out as an elite category of female samurai. They undertook the same training as their male counterparts, becoming skilled in the use of the bow, the *naginata* and the sword. They later became adept in the use of firearms.

Above: The legendary Empress Jingu setting foot in Korea. Painting by Tsukioka Yoshitoshi. She is shown carrying a bow with arrows in a quiver on her back and wearing a sword.

Tomoe Gozen

In the 12th-century chronicle *The Heike Monogatari*, an account of the Genpei War of 1180–1185, we are told of Tomoe Gozen, the female companion of Minamoto no Yoshinaka, a prominent general among Minamoto clan forces and first cousin of Minamoto Yoritomo (the first shōgun). The 'Gozen' part of her name is an honorific title which should be read as 'Lady'. This will be seen in other female warriors. Tomoe is described as 'a fearless rider whom neither the fiercest horse nor the roughest ground could dismay, and so dexterously did she handle sword and bow that she was a match for a thousand warriors and fit to meet either God or devil'. When it came to the battles of the war, she was not simply a soldier. Yoshinaka sent her out as his first captain and she performed more deeds of valour than

Above: Tomoe Gozen in an 18th-century woodblock print at the Battle of Awazu. There she fought alongside Minamoto Yoshinaka.

Right: Hangaku Gozen by Yoshitoshi.

any of his other warriors. Her fate is unknown. Some accounts say she fought to the death on the battlefield, others that she escaped on horseback carrying an enemy head and disappeared.

Tomoe Gozen is undoubtedly the stereotypical *onna bugeisha* and is the most famous of all samurai warrior women in battle. She is represented in many of Japan's historical festivals, usually as a beautiful armed and armoured girl who always wore long black hair on the battlefield.

Hangaku Gozen

Jō Hangaku (Lady Hangaku) was a member of the Taira clan and took a prominent role in the Kennin Rebellion, an uprising against the Kamakura Shōgunate in 1201. Hangaku was noted for her leadership and bravery during the three-month-long defence of Torisaka Castle. Hangaku commanded 3,000 soldiers against an army of 10,000 loyal to the Hōjō clan, a family

of hereditary regents to the shōgunate of Japan who exercised actual rule from 1199 to 1333. Ultimately, she was wounded by an arrow and captured. Hangaku is said to have been 'fearless as a man and beautiful as a flower'. She was a skilled archer and was said to have wielded a *naginata* in battle.

Hōjō Masako, the political leader

Hōjō Masako (1156–1225) was the wife of Minamoto Yoritomo, the first shōgun of Japan. She is known for her iron will and her political coolness when it came to maintaining power. She was not a warrior of arms, but she is seen as a type of warrior woman who took charge of the shōgunate after the death of her husband in 1182. After being widowed she decided to continue her life as a religious woman and was called the shōgun nun.

Ōhōri Tsuruhime

The daughter of the head priest of the shrine of Ōyamazumi at Ehime on the island of Omi. This shrine is dedicated to Ōyamazumi Kami, founding deity of Japan and one of the most historically significant shrines in Japan. She was born in 1526, at a time when the island of Shikoku was under invasion from the daimyō of Suo, Ōuchi Yoshitaka, the head of the Ōuchi clan. Tsuruhime's two elder brothers were killed in action, but when the Ōuchi returned to her island on a raid, she led an army into battle and drove them away. Some months later, when the invading army came back, Tsuruhime launched a daring raid on their attacker's ships using firebombs. Many vessels were destroyed, forcing the fleet back to Yamaguchi on the mainland.

Tachibana Ginchiyo

Ginchiyo (1569–1602) was for a time the head of her Tachibana clan during the Sengoku period. She recruited women to become her elite guard and trained all the young women of the castle in the art of warfare to intimidate visitors and to fight off attacks on her domain (a domain being the land controlled by a daimyō). She became the daimyō of the Tachibana clan after her father's death. In 1586, the Shimazu clan of Satsuma Domain marched with their troops to conquer Kyūshū and attacked Tachibana Castle. When

Right: Hōjō Masako by Yoshitoshi.

Left:
Ōhōri Tsuruhime portrait.

women fighting side by side with male samurai at the Battle of Aizu on 10 October 1868. Aizu women were taught the same values as their male counterparts and were instructed to protect the honour of their family, themselves and, most importantly, their daimyō. On the day of battle, Takeko and her cohort of 20 volunteer women warriors disregarded the orders of their male officers and engaged Tosa, Ogaki and Choshu troops in hand-to-hand combat. They proved to be a formidable force, defeating many of the imperial soldiers who had become overconfident when they realized that they were fighting women. Takeko, who like all of her female colleagues was skilled in the use of the *naginata*, personally slew six men before being shot in the chest. Her group of fighters was later known as the *Jōshitai* (Girls' Army).

Although Takeko and her comrades ultimately died in the Battle of Aizu, their story represents the virtues of Bushidō: loyalty, courage, sincerity, and benevolence.

the Shimazu commanders arrived close to Tachibana Castle, Ginchiyo armed her women with matchlock firearms to defend the main gate.

After the Battle of Sekigahara in 1600, the Tachibana family, having supported the losing side, was deprived of their domains and Ginchiyo was put under protection of Katō Kiyomasa with other retainers of Tachibana clan. Ginchiyo died of illness on 30 November 1602. She was only 33 years old.

Nakano Takeko: Aizu female warrior

Nakano Takeko (1847–1868), the daughter of an Aizu officer, fought for her clan's independence against the emperor's forces in the Boshin War and led a troop of

Below:
Nakano Takeko photographed in 1867.

Yamakawa Futaba
(1844–1909)

As the daughter and the wife of shōgunate officials in Aizu, Yamakawa Futaba was trained to fight and consequently participated in the defence of Tsuruga Castle in 1868 against the emperor's forces during the Boshin War (see page 183). After a month-long siege, the Aizu region surrendered, ultimately leading to the end of the shōgunate. Its samurai were sent to war camps as prisoners and their domains were divided up and redistributed to imperial loyalists. When the castle's defences were breached, many of the defenders committed *seppuku* (ritual suicide). However, Yamakawa Futaba survived and went on to lead the drive for improved education for women and girls in Japan.

Yamamoto Yaeko (also called Niijima Yae)

Another of the Aizu region's female samurai defenders was Yamamoto Yaeko (1845–1932). Her father was a gunnery instructor for the daimyō of the Aizu Domain, and young Yaeko became a highly skilled shooter under her father's training.

In the autumn of 1868, Aizu clan was caught up in the Boshin War (1868–1869), fought between forces loyal to the shōgunate and those who supported a return to imperial rule. The fighting culminated in a month-long siege of Tsuruga Castle in Aizu-Wakamatsu.

After the final defeat of the shōgunate forces in 1869, Yamamoto Yaeko moved to Kyoto to look after her brother, Yamamoto Kakuma. He was taken prisoner by the Satsuma clan in the closing days of the Boshin War and presumably received harsh treatment at their hands. Yaeko served as a nurse during the First Sino-Japanese War of 1894–1895 and the Russo-Japanese War of 1904–1905. She helped to found Doshisha University, a Christian school in Kyoto.

Above: Yamamoto Yaeko. Photographed around 1890 wearing katana and holding a spencer rifle. At her side is a poem written when she was under siege. It reads 'Tomorrow night, who from what country will be gazing at the moon's shadow remaining on my beloved castle?'

These accounts of the battle demonstrate how the women of the Aizu Domain embodied the unflinching 'brave heart' of warriors past, not only through physical combat but also through nurturing an inner sense of duty and benevolence, assisting as caretakers who calmly treated the injured, fed soldiers amid the battle and, above all, served the clan with fearlessness and nobility.

CHAPTER 2

The Coming of the Shōgunate

The Taira, having positioned themselves strategically throughout the court and with large land estates, held the upper hand. The Minamoto, stained by their support of a losing contender for the throne, had been exiled from the capital and faced a precarious future. In 1180, the Minamoto and Taira clans became involved in conflict with a power struggle, both sought control of the Imperial Court, aiming to dominate the nation. This resulted in the Genpei War (1180–85), which brought about the rise of the Minamoto clan and the fall of the Taira clan. Minamoto Yoritomo established Japan's first shōgunate at Kamakura in 1192, setting the stage for samurai dominance in Japan's politics for centuries to come.

The Fujiwara have reached their peak and are effectively running the government in the capital, Kyoto and yet the imperial house still retained some control and influence. However, things came to a head in 1156, when the retired Emperor Sutoko disputed the succession of the new emperor, Go-Shirakawa. The civil war that followed was known as the Hogen Rebellion and it saw the Fujiwara clan side with Sutoko, who called in support from the Minamoto and Taira clans headed by Minamoto Tameyoshi, while Shirakawa was supported by Taira Kiyomōri, the head of the Taira clan, and Minamoto Yoshitomo.

The war was a complex affair, not least because men from each clan fought on both sides in the conflict. This was not unusual, as it ensured that, whoever emerged victorious from a dispute, a clan could claim it had supported the 'right' side. In essence, though, the Minamoto and the Taira were predominantly in the new emperor's camp, with the Fujiwara backing the old emperor. On the night of 29 July 1156, Taira Kiyomōri and Minamoto Yoshitomo, leading around 600 mounted samurai, attacked the enemy palace defended by Yoshitomo's brother and father, Minamoto Tametomo and Minamoto Tameyoshi. In what was known as the Siege of Shirakawa-den, Kiyomōri and then Yoshitomo both attacked the West gate defended by Tametomo, but were repulsed by his archery units. A fierce battle followed that lasted long into the night. Eventually, the new emperor's supporters managed to set the imperial palace on fire, causing its defenders to flee. After Kiyomōri's victory, Yoshitomo was ordered to kill his father for leading the opposing side. He refused, but another Minamoto officer, saying it would be a disgrace to allow a Taira to execute Tameyoshi, performed the deed. As the supporters of the new emperor, the Minamoto and the Taira became the leading military force in Japan; the Fujiwara, having fought for the now-exiled old emperor, saw their power base destroyed.

The Hogen Rebellion, being directed by the military clans, created the foundation upon which the dominance of the samurai would be based. The imperial family had lost all authority and the military clans now controlled the political landscape. This short civil war is now considered the inciting incident of a chain of events that would produce the first of Japan's three long-lasting samurai-led dynastic governments.

It was Taira Kiyomōri who emerged as the ascendant power in Japan following the downfall of the Fujiwara. He would remain in command for the next 20 years. During this period, escalating rivalry between the dominant Taira clan and the sidelined Minamoto clan erupted in 1160. This came when around 500 Minamoto samurai attacked the imperial palace in an attempt to regain some of their earlier power. Kiyomōri put down this uprising after a month of fighting and then embarked on a brutal programme of retribution that saw every Minamoto adult executed. The Minamoto children, meanwhile, were exiled to monasteries or adopted into households of other families on the assumption that they no longer presented a threat. This proved to be unwise; Minamoto Yoritomo, the son of Yoshitomo, having been spared in this way was later able to take advantage of growing dissent over Taira rule and organized a new revolt.

Left: Detail of the Hogen Rebellion screen. Red banners of the Taira and white banners of the Minamoto.

Above: *Minamoto Yoritomo's Night Attack on the Shirakawa Palace in the Hogen Rebellion,* Yoshitora, 1850.

Since taking power, Kiyomōri had consolidated his position by marrying his daughter, Taira-no Tokuko, to the emperor, Takakura. In 1180, Taira-no Tokuko gave birth to a son, and Takakura abdicated so that the infant, named Antoku, could become emperor. The thought of Kiyomōri's grandson sitting on the imperial throne was too much for many, especially as the warlord took advantage of his greatly enhanced power by filling no less than 50 government posts with his relatives and exiling 45 court officials not deemed loyal enough to him personally. Opposition to Kiyomōri rallied around Go-Toba, another infant son of Takakura (and Antoku's half-brother – but, crucially, not Kiyomōri's grandson). Minamoto Yoritomo, by now the leader of his clan, championed Go-Toba's claim to the throne and this led to the Genpei War that would last for the next five years.

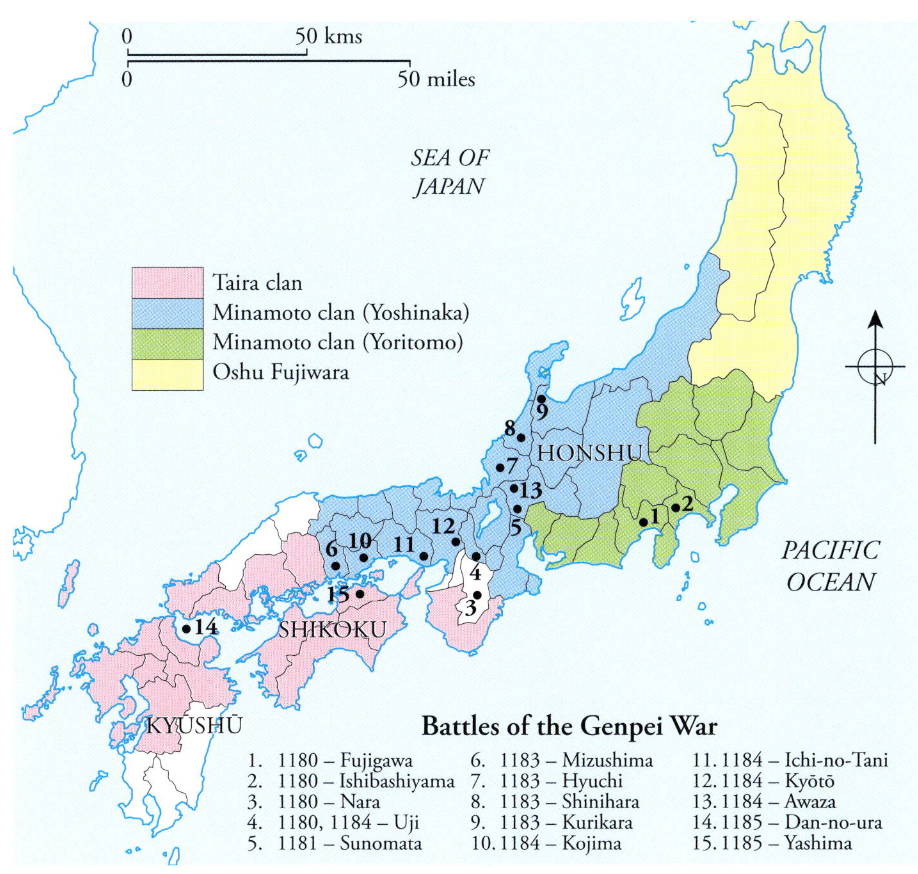

Right: Map of Japan in 1183 (Heian period) during the Genpei War (1180–1185). It shows the domains of the Taira, Minamoto and Northern Fujiwara clans with provinces and important battles.

The Battles of Fuji River and Kurikara Pass

Left: The Battle of Fuji River, Suruga Province, Genpei War, by Kuniyoshi.

Hostilities commenced in September 1180, when Taira Kiyomōri sent a massive army to engage Yoritomo and hopefully crush the burgeoning rebellion. With the open support of the Hōjō clan, Minamoto Yoritomo gathered a small force of around 300 and, expecting further reinforcements, advanced toward Ishibashi Yama, a mountain in the east of Honshu. However, severe weather and flooding prevented the additional troops from arriving and Yoritomo was intercepted by a Taira force of 3,000 samurai, with a further 300 troops attacking from the rear. The Minamoto fought courageously but were eventually overwhelmed, resulting in heavy casualties. Yoritomo managed to escape and was later able to establish a base in Kamakura. Hōjō Tokimasa, an influential daimyō who was to become the first regent of the Kamakura Shōgunate, convinced the Takeda clan of Kai and the Nitta clan of Kotsuke to join Yoritomo against the Taira. These, together with more clans in the region, launched a night attack on the Taira camp at the Fuji River. The Taira forces were surprised and became disorientated when a flock of disturbed waterfowl flew over their camp. In the confusion that followed, the larger Minamoto army was able to attack and overwhelm them. This would not be the only time a group of animals would come to the aid of the Minamoto, as we will see. To add to the Taira's woes, Kiyomōri died suddenly of illness in 1181. This was followed by the outbreak of a severe famine throughout the country, which further weakened the Taira's hold on power.

In 1183, as Yoritomo's cousin Minamoto Yoshinaka advanced down country with a large army, Taira Munemōri, Kiyomōri's son, decided to form an expeditionary force of 100,000 men against the Minamoto and placed it under command of his nephew, Taira Koremōri. After several minor successes against Yoshinaka, Koremōri, who was not an experienced military leader in the field, split his force when approaching the mountain passes connecting western Honshu to the east. The greater part of his army, some 70,000 samurai, headed for the Kurikara Pass on 2 June. As they did so, Yoshinaka, who was already in a well-prepared position, used banners to trick his enemy into misreading his position and then set a herd of oxen with flaming torches tied to their horns upon Koremōri's troops. In the confusion that

followed, thousands of the Taira perished, including many leaders, as the Minamoto scored a great victory.

Other victories soon followed, including the Battle of Ichinotani in March 1184, where Minamoto forces led by Yoritomo's younger brother Yoshitsune attacked the Taira down a steep slope and drove them into the sea. The Minamoto then captured successive Taira bases to open the road to Kyoto. After years of warfare, the Taira were driven from the capital and fled west, taking the child emperor Antoku with them.

With the Taira vanquished, the Minamoto installed Emperor Go-Toba on the throne, but only as a figurehead. Yoritomo was now firmly in control of the military government, the bakufu, and he set about appointing military constables, or *shugo*, to rule over the provinces and stewards to supervise public and private estates. Yoritomo subsequently focused on dismantling the influence of the powerful Fujiwara clan.

In 1189, Yoritomo led a large army to subdue the country's semi-independent northeastern Toho Region, where the fourth leader of the Northern Fujiwara, Fujiwara Yasuhira was defeated. This campaign had given Yoritomo a perfect opportunity to mobilize his *shugo* followers and brought him a good deal of new land with which to reward them. Three years later, in 1192, Yoritomo was granted the title of *Sei-i-taishōgun* by the Imperial Court, a designation that would later be simply referred to as 'Shōgun'. The word 'shōgun' means 'chief commander who defeats barbarians' and it was previously a title assigned to a military leader for the duration of a specific campaign. Now, though, it became permanent and the person who bore it ranked officially as the second person in the country after the emperor. It was at this point that the Kamakura bakufu as we know it reached its completion in name as well as in substance.

Before the Genpei War, there was no fixed identity of what a 'samurai' was, and warriors or soldiers were referred to in general as 'bushi'. During Emperor Shirakawa's period as retired emperor, he established the *'Hokumen Nobubushi' (northside bushi),* a group of warriors responsible for guarding the north side of his residence and compound, but who would

Below: *Yoshinaka at the Great Battle of Kurikara Valley*, Yoshitora, 1853. Dramatic scene from the Battle of Kurikara in 1183 illustrating a famous incident when Minamoto no Yoshinaka and his men tied flaming torches to the horns of oxen and stampeded them into a division of Taira caught between mountain passes.

The Battle of Dan-no-ura

As success followed success, Minamoto Yoshitsune grew more confident. He had spent the entire war avoiding sea battles but, having gained the support of a number of samurai who were expert sailors, he decided to engage the Taira at sea.

The Taira were undoubtedly more experienced than the Minamoto in naval warfare, but Yoshitsune had the larger fleet thanks to his new allies – approximately 700–850 ships, compared to the 500 operated by the Taira. These ships were mostly small boats, fitted with wooden platforms to ensure that the samurai didn't fall into the water. Most of the combatants were armed with simple bows and arrows.

On the eve of battle, the Taira fleet under the command of Taira Tomomori moved out from its base at Hikoshima, sailing eastwards through the Shimonoseki Strait. By the morning of 25 April 1185 it was in position to engage the Minamoto fleet, which had sailed westward from the island of Shikoku. Taira Tomomori made a heartfelt speech to the members of his clan, reminding them that this time there would be no opportunity for them to retreat and that they should fight as bravely as possible. As a precautionary measure, six-year-old Emperor Antoku was hidden on a simple boat, while a larger and more elaborate vessel was hung with pennants and insignia to make it look like the royal yacht.

With the Minamoto ships arranged in a line and the Taira divided into three squadrons, battle was joined at some time between 6 and 8 am in

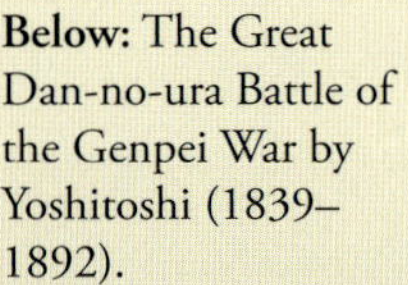

Below: The Great Dan-no-ura Battle of the Genpei War by Yoshitoshi (1839–1892).

Right: The Battle of Akama Strait at Dan-no-ura in Choshu in 1185 by Utagawa Sadahide.

the waters off a beach on Honshu known as Dan-no-ura. It began with archers from both sides exchanging long-range fire. Then, the Taira used their superior knowledge of local tides and currents to try to surround the Minamoto. As the ships closed around each other, the battle descended into hand-to-hand combat. Gradually, the Minamoto gained the advantage, despite a brief fright when one enemy warrior, Taira Noritsune, managed to board Yoshitune's vessel and tried to attack him.

As the fighting continued, Yoshitsune cleverly ordered his archers to target the oarsmen and helmsmen on the Taira's ships. Soon, many Taira vessels were drifting helplessly on the current. At the same time, a Taira traitor revealed to Yoshitsune on which boat the young emperor was hidden. He was a sitting duck. Realizing that all was lost, Tomomori boarded the emperor's vessel and advised him that the only way out was suicide. The emperor's grandmother took the young sovereign by the hand and led him to the side of the ship. Here, after offering prayers to the Great Goddess in Ise and to the Buddha, and then reciting the words 'There at the bottom, under the waves, we will find another capital', they jumped into the waves.

This initiated the most tragic mass suicide in samurai history. Emperor Antuko's mother tried to rush into the sea after him, but was caught by one of the Minamoto samurai, who hooked her by the hair with a war pitchfork. A lady-in-waiting was about to throw herself into the water, but an arrow nailed the hem of her clothes to the side of the ship, forcing her to drop the box she was carrying. It turned out that it contained a sacred mirror, one of the three imperial regalia. These represented the three primary virtues: valour (the sword), wisdom (the mirror) and benevolence (the jewel). The sacred sword had already been thrown into the sea. Taira Norimori and his brother Taira Tsunemori tied a heavy anchor to their armour and jumped into the sea, holding hands.

A similar action was taken by others, including Arimori and Yukimori, two members of the Sukemori family. Taira Munemori, however, was less decisive. At least he was until one samurai pushed him into the sea, ashamed of his weak spirit. Munemori turned out to be a good swimmer, though, and managed to hold on until the Minamoto took him prisoner. The last to die that day was Taira Tomomori, who donned two sets of armour, tied himself to an anchor, and threw himself into the water.

O sorrowful one view! Scarlet banners, scarlet banners, abandoned, torn, floated into the sea, like the crimson maple leaves that cover the waters of the Tatsuta River, torn off by gusts of storm. The white foam waves were painted scarlet, raiding on the shore. Empty ships, having lost their helmsmen, persecuted wind, carried away by the current, swayed on the waves and were carried away into the unknown sea distances...

Heike Monogatari, Volume 11

The battle at Dan-no-ura ended with the complete destruction of the Taira clan. Hardly any members of the family survived the engagement. After Dan-no-ura, the Taira name disappears from the pages of Japanese history. No victory in the history of the samurai was as complete as this.

Ever since the battle, sailors and fishermen in the waters off Dan-no-ura have reported the sights and sounds of restless Taira spirits haunting the sea, seeking a rest they will never find.

also grow to form the backbone of his and his successors' practical military strength. In addition to their guard duties, one of their prime uses was something that could be described as riot control, protecting against the followers of Japan's great temples. The temples of this era had begun to form bands of warrior monks, known as *Sohei*, from a combination of their young, low-ranking priestly members and any opportunistic mercenaries whom they could recruit and their challenges to imperial authority were increasingly bold and aggressive.

The hierarchy of the temples would send these bands out to march on Kyoto to make petition demands against the retired emperors or the imperial court. One of the largest offenders was the Temple of Enyaku-ji, just on the outskirts of Kyoto. The monks would carry a Mikoshi (divine palanquin) containing holy relics to play on the emperor's religious devotions. The hokumen bushi were not directly engage in combat with the warrior monks, but rather to act as a deterrent against them entering the city of Kyoto and causing disturbances. These group of warriors would be known in a loose way as samurai, this term was also applied to aristocratic warrior families (Buke).

This situation changed with the accession to power of Minamoto Yoritomo, who based himself not in Kyoto close to the emperor but in his headquarters in Kamakura, hundreds of kilometres to the east. Here, he established the country's first warrior-based government, the Kamakura Shōgunate (1185–1333). This development allowed for a samurai culture to develop, slowly at first and in an unstructured way, but, over the next few centuries, the identity of this warrior class would become increasingly fixed.

As military dictator, Minamoto Yoritomo ruled directly and the emperors in Kyoto became mere figureheads. He had become the country's dominant leader thanks to the actions of his samurai and there was no doubt that true power in Japan now lay in the hands of the warrior and in the symbol of his strength, the samurai sword.

Armour of the Nara and Heian periods (710–1185)

As we saw when it established its new capital city at Nara in 710, Japan absorbed significant Chinese influences from the early 8th century. This did not stop at town planning, but included weaponry and warfare too.

The emergence of the samurai class in the 10th-century Heian period marked a further, and pivotal, shift in military culture. These initially hired retainers developed their own distinctive armour and fighting styles.

As the power of the military grew and border conflicts intensified, there was a corresponding demand for superior equipment. Better swords were forged, and stronger bows were developed that were much more powerful than those of the past. Similarly, there was a requirement for armour to be strong and fit for purpose. Long, powerful and laminated bows (*yumi*), curved bladed glaives (*naginata*) and long swords (*tachi*) were the preferred options. The armour of this period can be classified into the two kinds: *ō-yoroi* ('great armour') and *haramaki* ('belly wrap'). *Ō-yoroi* was used by generals (*taisho*) and others on horseback; *haramaki* was reserved mainly for foot soldiers.

The first notable feature in the construction of the *ō-yoroi* is that there are attached at both shoulders flexible lames of scales spreading downward called *ōsode*. Since mounted warriors used both hands for loosing arrows and could not hold a shield at the same time, *ōsode* developed as a shield substitute. They become quite large and were attached to the cuirass (*do*) by four plaited cords so they could move backward and forward. To accommodate the demands

Right: Modern reproduction of aka-ito (red-laced) armour.

of horseback riding, the lower part of the cuirass was widened, allowing for increased leg movement. The plates from which the cuirass was made were usually not visible on the chest, since they were covered by a large piece of tanned and patterned leather. This was so that the bowstring of the bow could slide freely over the cuirass and not catch on the metal plates. The skirt section below the cuirass was divided into four sections called *kusazuri* to provide front, rear and side protection.

Ō-yoroi armour was constructed using small, stiffened plates or scales made from cowhide or iron and coated in lacquer. These components were interlaced with plaited silk braids or dyed chamois leather straps. Despite being composed of plates, the armour offered limited flexibility. Occasionally, ornate copper scales, sometimes coated in precious metals, were added for decorative purposes.

The art of lacing armour evolved significantly over time. By incorporating solid colours or patterns into the lacing, samurai could easily identify their comrades. Some believe this practice of clan-specific armour colours began during the reign of Emperor Seiwa (856–876), with the Fujiwara, Taira, Minamoto and Tachibana clans adopting light green, purple, black and yellow respectively. White lacing, traditionally associated with mourning, signified a warrior's determination to die in battle or fight for a lost cause. Consequently, many Heian period and later armours were as much works of art as instruments of war.

The earlier 'beaked' helmet developed into the *ikaboshi kabuto*, featuring a radial segmented design with prominent rivet heads. A large, hanging neck guard, or *shikoro*, shielded the rear, while wing-like, outward-turned cheek guards, known as *fukigaeshi*, deflected sword blows from the neck. The kabuto was worn over a material *eboshi* cap, uniformly of black cloth, usually hemp or similar, and later versions even used paper, which provided additional head protection. The entire armour set weighed approximately 30 kg (66 lb).

The *ō-yoroi*, while providing exceptional protection, was both cumbersome and costly to produce. In contrast, the *haramaki* offered greater mobility for footsoldiers, utilizing similar materials but with a more fitted design. Featuring more skirt plates, the *haramaki* opened at the back and fastened with cords. Initially worn by lower-ranking samurai, its practicality led to its adoption by higher-ranking warriors during the 15th century as battlefield mobility increased.

Right: Haramaki amour.

CHAPTER 3

The Kamakura period

The Kamakura period (1192–1333) marked Japan's transition into the medieval era. Named after the city where the Kamakura Shōgunate was established, this period witnessed the rise of a military government that exercised significant control over Japan. The shōgunate laid the foundation for the new feudal system and introduced a new legal framework that would shape Japan for centuries. In 1232, a legal code was enacted emphasizing loyalty between master and servant to address declining moral standards. During this time, Japan faced two Mongol invasions from Kublai Khan (1274 and 1281), which were successfully repelled by a combination of Japanese forces and the elements.

During the late Heian and early Kamakura periods, mounted samurai archers comprised a significant portion of the military. The Mongol invasions, however, prompted the development of new samurai weapons and tactics. The Sagami province became renowned for its skilled swordsmiths, producing blades of exceptional quality. Unfortunately, this era also saw the gradual erosion of the samurai's austere lifestyle, giving way to luxury and corruption. Ultimately, Emperor Go-Daigo, aided by the Ashikaga clan, overthrew the Kamakura Shōgunate, temporarily restoring imperial authority.

After Minamoto Yoritomo's victory at the Battle of the Fuji River in 1180, he established an institution known as the Samurai-Dokoro. This would specifically exist to manage the warriors who had sworn allegiance to him and confirmed a bond of loyalty and allegiance. He then followed this up by establishing two more agencies, one to handle administrative and financial affairs, and the other to look after legal matters. He gave jobs in them to some of his aristocratic friends. Finally, he appointed the most powerful of his vassals to rule the provinces. Their positions were equivalent to those of law enforcers or Constables (*shugo*) and they had the authority to arrest illegal traders, thieves and murderers, and to supply warriors for guard duties in Kyoto. These men would eventually evolve into provincial daimyō.

In 1199, at the age of just 51, Yoritomo died from the injuries he incurred in a horse-riding accident and the future of the organization he had spent the last two decades building suddenly became full of uncertainty. He was succeeded as shōgun by his eldest son, Minamoto Yoriie, who found it difficult to fill his late father's shoes. Most of his actual power as leader of the bakufu was quickly transferred to a council of 13 of his most powerful vassals.

With Yoritomo's death, the balance of power within the bakufu shifted dramatically. The Hōjō family, connected to Yoritomo through his wife Masako, rose to prominence. This culminated in 1203 with Hōjō Tokimasa, Masako's father, assuming the role of regent (*shikken*), effectively becoming the de facto ruler (this position remained within the Hōjō family for nine generations, lasting until 1333). The Hōjō consolidated their power by capitalizing on divisions among Yoritomo's generals, strategically eliminating their rivals and ultimately leading to the extinction of Yoritomo's direct line of succession.

The next council member to find himself standing in the way of the Hōjō path to progress was one Wada Yoshimōri. He oversaw the management of all the shōgun's vassals and as such could be regarded as the senior military official of the shōgunate. In 1213, two of Yoshimōri's sons and one of his nephews were implicated in an alleged treason plot against the shōgun. Yoshimōri was offended by the punishments handed out and, unwisely, led troops into Kamakura.

Left: A mounted samurai, fully armed with a bow and supply of arrows.

Above: Yoritomo falling from his horse. Rokuhara Battle Scroll by Kano Yoshinaga, Toyama Memorial Museum.

HATAKEYAMA SHIGETADA (1164–1205)

Hatakeyama Shigetada was a military commander from the end of the Heian period to the early Kamakura period. He became a retainer of Minamoto Yoritomo and played a major role in the Kamakura Shōgunate as a vassal.

Legend has it that in 1184 Shigetada and Minamoto Yoshitsune attacked the undefended side of the castle of Ichinotani. While descending the steep slope of Hiyodorigoe pass, Shigetada's horse was injured and, in order to avoid defeat and dishonour, he carried the animal on his back before successfully staging a surprise attack.

In a historical chronicle of the Kamakura Shōgunate he is described as being a handsome and talented musician. He was highly acclaimed for his bravery during his lifetime and was called 'the model of the Kantō samurai' for his upright and honest character.

After the Battle of Awazu in 1184, Shigetada was known for failing to capture the female samurai Tomoe Gozen.

Right: Hatakeyama Shigetada carrying a horse.

Samurai Family Crests

The use of the mon as a family symbol emerged during the Heian period (794–1185). This era witnessed the creation of many iconic crests, including some of the most stylish designs.

Below: A sake bottle from the Edo period decorated with the Tokugawa family *mon*.

In the 12th century, Japanese emperors established the chrysanthemum as their exclusive emblem. Gradually, the chrysanthemum became an unofficial state symbol, representing the imperial house. The practice of passing specific mon designs through generations solidified their association with families, reinforcing traditional hierarchies.

The *mon*'s position as a family symbol quickly extended to military application. During the Taira-Minamoto conflict, opposing armies were distinguished by red (Taira) and white (Minamoto) banners adorned with specific emblems. The Taira adopted a stylized black butterfly, while the Minamoto chose a gentian flower motif. As warfare evolved from individual duels to organized unit battles, clear identification became crucial for command and morale. Families adopted new *mon* to align with political affiliations, and the practice of awarding *mon* for distinguished service led to variations within the same family lineage. The scale of battles during the feudal era necessitated the clear identification of combatants. The Kodama clan, for example, adopted a war fan emblem, which later became their official *mon*. Other families, like the Nitta, Ashikaga and Miura, derived their *mon* from their battle flags, often featuring a simple circular bar design. Even families with established *mon*, such as the Kumagai, who traditionally used a dove pattern on their robes, adopted new emblems based on their battlefield identification.

By the time of the Mongol invasions in the late 13th century, the *mon* had become a firmly established symbol among military families. During the feudal era, the privilege of using a *mon* was restricted to royalty, daimyō and samurai families. However, in the 18th century, wealthy merchants began adopting *mon*

Right: Samurai family *mon*.

Imperial Crest | Tokugawa | Toyotomi | Ashikaga

Hōjō | Mori | Takeda | Satsuma

Sanada | Satake | Hosokawa | Kato

Honda | Akechi | Fujiwara | Mori (2)

as company emblems. Additionally, some prominent Kabuki actors incorporated *mon* into their attire.

The Edo period, beginning in 1600, marked a further stratification of society. The privilege of carrying two swords and displaying a *mon* became exclusively associated with the samurai class. In the peaceful Edo period, there was no further use for the battle flags and banners of the Age of the Warring States, but the display of heraldry *mon* persisted in the processions of daimyō, who were required to alternate their residence between their domains and the city of Edo under the Tokugawa Shōgunate's policy.

With the long peace under the Tokugawa came the finalization of the heraldic system of signs and colours and the transformation of the samurai costume into a kind of military uniform. The shōgunate carefully regulated the *mon*, their colours, and the number of flags a daimyō could wield, reflecting the meticulous control exercised over all aspects of samurai life during this era.

Mon designs were myriad, with flowers, birds, animals, mountains, water, clouds and lightning all being utilized. Religious symbols, weapons, coins, tools, heavenly bodies and Chinese characters all found their place. *Mon* are now found on kimono, building decorations, restaurant signs and trade signs.

After a long and bloody struggle and the first real battle to ever take place within the city itself, he was defeated and killed by bakufu troops under the Hōjō. So it was that Hōjō Yoshitoki, in addition to his role as Shōgunal Regent, assimilated control of both the legal and military branches of the Kamakura bakufu. In 1219, Minamoto Sanitomo was assassinated at a ceremony at the Zirugaoka Hachimangu Shrine in Kamakura by the shrine's chief priest. As he had no children to succeed him, this ended the Seiwa Minamoto Clan.

Despite their dominance, the Hōjō's relatively low social standing barred them from claiming the title of shōgun. Therefore, retired Emperor Go-Toba installed two-year-old Kujō Yoritsune, a member of the Fujiwara clan with a distant connection to Yoritomo, as the fourth shōgun of the Kamakura Shogunate. However, it was Hōjō Yoshitoki who truly governed, and subsequently, the Hōjō controlled the appointment of shōguns, always selecting them from the prestigious Fujiwara or imperial families to maintain an aura of legitimacy through lineage.

Left: Portrait of Hōjō Yoshitoki.

In June 1221, Emperor Go-Toba perceived the weakening of the Minamoto clan as an opportunity to restore imperial power. He issued a mandate calling for the overthrow of Shōgunal Regent, Hōjō Yoshitoki. For the samurai warriors of this time, both the Imperial Court and the Kamakura Shōgunate were important patrons to whom they rendered service, and deciding whom to side with in the impending conflict became quite a dilemma for many. However, few warriors responded to his request for support.

Left: Samurai with retainers, mounted samurai and light-foot (*ashigaru*) troops preparing to battle.

Right: A mounted archer at the Kyoto Jidai Matsuri festival. See the coloured silk patterning on the shoulder pads (*sode*), a common feature in the Kamakura period.

According to legend, Hōjō Masako called the most prominent warriors together and implored them to remember their late great leader, her husband Minamoto Yoritomo, and the debt which they owed to him for uniting them and defending their rights. The shōgunate responded with lightning speed, dispatching an army to the west just seven days after the retired emperor had issued his decree against the Hōjō. At first, the Hōjō considered taking a defensive position. By closing mountain passes, they could block an attack on Kamakura by Go-Toba's samurai. Instead, the regent's forces set out toward Kyoto.

The ex-emperor Go-Toba in truth possessed a small army of nervous and inexperienced troops and together with clans in the region, who had never accepted the authority of the Kamakura Shōgunate, fought enthusiastically against the advancing bakufu army. On 5 July 1221, the forces of the ex-emperor made their stand, attempting to defend the bridges over the Uji river. They failed and, despite heavy losses, the regent's troops forced their way across. The bakufu army won a quick succession of victories against the imperial forces and captured Kyoto within a month. Hōjō's strategy of a swift attack had paid off. There had been little time for dissatisfied lords to gather their forces and join the emperor, or for Go-Toba to talk more clans into joining his revolt. The emperor's attempt to reassert imperial authority had proved unsuccessful.

Emperor Go-Toba was arrested and subsequently banished to the remote island of Oki. This conflict, known as the Jōkyū War (named after the Jōkyū era, which spanned 1219–22), had significant consequences. The bakufu established a headquarters in Kyoto, allowing them to directly supervise the imperial court and manage the administrative and legal affairs of the western provinces. Furthermore, the bakufu confiscated the numerous estates belonging to the court aristocracy and warriors who had supported Go-Toba, redistributing these lands to their own Kamakura vassals as a form of reward and further solidifying their control. This marked a significant expansion of the bakufu's political power.

The Hōjō had shown that, even without a shōgun to give their power a degree of legitimacy, they could keep Japan under control. Much of the confiscated land was in central and western Japan, meaning that, overnight, the authority of the bakufu now covered the entire country. Until this point, it had mostly been an organization in charge of the Eastern Kantō Region. This struggle, known as the Jōkyū War, is often overshadowed by the longer and more impressive Genpei War that preceded it. But in terms of its historical significance for Japan's warrior class, it was just as important, if not more so. Its greatest consequence at the time was the impression it left on the hearts and minds of the people of Japan, who had now witnessed for the first time the emperor and leader of the aristocratic world being directly challenged and defeated by his social inferiors.

The Way of the Warrior

'The way of the samurai is found in death.'
Hagakure *by Tsunetomo Yamamoto, 1716.*

Francis Xavier, a Spanish Catholic missionary and saint, reached Japan in 1549 and landed in Kyūshū. He launched a brief yet successful missionary which ultimately led to the expulsion of all foreigners and the closure of Japan to the West. As one of the earliest European visitors, he wrote to his Jesuit colleagues in Europe about Japanese life:

Below: A posed photograph of samurai conducting *seppuku* from 1880.

'The Japanese are very ambitious of honours and distinctions, and think themselves superior to all nations in military glory and valour. They prize and honour all that has to do with war, and all such things, and there is nothing of

which they are so proud as of weapons adorned with gold and silver. They always wear swords and daggers both in and out of the house … in short, they value arms more than any people I have ever seen.'

The Life and Letters of St Francis Xavier by H. J. Coleridge of the Society of Jesus. Volume 2. Burns & Oates, London 1872

The samurai class had customs that, from an external perspective, often contradicted their professed ideals of honour. Several practices stand out as particularly disturbing. One such custom was the perceived 'right' of a samurai to strike down a member of a lower social class if they felt dishonoured. Another was *seppuku*, ritual suicide (see page 127), considered an honourable way to die and avoid disgrace. The display of severed heads of slain enemies was also a common practice. Furthermore, historical records indicate that samurai administered various cruel and unusual punishments to criminals, punishments that would have been deemed unacceptable in Western societies. Perhaps the most extreme example of these practices was *tsujigiri*, which involved using a newly sharpened katana to summarily decapitate or otherwise mutilate an unsuspecting person, effectively testing the blade's sharpness on a living victim. This brutal practice was eventually banned during the Edo period.

It is accurate to state that throughout the classical, medieval, and early modern periods of Japanese history, honour and reputation were absolutely fundamental to a warrior's sense of self. These concepts provided the framework within which all warrior behaviour was judged and understood. A samurai's reputation, honour, and personal pride were considered almost tangible possessions, taking precedence over virtually every other duty or responsibility.

From the origins of the samurai class and the establishment of the lord/vassal bond in the 10th century through to the end of the 16th century, the ties between a master and his retainer were fundamentally contractual in nature, based on a clear exchange of mutual interest and advantage. This meant that medieval samurai maintained their loyalty to their lords only as long as it served their own personal or familial interests. They were not bound by an absolute or unwavering sense of fealty and could, and frequently did, readily switch their allegiances when the situation presented a more favourable opportunity. The frequency of defections, often taking place in the heat of battle, in many of the most important battles in Japanese history serves as a stark illustration of this pragmatic approach to loyalty.

Medieval Japanese notions of honour and honourable conduct in battle were far more flexible than the strict standards imposed by the later Tokugawa shōgunate. This flexibility allowed successful warriors to rationalize a range of behaviours that would have been strongly condemned under Tokugawa rule. Although the concept of a samurai code emerged centuries earlier, during the Kamakura period, it lacked a unified definition or set of rules. Before the 17th and 18th centuries, there was scant written discourse on proper warrior conduct, and samurai prioritized practical effectiveness on the battlefield.

The word that we in the West understand to be the samurai code is Bushidō. Yet the term was scarcely used at all before modern times until the publication of Nitobe Inazō's 1899 small book *Bushidō: The Soul of Japan* and this was 30 years after the end of the samurai as a class.

The modern interpretation of Bushidō as illustrated and explained in Nitobe Inazō's book would be based on seven principles: Righteousness, Loyalty, Honour, Respect, Honesty, Courage and Consistency.

THE SEVEN PRINCIPLES OF BUSHIDŌ

義	忠義	名誉	礼	誠	勇	真
Righteousness	**Loyalty**	**Honour**	**Respect**	**Honesty**	**Courage**	**Consistency**

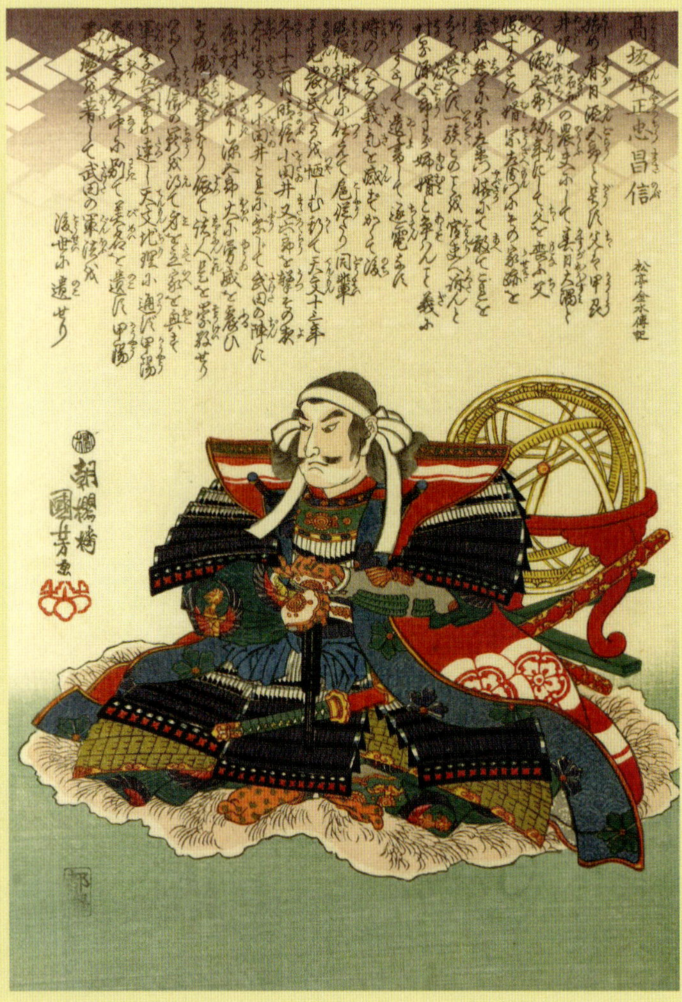

Left: Kōsaka Masanobu (1527–1578), the first to write about bushidō in his work.

The first mention of the term bu-shi-dō is in the work by Kōsaka Masanobu (1527–1578) written in 1616 for the Takeda-Ryū (martial arts school). This contains the history of the Takeda family and their military tactics and exploits in battle. It emphasizes that bushidō lies only in 'becoming as a spear' on the battlefield and it is waste of talent when a bushidō practitioner takes on administrative roles in government or financial affairs. These notes were spread throughout the samurai schools and helped popularize the term.

The Tokugawa Shogunate's 'Laws for the Military Houses,' first issued in 1615, had a profound impact on the relationship between daimyō and their samurai retainers. These laws, along with subsequent regulations limiting retainer numbers, fixing tax rates, and controlling daimyō incomes, effectively eliminated the possibility for samurai to find alternative employment. This lack of economic mobility created a situation where samurai were entirely dependent on their daimyō for their livelihoods. Consequently, daimyō were in a position to demand and receive unwavering, unqualified loyalty from their retainers, as there were no other viable options for these warriors. This system of enforced loyalty was a direct result of the shōgunate's efforts to centralize power and control the warrior class.

During the early 17th century, the samurai underwent a significant transformation, evolving from an occupational group defined by specific martial skills into a legally defined, hereditary social class. This shift was accompanied by the removal of samurai from the land, as daimyō sought to create more efficient and centralized military forces. Consequently, the image of the daimyō also changed, shifting from that of a charismatic 'warlord' who attracted followers through personal qualities and achievements to that of a bureaucratic leader overseeing an organization of employed retainers.

Under these conditions, ideas about samurai honour and behaviour became formalized at the same time as losing their original role as warriors. Most samurai of the Edo period were sword-bearing bureaucrats whilst playing a central role in the policing and administration of the country.

Opposite: Miyamoto Musashi fighting Sasaki Kojiro in 1612, from an ukiyo-e print by Yoshifusa Utagawa.

By the mid-17th century, a significant transformation had taken place within the samurai class. The majority of samurai had relocated to castle towns, no longer deriving their income from rents and taxes collected from their former land holdings, but instead subsisting on stipends provided by their overlords. This trend intensified, and by 1700, over 90 per cent of samurai lived in this manner. This shift in economic dependence also led to a change in the focus of their loyalty. Rather than personal allegiance to a specific lord, loyalty became directed towards the domain as a whole, as symbolized by the daimyō. This marked the emergence of a form of collective identity more akin to modern patriotism than the traditional, personal bonds of feudal loyalty. The bushidō literature of this time contains much thought relevant to a warrior class in search for the proper role of a warrior order in a world without war and reflecting on Japan's long history of war.

The senior sengoku daimyō, Kuroda Nagamasa (1568–1623) noted that '*The art of peace and the art of war are like the two wheels of a cart, which lacking one will have difficulty standing.*'

The famous swordsman and writer, Miyamoto Musashi (1584–1645) describes the general framework of bushidō '*...to apply skills in any situation, always carry two swords, learn how to effectively use the lance, naginata, bow and arrow, and guns. A daimyō should know the strength of his troops and how to properly deploy them.*'

Although the Meiji Restoration in the 1870s formally abolished the samurai class, their legacy continued to shape Japanese society. While they were transitioned into new roles in professional, military, and business fields, their influence persisted due to their continued presence in important positions. The former samurai and their descendants remained a powerful force in Japanese society long after their formal class status was dissolved.

For the first time in their history, Japan's samurai warriors were the undisputed masters of the country. The emperor was in exile and the aristocracy was under their control.

The next 40 years was to see changes in the Hōjō regency. In 1233, a code was introduced that governed the behaviour, morals, civil affairs, lawsuits and punishments applicable to the Hōjō's vassals. The country's first military code of law, it reflected Japan's well-thought-out transition from court to militarized society. Although purposefully made for the shōgunate's retainers, other warriors began to adopt it. In this way it was to develop into a doctrine of 'The Way of the Warrior'.

In addition to their duties as land managers, the Kamakura *bushi* placed a great deal of emphasis on the arts of war. These samurai had now consolidated themselves as a distinct warrior social class. This appeared in their daily lives through the practice of what were military sports that focused mostly on the training of archery and horseback riding skills. These included things such as organized hunts and a mounted archery target practice sport called *yabusame*. According to traditions which survive in the literature of the time, individual combat would commence with horseback archery after announcing their name and heritage. The use of swords at this time was not regarded as being of a great skill.

These decades also saw the main line of the Hōjō gradually establish itself as a sort of pseudo royal family within the context of the shōgunate; by the 1260s, the Kamakura shōguns were little more than puppets, and the position of Shōgunal Regent was the undisputed property of the Hōjō family.

In 1268, Japan's leaders were sent a message from a young empire to the west that had been vigorously expanding for the last few decades. It read:

We have received the mandate of heaven and become masters of the universe; we wish to open relations with your country and become good friends. We see this world as a great family, but such a family cannot exist without mutual communication. We would hate to have to resort to force of arms.

The Kamakura Shōgunate had just received its first correspondence from the Mongol Empire, one of the greatest conquering forces in human history. The letter had been dictated by Kublai Khan himself and it strongly urged the Japanese to become a tributary state of the Mongol Empire. The retired emperor's council, however, opted not to send a reply. The Kamakura Shōgunate followed suit, urging the warriors of western Japan to be vigilant in anticipation of a possible Mongol threat. The following year, an irritated Kublai sent a second message to the Japanese. This time the increasingly

Below: The samurai boats attacking the Mongol ships.

Above: Image of a *wakō* as a bearded pirate in a short-sleeved kimono, barefoot and wielding a katana sword. *Wakō* pirates came from across the sea to plunder villages.

nervous Imperial Court drafted a politely negative reply, but the bakufu stepped in and vetoed it. Japan would have no words at all for the Mongol Emperor.

The leader of the Kamakura bakufu at this time was 18-year-old Hōjō Tokimonne, and in 1271 he and the bakufu received a final messenger from the Mongols to which they yet again failed to respond. Instead, the bakufu ordered any eastern samurai warriors possessing land in Kyūshū to prepare to defend their southern territory from foreign invaders. In 1274, Kublai lost patience and launched an invasion of Kyūshū, with an army of around 20,000 Mongols and 10,000 Koreans. The force brutalized the islands of Tsushima and Iki and plundered along the coast of Bizan province, before finally attempting a fully-fledged landfall at Hakata Bay, where they were met by bakufu forces. The samurai warriors struggled against the Mongols' organized fighting style and advanced weaponry, which even included an early type of hand grenade, and they were forced to retreat to the city of Dazifu, the western capital of Kyūshū, and allow the Mongol army to temporarily occupy Hakata. That night, however, the Mongols surprisingly headed back to their ships and the next day sailed back to Korea. This marked the end of the first Mongol invasion of Japan – which, it is thought, had been launched as a reconnaissance and intimidation mission rather than a full-scale invasion.

Interestingly, the Mongol invasions of the 13th century are often cited as the first instance of Japan's samurai warriors engaging in battle with a foreign enemy. But there had been a clash more than 250 years earlier, in 1019, when a fleet of around 50 pirate ships from the Korean Peninsula launched an attack on southern Japan and took the islands of

Tsushima and Iki. After the garrison of 147 soldiers on Iki was wiped out, the pirates slaughtered all of the island's men and seized the women as prisoners. These pirates, from an ethnic group known to the Japanese as the Toyi, spent roughly two weeks ravaging the provinces of Northern Kyūshū. By the time the attacks ended, more than 300 civilians were dead and a thousand had been taken captive. Close to 400 cows and horses had been stolen or killed. The government of Kyūshū struggled to scrape together the ships and soldiers needed to repel the invaders, and the day was instead saved by the local *bushi* warriors who stepped up to meet the pirates in battle. Once the pirates returned to the mainland they were finally defeated by Korean forces, who also returned several hundred civilian captives to Japan, for which they were rewarded with a gift of gold.

More than two centuries later, Kublai Khan set his sights on Japan and in 1275 he sent yet another embassy to see if the country's leaders had learned their lesson. They hadn't. Instead, the stubborn Hōjō Tukimune decided to give Kublai a hard rebuttal and had his messengers beheaded in Kamakura. The bakufu then began preparing for the now remarkably high possibility of a second invasion, establishing a guard duty system in Kyūshū, the Foreign Defence Service Rotation, and building a series of earth and stone walls along the coast of Hakata Bay. The army Kublai Khan mustered for his second invasion of Japan in 1281 is said to have been a massive 140,000 men, much larger than his first force. For the purpose of travel, it was split into two main contingents: the Eastern Route Army (*Dongro Army*) and the Southern Route Army (*Gangnam Army*). The former army was the smaller of the two, at about 40,000 men and 900 ships, and was made up of a combination of forces from the Yuan Dynasty and Goryeo Kingdom of Korea; the latter army of 100,000 troops

Left: Samurai warriors charging to the defences during the Mongol Invasion, from the late *Mōkō Shūrai Ekotoba* handscroll.

Left: Manning the coastal stone defences, from the Mongol Invasion Scroll, 1293.

Below: The defeat of the Mongol army in 1281. This illustrates the devastation on the Mongol fleet by the strong winds (*Kamikaze*).

comprised soldiers from newly conquered Song China. Hence, the 'Mongol' force comprised very few actual Mongol fighters, which would have lifted the morale of the Japanese. So too would the fact that, while the Dongro Army sailed off for Japan on schedule in late May, the larger Gangnam Army was delayed by roughly six weeks due to its commander suddenly taking ill. In terms of numbers, the Gangnam Army was much larger, but in reality, the ships were loaded with agricultural tools such as hoes and shovels and seeds, rather than weapons, and most of the soldiers were conscripted in a hurry and were not properly trained, so it was the weakest

Above: The *Mōko Shūrai Ekotoba*, or *Mongol Invasion Scrolls*, painted in 1293. This shows the samurai, Takezaki Suenaga (1246–1314), a retainer of the Higo province, who commissioned the original work to indicate his part in resisting the invasion.

group among the Southern Song Army. The main force, of course, had to be the Dongro Army.

The Dongro army attempted to make landfall in Japan unsupported, but the warriors of Kyūshū, aided by their new coastal defence embankments, forced the Mongol soldiers to retreat before they were finally able to secure a foothold in Hakata Bay. The Gangnam army, meanwhile, eventually made it out to sea in early July, and by early August had linked up with the battered Dongo army and relocated to an island called Takashima off the coast of Kyūshū to begin preparing for a full strength second attack on the Hakata area. However, on the night of 15 August 1281 they were hit by a massive summer typhoon – an event that was later ascribed to providence, or a 'divine wind' (*kamikaze*), protecting Japan from foreign invaders. The Mongol fleet was devastated by the storm, and the opportunistic Japanese warriors seized the chance the next day to attack what was left of it by harassing the remains of the invading armada in scores of small boats. It is said that only about 10–20 per cent of the great Mongol army made it back to mainland Asia.

During the chaos of the Mongol invasions, several personnel changes were made in the military governor (*shugo*) appointments to Japan's southwestern provinces in the name of better responding to the foreign threat. In effect, Hōjō clan members took control of more and more positions of power. By the end of the Kamakura period, the greater Hōjō clan held more than 30 of Japan's 68 provinces. With the establishment of the Hōjō's undisputed supremacy over the Kamakura bakufu and, by implication, the country, a powerful new political force emerged. The personal retainers of the Hōjō clan enjoyed unprecedented levels of power and prestige, even though many of them were of low status.

In December 1285, after the death of Hōjō Tokimune, his 14-year-old son Sadatoki succeeded him as regent. At this time, a power struggle broke out between the senior vassal Adachi Yasumōri and Taira Yoritsuna, the head of the Tokusō Family (the main branch of the Hōjō clan). Confrontation and rivalry became intense and Yoritsuna's samurai made a pre-emptive assault that killed Yasumōri as he arrived at Sadatoki's residence in the middle

of Kamakura. The attack killed some 30 people and injured 10 others, triggering a massive and chaotic street battle. This ultimately led to a fire that spread to the shōgun's palace and claimed the lives of about 500 high-ranking *shugo*, including many key members of the Adachi family. This incident resulted in similar anti-Adachi purges in other parts of the country. The conflict split the bakufu into two large sections: those who supported Yoritsuna and those backing Yasumōri's clan. This, the most vicious internal conflict of the Kamakura period, is remembered as the Shimotski Incident.

Taira Yoritsuna would exert his full control over the bakufu in the country for the next eight years as the chief steward, ensuring that power and wealth continued to be concentrated in the hands of the Hōjō. However, Yoritsuna's reign came to an end when Hōjō Saratoki decided to regain his powers from his lowly retainer and had him killed.

The Hōjō had appeared to be living out a golden age as the undisputed masters of the country. But however grand the house that Tokimasa had built may have appeared on the surface, corruption and nepotism were seriously beginning to rot its foundations and it had become brittle enough that a robust push from an outside force could bring the whole organization crashing down. That push would come from a place that the bakufu leaders had long considered to be a neutralized threat: the imperial court.

Emperor Go-Daigo came to the throne in 1324 and proceeded to oppose the bakufu, recruiting disgruntled monks and samurai to his cause. The bakufu fought back and dealt harshly with the participants, with the exception of the emperor himself. Emperor Go-Daigo was not one to be deterred by failure and within a few years had already formulated another plan to topple the Hōjō, making diplomatic visits to the great temples and shrines around Kyoto and Nara to build friendships and calling on the gods to destroy the bakufu. At the end of 1331, however, the emperor's plans were leaked to his enemies and this time the bakufu was not so lenient in its response, executing two of Go-Daigo's closest aristocratic confidants. The emperor fled to Mount Kasagi, south of Kyoto, and gathered some troops. The bakufu dispatched a large army of its samurai and surrounded the mountain. Despite the defenders' best efforts, they were overwhelmed by the much greater force and the emperor was taken into captivity. He was forced to abdicate and exiled to the remote island of Oki.

The Japan of the early 14th century was a far different place than it had been the first time the bakufu had dethroned an emperor. The country was now full of people who were sick and tired of Hōjō tyranny and a bakufu that had failed to help its core constituents as they had slowly slid into poverty and ruin. The emperor's defiant stand against the bakufu had created ripples that were now radiating throughout the country.

Right: A contemporary painting of Emperor Go-Daigo.

Armour of the Kamakura period

1186–1333

Armour design remained largely unchanged during the first half of this period, reflecting the continuity of warfare tactics. However, subtle developments emerged in areas such as helmet construction.

The hallmark of samurai armour during this period was its meticulous craftsmanship and attention to detail. While earlier armours often relied on leather for protection and fastening, a gradual shift toward the use of iron and silk became evident. Helmets (*kabuto*), once constructed from a single piece of metal, evolved into intricate assemblages of multiple plates fixed together by a larger number of rivets with smaller heads, so offering increased protection and flexibility. Simultaneously, the shape of helmets transformed, becoming lower and rounder to deflect blows more effectively. The traditional top hole, once accommodating the hair queue, was reduced in size and transformed into an ornamental feature adorned with layered floral washers. Warriors now wore their hair loose, covered by a soft cap (*eboshi*) and secured with a cloth headband. During the late Heian and early Kamakura periods, generals (*taisho*) adopted the practice of adorning their helmets with decorative horns, typically crafted from iron or gilded copper. By the end of this period, these horns had become a common helmet adornment.

Decorative elements also played a significant role in armour design. Elaborate patterns, often incorporating natural motifs like chrysanthemums or cherry blossoms, adorned helmets and armour plates. These embellishments were not merely aesthetic; they frequently held symbolic meaning within the warrior culture. The nobility had started to incorporate a family recognizable design on their palanquins and banners, rather than the Red or White Banners seen in the Genpei Wars, these family crests were to become known as *kamon*. The samurai class soon adopted a similar marking system using designs in a circular pattern, these non-family designs were to be known as *mon* and would appear on clothes as well as armour (see pages 38–39).

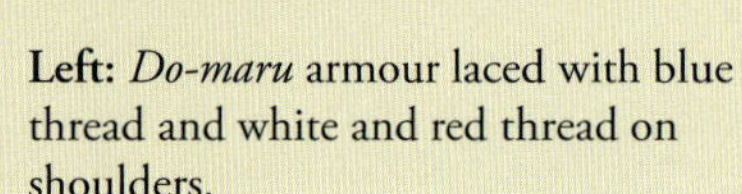

Left: *Do-maru* armour laced with blue thread and white and red thread on shoulders.

Left: Helmet 28-piece *hoshi* (*nijuhachiken-no hoshikabuto*). Kamakura period, 13th century.

The main development in armour came in the form of the *do-maru*, meaning 'around the body'. Similar to the *ō-yoroi* but lighter and more form-fitting, it was designed for use by samurai on foot. Thus, it needed to be more flexible. The midsection of the *ō-yoroi* overlapped under the right arm, eliminating the necessity for a separate plate. Since the armour was designed for foot combat rather than for archery, there was no need for the decorative and practical sheet of leather over the front. To allow the wearer to walk and run, its lower portion was divided into many sections, typically seven or eight. The *do-maru* was fitted with huge shoulder guards, known as *sode*, as was the *ō-yoroi*. Some *haramaki* armours were provided with small shoulder guards or, more commonly, with solid plates that hung over the point of the shoulder.

The main factor that distinguished the *haramaki* from the *do-maru* was that the opening ran down the centre of the back rather than under the right arm. The gap was similarly protected with a separate narrow plate.

As warfare on foot became more common, the *ō-yoroi* was largely abandoned by the late 14th century in favour of higher-quality *do-maru* and *haramaki*, worn together with a helmet and limb defences. Armour became more refined, with smaller scales and lacing often done in stripes or blocks of different colours. The earlier fastening methods employed leather or cotton, but these were replaced by silk cords. A large, ornamental cord bow was secured to the back of the armour, serving as an attachment point for cords connected to the *sode*, preventing them from shifting during movement. A smaller version of this cord bow was attached to a ring on the back of the helmet, originally to accommodate a streamer-like badge, and added a decorative element.

Thigh armour (*haidate*) in the form of a split apron of scales, appeared in the mid-13th century. It was slow to catch on but would eventually become the dominant form.

Foot soldiers were primarily equipped with the *naginata*, the long-handled spear with a curved blade, while cavalry relied heavily on the bow. However, the samurai sword was gaining prominence as mounted warriors increasingly dismounted for combat. This shift from swift cavalry engagements supported by foot archers towards more entrenched, infantry-focused battles elevated the importance of the foot soldier. While shin guards (*suneate*) were standard for mounted warriors, foot soldiers typically wore only cloth leggings.

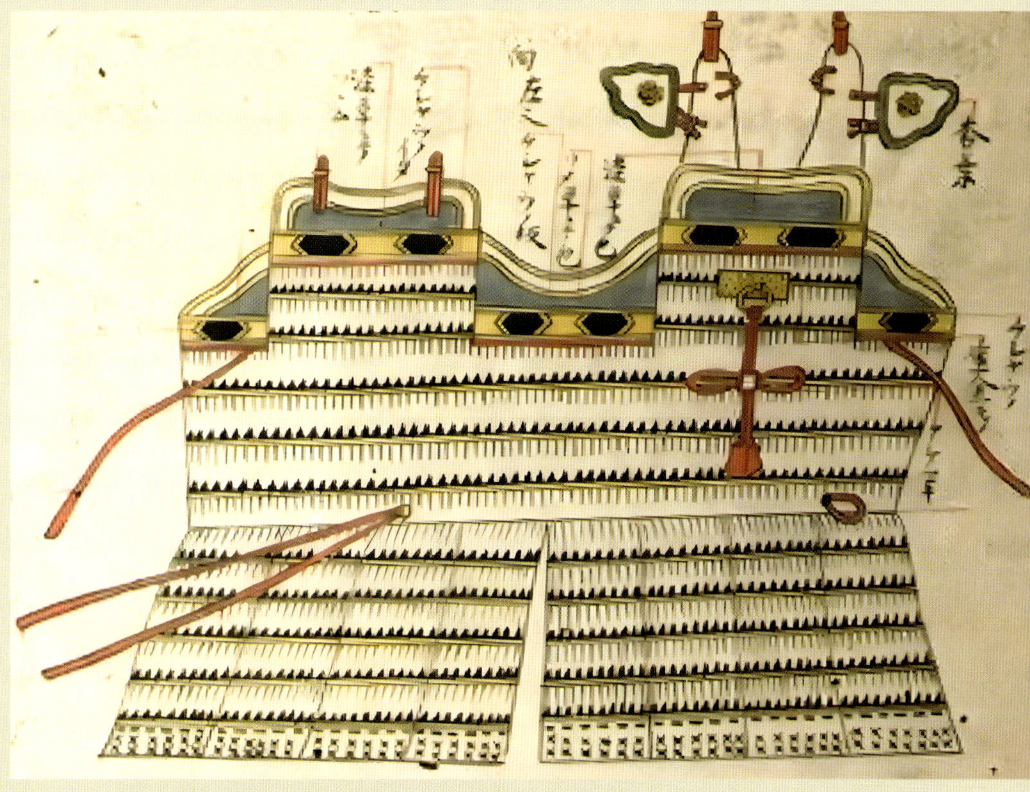

Right: Illustrations from an antique book on armour showing *haramaki* construction.

CHAPTER 4

The Muromachi Period

Emperor Go-Daigo's reign and his determined attempts to restore imperial power were crucial in shaping the course of Japanese history. His bold endeavour to reclaim power from the Kamakura Shōgunate and fully re-establish imperial rule ensured his land would be caught in the grip of turmoil, political intrigue and warfare. This situation of transition from rule by courtiers to rule by warriors or its inverse reached its climax in the Kenmu Restoration of 1333–1336 and the ensuing 'War of the Dynasties' that lasted from 1336 to 1392.

On 8 April 1333, Emperor Go-Diago escaped from his island of exile. One of the women of the court was due to deliver a child and, as was the tradition, in celebration large quantities of sake were consumed by all – including the emperor's guards. When the time came to remove the pregnant woman to where she was to be sequestered, a palanquin was called and she was placed inside. Alongside her, however, was the emperor, who managed to evade the drunken troops watching over him. After spending the night resting in the village, at daybreak the emperor and a small group of retainers set out on foot for the nearest seaport and embarked on a fishing boat. After a five-day voyage, the emperor made landfall in Katami, in Hoki province, where he was welcomed by the lord, Nawa Nagataka. It is recorded that on the first stage of his journey to a safe residence in the mountains the emperor had to be carried on the back of Nawa Nagataka's brother, Nagashige, no other form of conveyance being available.

Emperor Go-Daigo established Hoki as his primary stronghold in the initial stages of his rebellion against the Kamakura Shōgunate. Soon many loyal samurai, including Kusunoki Masashige, flocked to the Imperial cause and rebelled against the shōgunate. Masashige had been a vassal of the bakufu but had supported Go-Daigo in his earlier rebellion. Within a month of the emperor's exile, Masashige raised troops and openly carried out anti-bakufu actions.

Emperor Go-Daigo's renewed challenge to the shōgunal authority highlighted the Hōjō's inability to hold the allegiance of some of their most powerful vassals. There had been growing dissatisfaction with Hōjō authority and severe strains in the warrior society. This was because of the continuing Mongol invasion threat and the financial burden imposed by defending against it. Added to this was the fragmentation of main and branch samurai families and the exclusion of many vassals from the inner circles of power around the Shōgunal Regent. To deal with the rapidly worsening situation, the bakufu dispatched a massive army into central Japan to put down the insurgency.

The bakufu army co-commanded by Ashikaga Takauji initially cooperated with allied forces in engaging the imperial sympathizers in the provinces west of the capital. But when Takauji's co-commander was killed in battle and he was left in sole charge of the army, he used the situation to his advantage by switching his allegiance to the deposed emperor. This betrayal was a devastating blow to the Hōjō, as Takauji's high status as a member of the Minamoto bloodline was all the excuse needed for many disgruntled *shugo* to abandon the Hōjō.

Left: Emperor Go-Daigo escaping from his captivity on Oki Island dressed as a lady ready to give birth.

With Takauji's forces reinforcing the existing imperial samurai supporters, Kyoto was captured. Many bakufu survivors fled and around 500 committed ritual suicide (*seppuku*).

At the same time, Nitta Yoshisada, another eastern lord, rebelled against the shōgunate back in the Kantō Region and began bringing the battle to bakufu loyalists in Kamakura. Within just a couple of days he had beaten them in several key engagements, as the Hōjō and their close retainers struggled desperately to hold the city. After a day of street-to-street fighting, it became clear that the anti-bakufu forces had won the day. Hōjō Takatoki and his family members and closest associates gathered in the Temple of Toelsho-ji on the northeast side of the city and, when they realized that all hope was lost, set fire to the temple and died as the flames engulfed the building around them.

Above: Ashikaga Takauji (1305–58).

Left: Nitta Yoshisada allied himself with the emperor and raised an army to fight the Hōjō clan. As they marched on the Hōjō stronghold in Kamakura, they found themselves trapped on a narrow stretch of sand, between high cliffs and Hōjō boats full of archers. Yoshisada prayed to the gods of the sea and cast his sword into the water to show his sincerity.

The Samurai Who Cut Off His Own Head

Nitta Yoshisada was daimyō of the Nitta Clan, a group whose support of the restoration of the Emperor Go-Daigo was crucial in destroying the Kamakura Shōgunate that governed Japan from 1192 until 1333.

Left: Nitta Yoshisada dies in the Battle of Fujishima in Echizen, from the *Chronicles of the Great Peace* (the Taiheiki), an 1884 print.

In 1336, dissatisfied with the way that the government was being run, Ashikaga Takauji established his own military government in Kyoto. He named himself as shōgun and seized power from Go-Daigo, effectively overthrowing the Kenmu Restoration. He established the Ashikaga Shōgunate, which marked the beginning of the 'Northern and Southern Courts' period.

Emperor Go-Daigo gave Yoshisada the imperial banner and ordered him to pursue Takauji and his followers. After some months of inconclusive fighting, on 17 August Nitta Yoshisada led his army to engage in battle with shōgunate forces on the Ashuba River. As it crossed the river, the horse of the samurai responsible for holding the imperial banner stumbled and unseated its rider, who dropped his standard into the water. This may have been an omen.

After crossing the river, Yoshisada led his personal mounted samurai in support of a cohort of warrior monks attacking Kuromaru, the 'Black Fortress' of Shiba Takatsune, the local *shugo* who supported the rebels, in what would come to be known as the Battle of Fujishima. When the warrior monks were bribed to change sides, the engagement turned in favour of Yoshisada's enemies and he was forced to break off the attack, during the course of which his forces were ambushed by around 300 archers as they withdrew. Fifty imperial mounted samurai were killed or wounded and Yoshisada himself was pinned under his own horse, which had been felled by an arrow. Unable to move, Yoshisada was an easy target for the enemy archers and was blinded by an arrow to the forehead. He knew that all was lost and decided to commit *seppuku*. He could not reach his abdomen, however, so instead put his sword against his neck and drew it hard across his throat. On hearing of Yoshisada's death, three of his retainers, Nakano Munemasa, Yuki Chiki and Kanamochi Shigenoki, also took their own lives. The rest of his cavalry rushed into the enemy formation and were killed by the superior force.

After the news of Yoshisada's suicide spread, his troops fled and this army's defeat resulted in the end of the imperial restoration and the complete rise to power of the Ashikaga family, which would dominate Japan until 1573.

The story of Yoshisada's end, as chronicled in the 14th-century historical epic *Taiheiki*, says that, 'the brave warrior then took his short sword and used it to cut off his own head'. Practically speaking, he would probably have slit his own throat rather than remove his own head. Yoshisada's head was sent to Kyoto, where it was said to have been hung inside a prison containing some of his captured samurai, who were thus forced to contemplate their leader's fate.

Japan's first warrior government, the Kamakura Shōgunate, had truly gone up in smoke. On the surface, at least. What had been destroyed was the Hōjō clan and its direct retainers. The majority of the *shugo* in the provinces had already by then abandoned the Hōjō cause.

Ashikaga Takauji, who had moved his allegiance from the bakufu to fight for the emperor, played a key role in Emperor Go-Daigo's successful campaign to dismantle the Kamakura Shogunate and return political power to the imperial court and then initiated the relocation of the capital from Kamakura to Kyoto, so restoring his authority. This action was known as the Kenmu Restoration. However, the reforms he initiated alienated many of his major supporters by

Opposite: The Battle of Minatogawa by Utagawa Yoshitora *c.*1848. Battle of the Minatogawa (1336) between the Ashikaga clan and forces loyal to the exiled Emperor Go-Daigo led by Kusunoki Masashige. Under fluttering banners and fringed standards, the samurai are brandishing swords and spears. Note the vast array of heraldry both with the troops and also on the sails of the ships.

Right: The legendary samurai Kusunoki Masashige greeting the arrival of the Emperor in the Imperial carriage. At the Battle of Minatogawa, Kusunoki led his men into the field on the emperor's orders, knowing that his side faced superior forces and almost certain death. Badly defeated, Kusunoki and his remaining men committed *seppuku*.

The Statue of Kusunoki Masashige (1294–1336)

Standing in the Kokyo Gaien National Garden, across from the Imperial Palace in Tokyo, is a bronze statue of a samurai mounted, armoured and reining in his spirited horse, expressing all the idealistic views associated with his warrior class.

Visitors from all over the world stop to admire the statue which, including its plinth, stands almost 8m (26ft) high.

He is Kusunoki Masashige, a samurai who lived toward the end of the Kamakura period and is celebrated for his unswerving loyalty to the Emperor Go-Daigo.

Everything about the work is richly detailed, from the determined expression on the samurai's face to the taut sinews of the splendid horse. An image of this statue once graced a Japanese banknote. Overlooking Nijubashi Bridge, a sightseeing spot, this is one of the most famous statues in Japan. Professor Chitora Kawasaki of Tokyo Fine Arts School was responsible for ensuring historical accuracy of the armour. He visited temples and shrines associated with Kusunoki Masashige, researched items said to have once belonged to him and completed the design of the armour. There was also a debate about the breed and type of horse. Seeking advice from equine specialists, it was decided to depict an idealized Japanese horse embodying the traits of the best horses from around the country. Painstaking research was undertaken to ensure the historical accuracy of Kusunoki Masashige's attire, weaponry and tack.

In 1331, the emperor escaped from exile after his plan to

Below: The statue of Kusunoki Masashige was erected near Nijubashi Bridge in 1900.

Right: The Tachi sword of Kusunoki Masashige, known as Little Dragon Kagemitsu (Koryū Kagemitsu).

overthrow the Kamakura Shōgunate was discovered. Kusunoki was one of the first to pledge his loyalty to the emperor and advised him that the main thing needed to unite the provinces was to rely on military power and strategic cunning.

Kusunoki went back to his home north of Kyoto, where he built a simple castle on top of a mountain and, with around 5,000 troops, made his stand. The shōgunate thought they could finish this little rebellion in a few short hours. However, it turned out to be not that easy to defeat Kusunoki, whose battle tactics were rather unconventional.

The reported 300,000 warriors of the opposing forces looking at Kusunoki's fortress saw an unimpressive structure and assumed it contained an insignificant enemy. The attacking samurai, eager to claim victory, jumped off their horses and ran forward toward the wooden fences.

In the castle, Kusunoki had 200 well trained archers, and on the mountain nearby were stationed 300 mounted samurai. The attackers were unaware of these defenders and in their haste to take the castle failed to take cover. In no time at all, at least 1,000 shōgunate troops lay dead or wounded under a hail of arrows. Then, Kusunoki's cavalry silently advanced through the forest, its banners showing chrysanthemums on the water waving silently in the wind. The shōgunate samurai saw them but thought they were their own troops. The horsemen then cried out the charge and crashed into the rear of the shōgunate forces, forcing them to flee in terror and confusion.

Having lost this battle, the shōgunate samurai decided to lay siege to the fortress, believing Kusunoki's men would soon be starved out. Ultimately, however, it took 100 days for the siege to end.

Kusunoki's tactical brilliance and the tenacious defence of his castle convinced Ashikaga Takauji, a general sent by the shōgunate, to change sides and this helped the emperor regain power. With the ending of the Kamakura Shōgunate, the rule from the Imperial Court was reinstated. However, the new regime soon became unpopular and Ashikaga pleaded with the emperor to do something before rebellion broke out. But his warnings were ignored and he turned on the emperor once more, leading an army against him.

Emperor Go-Daigo insisted that Kusunoki and the remaining loyalists take on Takauji's superior forces in battle. Kusunoki, in what would later be viewed as the ultimate act of samurai loyalty, obediently accepted his emperor's unwise command and knowingly marched his army into almost certain death. Kusunoki's army was defeated and the emperor overthrown by Ashikaga Takauji, ushering in the Ashikaga Shōgunate in 1336. Takauji installed members of reliable branch families as constables in as many provinces as possible. By the end of the 14th century, of the 67 provincial appointments recorded, 42 were held by Ashikaga kinsmen. This split the imperial family into two opposing factions: the Ashikaga-backed Northern Court in Kyoto; and the Southern Court based in Yoshino, led by Go-Daigo and his successors. This double imperial court was immersed in conflict until 1392, with both the Yamato and Kyoto courts claiming power. It was not until the rule of Ashikaga Yoshimitsu as third shōgun from 1368–94 that true control was fully restored by the Northern Court.

Although Kusunoki's role in Japanese history only lasted from 1331–36, he remains one the country's most popular samurai because of his loyalty and devotion to Emperor Go-Daigo.

Above: The Great Army of Ashikaga Takauji under Akiuji Hosokawa is defeated by the small force of Kusunoki Masatsura by Utagawa Yoshitora.

reasserting the primacy of the court nobles over the warrior class.

Takauji, along with many other samurai across the country, became increasingly disillusioned with Emperor Go-Daigo's rule, citing concerns over favouritism towards certain individuals and excessive spending.

In the meantime, Takauji had been tasked with quelling the last vestiges of Hōjō resistance in Kamakura. He achieved this in just a few weeks, but rather than hand over the city to the emperor he instead assumed the title of shōgun. This enraged the emperor, who proclaimed him a rebel and entrusted Nitta Yoshisada with apprehending Takauji and his followers. Actions went well initially for the imperial troops, but when a large contingent of imperial samurai from Kyoto, led by Enya Takasada, changed sides during a battle to support Takauji, he was able to shatter his opponents.

After regrouping, Nitta Yoshisada's remnant army joined with the forces of another two imperial military leaders, Kusunoki Masashige and Nawa Nagatoshi, and attempted to intercept the Ashikaga forces by arraying their forces to the west of the mouth of the Minato River in Settsu province. However, Ashikaga Takauji outmanoeuvred them when he attacked his enemy from the front while his ally, Hosokawa Jozen, surprised them with a seaborne landing from the rear. The engagement, which took place near modern-day Kobe, was a tactical disaster. Apparently, a proposal by Kusunoki Masashige to his emperor that the imperial troops attack Takauji's forces from two sides was ignored. So too was a suggestion by Kusunoki that the emperor make peace with Takauji and bring him back into the imperial camp. Forced to fight on Takauji's terms, Kusunoki found his army completely surrounded. Just 50 of his 700 mounted samurai survived the battle and Kusunoki, choosing to die with honour, performed *seppuku*.

Takauji made the decision to expel Go-Daigo from Kyoto and then installed Emperor Kōmyō as the new ruler and subsequently established himself as the first shōgun of what would become known as the Muromachi Period (1336–1573) and the Ashikaga Shōgunate.

There was a temporary revival of the fortunes of Japan's Southern Court in the 1340s, with Kusunoki

Masashige's son, Kusunoki Masatsura, being a primary leader and serving the new emperor, Go-Murukami, who had come to power in 1339 aged 11. Emperor and general developed a trusting relationship, as their fathers had, but they were hampered by a lack of resources. For several years their primary focus was defending their base at Yoshino. In 1347, Masatsura led an attack on shōgunate sympathizers in Kii province and gained additional supporters. When the shōgun's Northern Court sent Hosokawa Akiuji to stop him, Masatsura met Hosokawa and defeated him at Sakainoura. After several more campaigns against the shōgunate, Masatsura was killed at the age of 22 in 1348 at the Battle of Shijo Nawate.

This action was portrayed by the artist Kuniyoshi, in two different paintings, with the Kusunoki samurai dying in a hail of arrows. Masashige's grandson, Kusunoki Masakatsu continued the family tradition of supporting the Southern Court but was defeated in 1392 when Chihaya Castle fell and he fled to Totsukawa in Yoshino.

The final ascendancy of the Northern Court over its southern rival began in 1390, when Ashikaga Yoshimitsu foresaw trouble arising with the powerful Yamana clan. The Yamana clan, claiming descendance from Minamoto no Yoshishige and so from the rulers of the first shōgunate. At its peak, they held the position of Constable (*shugo*) in eleven provinces. With the advice and assistance of Hosokawa Yoriyuki, Yoshimitsu organized the Ashikaga forces into a high state of readiness.

At the end of 1391, Yamana Ujikiyo and Yamana Mitsuyuki took the field against the Muromachi bakufu under the Southern Court's imperial standard, made of a gold brocade, so giving them a legitimate cause to attack Kyoto in what was known as the Meitoku

Below: The final stand of the Kusunoki heroes with a fierce and gruesome impact in this scene that certainly feels like a nightmare. Drawn from the Taiheiki (Chronicle of the Great Peace), the 1348 battle at Shijo Nawate marked the last attempt of the Southern Court to overthrow the Northern court. Though wildly outnumbered, the Southern warriors fought to the bitter end. The artist, Utagawa Kuniyoshi focuses on three brothers of the Kusunoki clan: Wada Genshu takes the lead, followed by his younger brother Wada Shinbei Masatomo, and finally, their leader Kusunoki Masatsura. Both of these interpretations by Kuniyoshi. As the leader of the Southern forces leans against a slain horse and uses a human body for cover, the horror of the battle becomes unmistakable.

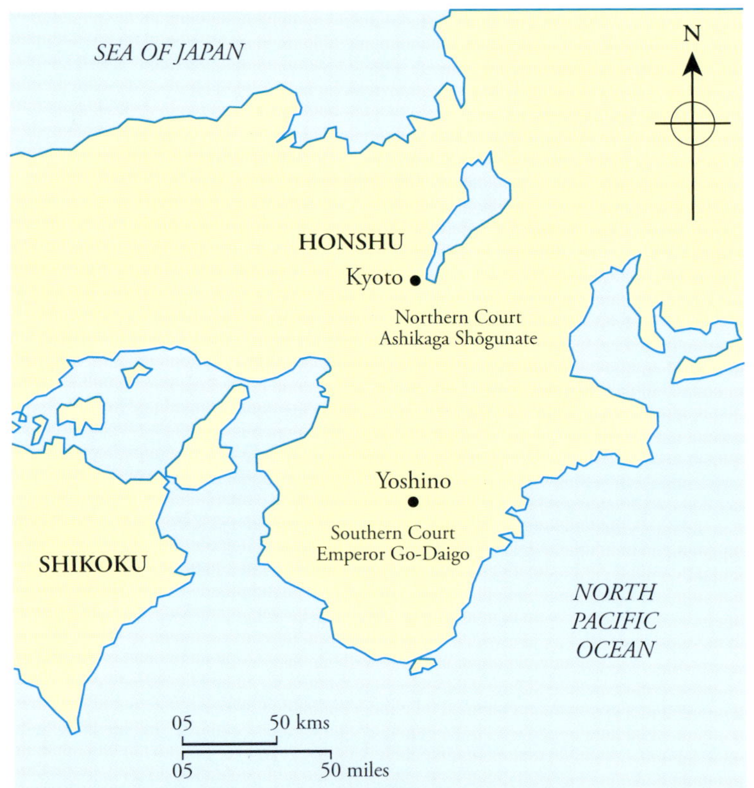

Rebellion. The Northern Court's army consisted of more than 5,000 mounted samurai of the Hosokawa, Hatakeyama and Kyogoku clans. In the fierce fighting, the Yamana leader was killed and his army completely routed. Thus, the Yamana clan was defeated in one day of battle. It was reported that there were 260 deaths from the Northern Court's forces and 879 deaths from the Yamana army.

Within a few months, the War of the Two Dynasties came to a close. The event that marked its end was the surrender to the Northern Court's

Left: Two imperial courts existed in Japan for over 50 years: the Southern and Northern courts. They fought many battles against each other. The Northern court usually was in a more advantageous position; nevertheless, the South succeeded in capturing Kyoto several times for short time periods resulting in the destruction of the capital on a regular basis. The Southern court finally gave in in 1392, and the country became emperor-wise reunited again.

forces of the important Kawachi Chihaya Castle in 1392, which had been built by Kusunoki Masashige and which, during the 60 years of conflict between Yamato and Kyoto, had remained unconquered. Having emerged victorious from the war, Yoshimitsu imposed the authority of his Northern Court over the rest of the country, despite his promises to share power with the Southern Court. He also empowered regional constables, laying the groundwork for the powerful daimyō. A complex power balance subsequently emerged between the shōgunate and these regional warlords.

Following Yoshimitsu's rule, the shōgunate's authority declined steadily as powerful daimyō and regional warlords consolidated their power, undermining central control. The shōguns never commanded a private army that could hold its own against the strongest of their major vassals, let alone against a combination of constables. The Ashikaga family became symbolic rulers, with real power held by the Deputy Shōgun, a position that rotated through each of the three main clans, the Hosokawa, the Shiba and the Hatakeyama.

Above: Kusunoki Masashige before the Battle at Minato River.

Opposite: The shōgunate's forces attacking Kusunoki Masashige's Chihaya Castle.

The Colour of War – Samurai Lacing

Samurai armour is more than just protective garb. It's a symbol of status, a reflection of personality and a canvas of rich symbolism. One of the most intriguing aspects of this armour is its colour. The choice of which was steeped in mythology, symbolic meaning and sometimes practical considerations.

Below: Coloured lacing on Tachi-dō Gusoku armour.

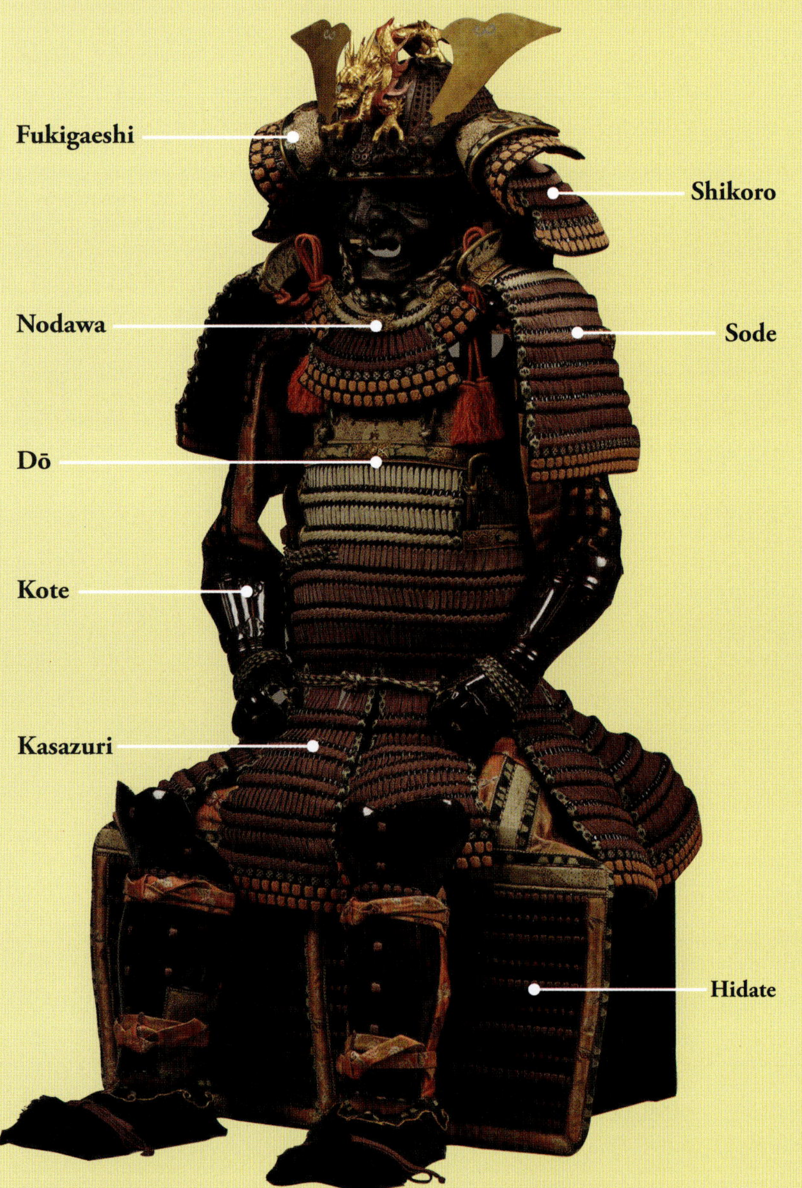

The distinctive appearance of the armour is defined by its lacquered metal components and colourful cords.

Lacquering, a specialized craft performed by skilled artisans, was an essential step in samurai armour production. *Urushi*, a type of Japanese lacquer renowned for its beauty, was commonly used for the armour's metal parts and created a lustrous finish after many specially applied coatings (although it was prone to scratches and fingerprints). Black and red were popular colours due to their rich, glossy finish. Other colours, which took more time to prepare, were lustrous brown, bronze or gold. These tones were achieved with the application of additional layers or metallic dusts over the base colour.

A distinctive feature of samurai armour is the coloured bindings that hold its various components together. The cords, known as *odoshi*, were traditionally crafted from silk, hemp, cotton or tanned deer skin and served both protective and aesthetic purposes.

Plant-based dyes provided the cords with a range of colours, often in contrast to the lacquer of the armour. The colours used varied, with dark blue, white, green, orange, pale blue and purple being common for silk ties. However, the use of the dyes could damage the material structure of the silk fibres used in the lacing, leading to its decomposition.

Left: Red and blue laced suit of armour from the Kii Tokugawa Family.

Surprisingly, the colour which suffers most over time is black. While red was a popular choice, dark blue was the most common colour for samurai armour lacing. Indigo-dyed lacing offered superior resistance to ultraviolet rays. Unlike some European heraldic practices, samurai did not associate specific colours with virtues or family allegiances.

Here are some possible colour interpretations, though it's important to note that these are not definitive and can vary depending on the specific historical context, the individual warrior and cultural nuances. The choice of cord colours was often a personal expression and could reflect a warrior's unique personality and beliefs.

Red: Often associated with courage, bravery and passion. It is the most used colour in existing national treasure armour. It might symbolize a warrior's determination and fierce spirit.

White: Representing a strong determination of will. It could suggest a warrior's commitment to a noble cause or a desire for harmony.

Green: Could symbolize strong vitality and hope. It was a favourite colour for young warriors during their first campaign. It might reflect a warrior's optimism and resilience.

Black: Often associated with strength and power. It could symbolize a warrior's unwavering determination.

Dark Sky Blue: May represent loyalty, trust and stability. A lucky colour, it could suggest a warrior's commitment to their lord or clan.

Below: Jidai Matsuri, the Festival of the Ages. A popular highlight of the festival is the afternoon parade of costumes when hundreds of participants dressed as samurai take to the streets.

Above: Example of 14th-century *ōsode* with white and pale earth coloured *odoshi*.

Indigo Dark Blue: Indigo dyeing has antibacterial and insect-repellent properties, making it a colour that wards off evil. Some national treasure armours still exist in this colour.

Purple: Historically associated with royalty and nobility, purple might symbolize high status and authority.

Individual sets of armour often featured intricate designs combining different colours and patterns. In reality, all parts of the armour had to have the same lacing pattern, whether it was an *ōsode* pattern or a *kusazuri* pattern. However, on the *do-maru* and *haramaki-do* armour, their *ōsode* could have one pattern, which was also repeated on the chest and back. On the *kusazuri* plates there could be a different one; most often, the darkest colour of the stripes on the *ōsode* was used.

The symbolism associated with different cord colours in samurai armour is complex and often debated. While there is no universally agreed-upon interpretation, certain colours may have carried specific connotations or suggestions based on cultural and historical context.

Some warrior families displayed a preference for certain colours. For example, the Fujiwara clan favoured green, while the Taira clan preferred purple. Many samurai also opted for multi-coloured lacing, known as *iro-irō odoshi*, which is very complex and striking, with the colour of each new woven stripe different from the one preceding it. This practice spread from the 12th century. *Susgo-odoshi* was a style where, starting from the upper white stripe and moving down, each line was darker than the previous one; very often, a yellow stripe was placed between the upper white colour and the darker colours at the bottom. If the light stripes were at the bottom and the dark ones were at the top, this style was known as *nioi-odoshi*. Both of these types of weaving were popular during the Genpei War Period.

A few more types of patterns:

Koshitori-odoshi: Where the cords of a different colour were placed at the bottom.

Dan-odoshi: Where the stripes alternated.

Katami-gawari-odoshi: A variant of *iro-irō odoshi* weaving, in which the colour of the stripe in the middle was replaced by another. The term literally means 'replacement of half of the body'. This type of weaving was very popular during the Muromachi era (1336–1573).

Saga-omodaka-odoshi: A form of chevrons that angle upwards.

Omodaka-odoshi: Another form of chevrons that angle downwards. Along with *saga-omodaka-odoshi*, it was a rarely used style.

Tsumadori-odoshi: A half-corner chevron pattern often used in the early Muromachi era.

Shikime-odoshi: Checkerboard weaving.

Tatewaka-odoshi: With the weaving lines in waves.

Fushinawa-me-odoshi: The zigzag pattern on the cords was popular during the Nanbokuchō period (1336–1392), the period of the southern and northern courts.

Family *mon*: The lacing could also depict the *kamon* (family crest) of the owner of the armour. For example, the depiction of the Japanese swastika *manju* (facing left) distinguished the Tsugaru clan, which dominated northern Japan.

The sixth Ashikaga shōgun, Yoshinori, came to office in 1428, having been elected from several suitable candidates. He belonged to a different category of men from his immediate predecessors.

He had attended a Buddhist school at the age of ten becoming a monk and became head of the Tendai sect in 1419. Yoshinori's shōgunate was to be defined by his aggressive pursuit of centralized power. He wasted no time in strengthening the shōgunate and his personal authority through various means including the authority of the Deputy Shōgun. Military reforms, including placing public security directly under his control, bolstered his military strength. He actively intervened in the affairs of shrines and temples and brought the troublesome Kyūshū region under control by installing the experienced Ouchi Mochiyo, a battle-hardened henchman, as military administrator. A major campaign against the consistently rebellious Kamakura prefecture further demonstrated his resolve. To ensure complete submission from the daimyō and elevate the shōgun's authority, Yoshinori resorted to a brutal reign of terror, systematically eliminating anyone who challenged his power, regardless of their status – from direct daimyō vassals and government officials to members of the court and imperial family.

He crushed the uprising of the military monks on Mount Hiei, put an end finally to Kamakura's intrigues, obtained control of the west and quelled his enemies in all directions. It was not all plain sailing for Yoshinori. He was notorious for his oppressive measures and unpredictable dictates, both of which made him powerful enemies. These included the over-strong sub-clans and branch families of the Ashikaga clan, and the Akamatsu family, with whom he incited a dispute over the allocation of High Constable positions in several provinces. The Akamatsu family was a descendant clan of the Minamoto, founded by Akamatsu Norimura in 1336 after he allied with Ashikaga Takauji to fight the Kamakura Shogunate. They were one of only four families who were eligible to head the Samurai *Dokoro*, a department given the leadership of the shōgun's retainers (*gokenin*), and to be in charge of the imprisonment of criminals during the Muromachi Shogunate.

However, even with this cruel reign of terror, it seems that it was already too much, and in the end, a cruel and miserable end waited for Yoshinori. In 1441, Yoshinori returned from a military campaign and was invited to a celebratory feast at the Kyoto residence of Akamatsu Mitsusuke. But, in the middle of the banquet, a number of horses suddenly burst from their stables and caused great confusion among the party. Mitsusuke had arranged this noisy diversion, and in the course of the pandemonium that followed he had Yoshinori struck down. With the shōgun dead, Mitsusuke and 700 of his Akamatsu followers rode off to their castle stronghold in Harima and called for revolution. This failed to transpire, and back in Kyoto the emperor ordered the bakufu to punish the Akamatsu. After three days, a coalition of 50,000 warriors that included fighters drawn from important *shugo* daimyō families including the Yamana, Hosokawa, and Hatakeyama defeated and killed Mitsusuke in battle and took his castle.

Although the Ashikaga line continued after Yoshinori's assassination, his death marked the beginning of a decline in the power of the shōgunate. The mere fact that assassination and treason had become a reality served to undercut the ethic of loyalty previously embodied by the warrior class. It was a precursor of the challenges to come.

Below: Ashikaga Yoshinori.

Armour of the Muromachi period
1336–1573

A surprising number of samurai armours from this period have survived due to the tradition of daimyō offering them to Shinto shrines in the Nara region.

Below: *Ō-yoroi* armour of Ashikaga Takauji, 14th century.

These ornate *ō-yoroi* armours, characterized by intricate lacing and decoration, epitomize the opulence of the early Muromachi period, predating 1400. The lacework exhibited an astonishing diversity of patterns and colours, each with its own distinctive name. Shoulder guards were often adorned with wave, triangular or family crest motifs.

Initially, lower-ranking samurai adopted both *do-maru* and *haramaki*-style cuirasses. The *do-maru*'s lighter weight made it a preferred choice, even among some higher-ranking samurai, who often wore it under their outer garments like an armoured vest. Early *do-maru* designs featured an open back, but this was later reinforced with a scaled plate similar in width to a *kusazuri* skirt panel.

The widespread adoption of *do-maru* and *haramaki* armour by samurai warriors coincided with the emergence of a new helmet style: the large, riveted and ridged *kabuto*. Initially, these helmets retained the low, rounded profile of their predecessors, but by the 1400s they evolved into a wider, slightly taller shape. Interestingly, the majority of *ō-yoroi* armour continued to utilize the traditional raised rivet helmet style with minimal changes until around 1400.

Around the mid-1300s, full armour underwent significant enhancements. The introduction of the *menpo*, a face mask and a protective throat guard, addressed a critical vulnerability. Additionally, chain mail inserts were added to the *kote* (arm guards) to reinforce protection. By 1400, the use of paired sleeves had largely replaced the single left sleeve, reflecting a shift in combat tactics away from archery.

Right: A suji-kabuto helmet, in the shape of *akoda-nari*, a style fashionable in Muromachi period.

gear by salvaging pieces from fallen enemies. The tumultuous Ōnin War accelerated this shift toward simpler, more practical armour designs. Elaborate construction gave way to solid plates, and complex lacing patterns were replaced by a simpler, wider spacing system.

Polearms for both foot and horse became more common. The handle of the curved *naginata* was made longer and straight-bladed *su-yari* were reintroduced. A further breakaway from tradition was the arming of infantry with bows.

Left: This type of armour was popular during the Muromachi period. It is designed for ease of movement, thus making it ideal for fighting on foot. The cuirass closes under the right arm, while the *kusazuri*, the skirt-like part protecting the waist and thigh area, is divided into several smaller sections. This dazzling design must have stood out magnificently on the field of battle.

Below: Samurai armour in the style of the Muromachi period *c.*1384.

The devastating Ōnin War (1467–77) radically transformed both warfare and military equipment. Increased foot combat necessitated the development of lighter shin guards incorporating mail and splints. Additionally, this period saw the emergence of thigh armour, a divided fabric apron secured around the waist and thighs, with scaled protection for the lower portion.

Late Muromachi period cuirasses featured smaller shoulder guards compared to earlier designs. The *do-maru* often incorporated a convex shoulder guard with a protruding cap plate, while the *haramaki*-style cuirass utilized long, convex shoulder pieces that closely fitted the shoulder and upper arm.

To bolster their armies, daimyō began recruiting *ashigaru* from the peasantry rather than the samurai class. Initially, many of these foot soldiers lacked proper armour, relying on spears and swords as their primary weapons. However, they often improvised protective

CHAPTER 5

The Age of Warring States

By the middle of the 15th century tensions were rising in the Ashikaga shōgunate. The daimyōs were growing increasingly powerful and were determined to further their own power. After the assassination of Yoshinori, issues continued to plague the regime. In 1467, the shōgunate was further damaged when the eighth shōgun, Ashikaga Yoshimasa, adopted his younger brother Yoshimi as his named successor. Yoshimasa was considering retirement and had no children, so this move was specifically aimed at preserving his family's rule. This backfired the following year, however, when he fathered a son, Yoshihisa. Yoshimi was immediately disinherited and this began a feud that evolved into the Ōnin War that lasted until 1477. This was the beginning of the era known as the Sengoku Jidai*, or the Warring States period.*

The Kamakura government of Ashikaga Yoshimasa had eased traditional control in Japanese society, resulting in the formation of new classes and new wealth. While the shōgunate's elite jockeyed for power in Kyoto, provincial magnates were consolidating their resources and increasingly defying central authority. Into this melting pot of family pride, disagreements and land possession came the controversy of who was to be the successor of Shōgun Yoshimasa.

As the significant families continued to extend their powers over their assigned provinces, they found the backing of the shōgunate advantageous and even necessary. At the same time, the bakufu grew in national influence to the point that it could strongly request most daimyō to take up residence in the shōgun's capital of Kyoto. With some exceptions, including the 11 Kyūshū provinces supervised by the deputy-shōgun, all the daimyō controlling provinces built official residences in Kyoto during this period. Since as many as seven daimyō were from more than two provinces, the number of daimyō residing in Kyoto was at most 21 or 22. Though not required to do so, Kyūshū daimyō, such as Shimazu Motohisa and Ōtomo Chikayo, built mansions in Kyoto, enabling them to have closer relations with the bakufu.

As the prime symbol of new wealth and status in the capital's society, the shōgun often called upon the daimyō to contribute large sums of money to finance special celebrations or repair palaces and religious structures. In addition to such contributions, the daimyō were also expected to finance the lavish entertainments expected for when the shōgun would occasionally call on them at their mansions. It is reasonable to conclude that daimyō who could survive such onerous financial burdens must have been men of considerable wealth.

Each of the daimyō was accompanied by a full retinue of vassals, relatives, household servants and others, amounting to several hundred persons. The shōgun freely availed himself of the manpower which the daimyō brought with them. When Yoshinori undertook the renovation of the shōgun's Muromachi residence, he commanded various daimyō to supply, among other things, quantities of large rocks needed for the garden. It is recorded that the labour force contributed by the Hosokawa house amounted to 3,000 men, and by the Akamatsu house 2,800 men. To return to one's province without the express permission of the shōgun was regarded as a rebellious act tantamount to treason. This regulation, which seems to have been established during the last years of Yoshimitsu's rule, was strictly enforced by his successors. In most cases, the primary reason for a daimyō's eagerness to return to the provinces was the desire to ensure his control over, and especially the flow of income from, his territories.

Opposite: Daimyō's samurai retinue procession travelling from their home province to Kyoto at Hakone by Lake Aiwa.

However, the shōgun did not consider this a legitimate excuse for wanting to leave the capital.

Some of these tensions between the shōgun and the daimyō came to a head in the Ōnin War that broke out following a succession dispute in 1467. This erupted when the childless eighth shōgun, Ashikaga Yoshimasa, adopted his younger brother Yoshimi as his named successor – and then dropped him when his wife Hino Tomiko unexpectedly presented him with a son and heir, Yoshihisha. Hino Tomiko came from a politically ambitious family, so it came as no surprise that the court was intensely divided by Yoshihisha's birth. One faction wanted Yoshimi to remain as his brother's heir, while another group favoured Yoshihisha's claim. Yoshimasa was ambivalent. He naturally wanted his son to succeed him, but he intensely disliked his wife's family and did not want them to wield too much power.

Hosokawa Katsumoto, one of the three vice-shōguns (*kanrei*) appointed by Yoshimasa, supported the shōgun's brother as successor – and this gave Hosokawa's father-in-law Yamana Sōzen an opportunity to resurrect his own personal animosity toward his daughter's husband. Yamana had a number of family and financial grievances against Hosokawa, so he sided with Hino Tomiko in advancing her son's claim on the succession. As tensions grew, Yamana and Hosokawa stationed troops close to Kyoto. The shōgun, meanwhile, interpreted this as an act of rebellion by both sides and mobilized his supporters to try to stop it.

The simmering hostility between the Hosokawa and Yamana clans escalated into open conflict in late spring 1467, when Hosokawa forces attacked a mansion belonging to one of Yamana's key retainers. Despite Shōgun Yoshimasa's attempts to mediate, the fighting raged for days, igniting a conflict that would devastate Kyoto. The fighting was primarily at close quarters, with the great rival Kyoto families calling in their supporters from the countryside. In the following weeks and months, people began to evacuate the city as the violence escalated. In the first stage of what would become known as the Ōnin War, the Hosokawa forces (the Eastern Army), numbering some 160,000 men drawn from 24 provinces, fought against the Yamana forces (the Western army), who mustered about 90,000 men from 20 provinces. In September, however, the powerful clan leader Ōuchi

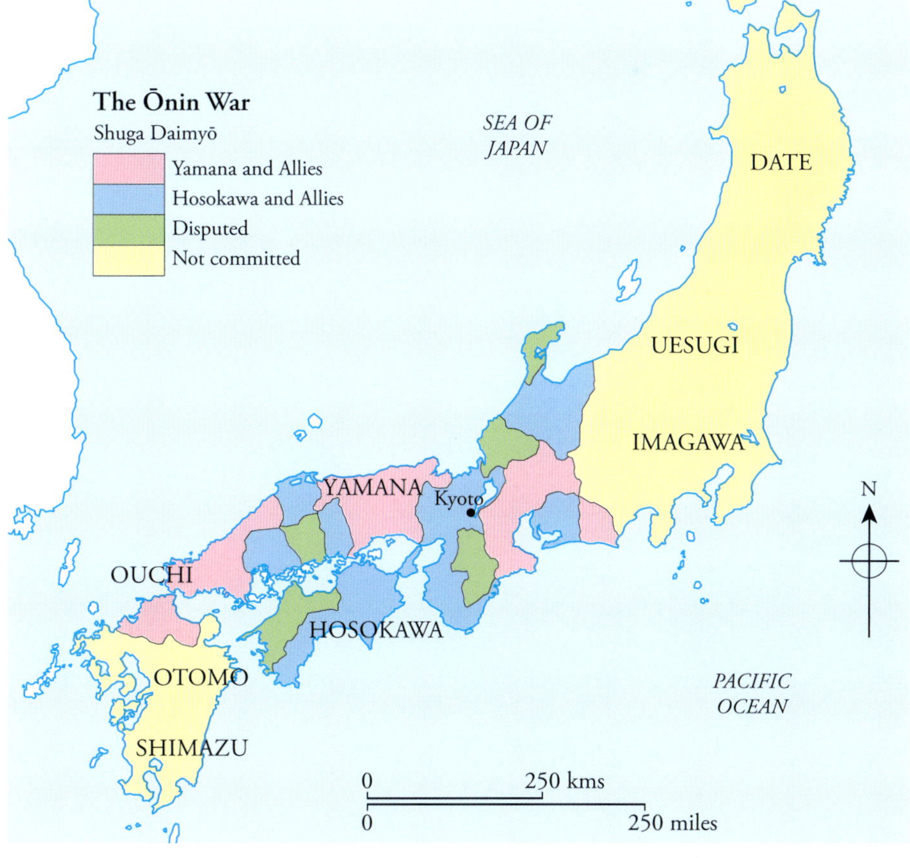

Right: The major players in the Ōnin War. The Yamana (Western Army) and the Hosokawa (Eastern Army).

Yasuhiro's 20,000-strong force joined the Western Army, turning the tide in its favour and allowing Yamana's men to surround the Hosokawa army in Kyoto. Later, however, a counter-force marched up to the capital to redress the balance, joining the Eastern Army and breaking the encirclement.

The fighting was initially confined to the city itself. During the first three months, much of northern Kyoto was reduced to ashes and rubble. Trenches had been dug in the city streets, watch towers built and barriers erected to prevent movement. These are all symptoms of what today are known as military operations in urban terrain (MOUT). Hosokawa forces controlled the main bakufu buildings, plus the clan's own mansion. The Yamana held territory to the south and west and controlled seven of Kyoto's eight gates, by which they hoped to starve the Hosokawa into submission. But this time, however, the fighting had extended beyond Kyoto. With the breakdown of all central authority, the Ōnin War unfurled throughout much of Japan.

The shōgun played little part in the fighting. Instead, he warned that whichever family had started the violence would be declared outlaws and then remained in his residence, enjoying the pleasures of life. In early July 1467, he emerged to officially declare Yamana Sōzen and his supporters rebels. This was a politically expedient move, as the Hosokawa clan had clearly instigated hostilities in Kyoto. Yoshimasa charged his brother Yoshimi with subduing the rebels and appointed Hosokawa Katsumoto as his commanding general.

Shōgun Yoshimasa's declaration of Yamana Sōzen as a rebel alienated some of his supporters. Simultaneously, the Hosokawa provoked unrest in Yamana's domains, forcing him to divert troops there for defensive purposes. Intense hostilities persisted until 1468, culminating in a protracted military occupation that left Kyoto in ruins. While open warfare in the capital subsided after that, political manoeuvring and proxy conflicts continued to plague the shōgunate. Fierce fighting persisted in the provinces, where powerful daimyō vied for control. In a dramatic turn of events, Yoshimi unexpectedly assumed command of the Yamana forces, transforming the conflict into a broader power struggle that pitted the shōgun against his own brother.

Large numbers of peasants were recruited as foot-soldiers (*ashigaru*), and bands of outlaws and displaced samurai (*rōnin*) preyed on whatever and whoever they could. It became increasingly difficult to follow any rational pattern in the campaigns, and in the end there was no clear-cut winner. Both Yamana Sōzen and Hosokawa Katsumoto died in 1473, and even then the fighting continued. With neither side able to figure out how to end the war, the complex array of factional armies simply fought themselves to exhaustion.

The Yamana clan's fortunes waned as the stigma of rebellion took its toll. Their general, Ōuchi Masahiro, eventually resorted to burning his own section of

Right: A photograph taken by the English photographer, John Paine, during his tour of the Far East in 1884–86 showing a mock battle in full armour of the late Muromachi Period.

Kyoto before retreating. After a decade of devastation, the capital was a lawless wasteland. Neither the Yamana nor the Hosokawa achieved their objectives beyond decimating their opponents. The conflict, far from contained, spread throughout Japan, leaving no corner untouched by its violence.

To extend its influence beyond its headquarters at Kamakura, the first shōgunate had become reliant on its network of constables and provincial commanders selected from among its *shugo* vassals. This had allowed it to maintain a degree of authority within the existing framework of imperial provincial governance. The Ashikaga Shōgunate, by contrast, operated differently. By consolidating their martial power with the authority previously held by provincial constables, daimyō under the Ashikaga were effectively transformed into regional military governors. The combined powers of the shōgun and the daimyō constituted a system that resembled a national government. Even though the Ashikaga Shōgunate dealt with a higher volume and a more complex range of administrative, legal and military transactions than the Kamakura Shōgunate, neither the shōgun nor the daimyō acquired the executive powers required to assert the authority they claimed. Ashikaga dominance depended critically upon the support of vassal houses and much less on its capacity to maintain a private armed force. The balance of political-military power on which the Ashikaga house rested its rule was weakened because many daimyō were as powerful as the Ashikaga house itself. The shōguns never commanded a private army that could hold its own against the strongest of their major vassals, let alone against a combination of powerful daimyō.

Opposite: Two scenes from the *Onin War Scroll* (1661), illustrating the fierce fighting between the two opposing sides of the Hosokawa and Yamana troops. It shows early trench warfare in Kyoto with barriers for urban fighting.

This era and the Sengoku period (1467–1568) that followed, were marked by intense political instability. This situation resembled a turbulent vat of sake, where the fermenting bubbles rise to the top to burst or merge together, forming a crust and an ever-changing surface. Clans rose and fell, forming alliances and splitting

apart. There are far too many ups and downs to chart in detail here, so what follows is just a simple outline of the main events of the era.

The Kantō is a region in central Japan where all the great daimyō of the warring states period (hereafter known as the Sengoku-daimyō) had their origin and where most of the 'action' took place. The region was formed of eight provinces – Sagami, Musashi, Kosuke, Shimotsuke, Kazusa, Shimosa, Awa and Hitachi. The Kantō Plain, often referred to as Japan's 'Rice Basket', comprises slightly more than 45 per cent of the region. The remaining land is composed of hilly and mountainous terrain that forms the area's natural boundaries. To travel from central Japan's Kantō region to Kyoto would mean travelling by one of two available routes through the mountains. The route to the north was mountainous and hazardous, the more popular was the coastal road to the south known as the Tōkaidō. These mountain ranges and the difficulty in traversing them formed a natural barrier between the Eastern Provinces and Edo and those of the West where Kyoto and Ōsaka are located.

In the struggle for the shōgunate between the Kamakura and the Kyoto branches of the Ashikaga clan, Ashikaga Shigeugi, after being deposed and driven out of Kamakura by Ashikaga Yoshimasa, escaped to Koga in Shimosa province and became known as Koga kubō, a position similar to that of a kind of local shōgun. He ruled there until he died in 1497, when Yoshimasa sent his younger brother, Masatomo, to rule in the Kantō. His two senior retainers were from the two powerful Uesugi families. These Uesugi families soon engaged in a hostile and long-running rivalry (see Chapter 6), becoming entangled with the succession of Masamoto's two sons.

Towards the end of its rule, the Ashikaga family held the daimyō territories of Mikawa and Kazusa and estates in the provinces of Shimotsuke, Kazusa, Sagami, Mikawa and Tamba. For its military forces, it could count on many branch families from those provinces. In Takauji's generation, the families included such names as the Hatakeyama, Niki, Hosokawa, Kira, Imagawa, Togashi, Isshiki, Shibukawa and the Shiba. Many other warrior families allied themselves with the Ashikaga in their struggle for dominance. However, in chaos and warfare, no allegiance can be guaranteed.

In 1485, out in the provinces, the farmers, whose tax burdens, food shortages and other sufferings were aggravated by the war, had had enough, as had the lesser poor samurai. They revolted against their provincial governors – sometimes while these were absent on campaign, but not always. Setting up their own armies (*ikki*), they forced clan armies out of their areas. The *ikki* became a powerful force, much more than simply an armed mob. In an extreme case in 1485 in Yamashiro province, south of Kyoto, the united farmers and ji-samurai (local sheriffs) presented an ultimatum to the warring local commanders from two branches of the Hatakeyama family, forcing both to withdraw from the province and setting up a provisional government which ruled Yamashiro for ten years.

Similarly, in 1488 in Kaga province, northeast of Kyoto, Buddhist *ikkō* monks allied themselves with Shinto priests, local nobles, disaffected farmers, merchants and peasants in what was called the *Ikkō-ikki* movement and successfully revolted against the province's lord. They established an independence that would last until the 1580s, when it was finally crushed by the nation's unifiers.

During the ten years of the Ōnin War, the authority of the shōgun was destroyed; the title still had useful

Left: The Kantō region.

Above: The battle of Azukiazaka, 1564, between Tokugawa Ieyasu and Ikkō-ikki rebels.

prestige, however, for those who needed a pretext for war, as had long been the case with the emperor. The war ground to an end in 1477. Hosokawa Katsumoto, one of the originators of the war, died, but his clan triumphed. The Western army, now led by Ochi Masahiro, left Kyoto. The emperor became a mere figurehead, controlled by a shōgun who wielded little actual power. Real authority rested with the Hosokawa clan, whose deputies effectively governed the nation. Actual authority in the land, then, was two steps removed from the throne. While the Hosokawa had gained control of the shōgun, the war had deprived the government of much of its power.

Several great clans had been wiped out during the war. The Yamana, Isshiki and Hatakeyama all disappeared. Other clans, such as the Takeda, Uesugi, Imagawa, Shimazu and Saitō, rose to take their place. Having seized power through force, they were not hesitant to employ violence again to maintain their dominance. Other powerful clans would not emerge for some time. There was to be no end of war; the chaos and disruption which it had sparked continued seamlessly throughout the so-called 'age of the warring states', or *Sengoku Jidai.* This period continued for well over a century and saw the locally based military class come to dominate at the expense of the imperial court. The force of arms took precedence over political ties. It was a period of revolt against the status quo, known as *gekokujo*, or 'the lower topple the higher'.

An example of this in action can be seen in the case of Asakura Toshikage, a lower-ranking retainer of the Shiba clan who had been allied to the Yamana during the Ōnin War. In 1471, Toshikage broke away from the Shiba and declared his support for the Hosokawa clan, creating his own Asakura clan and later defeating the Shiba and taking full control of Ichizen. However, a more famous and influential example of an early Sengoku-daimyō would be a samurai named Ise Shinkurō. In the late 1460s he was a low-ranking retainer of the Imagawa clan, a group that had previously been in the service of the Kamakura Shōgunate and was now allied to the Ashikaga Shōgunate, having enjoyed a prosperous rule over three provinces in south-central Honshu: Mikawa, Totomi, and Tsugura. Unfortunately, by 1480 the Imagawa clan was riven by a succession dispute between Imagawa Ujichika, the rightful heir to the clan, and his ambitious cousin, Oshika Norimitsu. Shinkurō sided with Ujichika and personally saw to the defeat of the upstart Norimitsu. In reward for his great service, Shinkurō was given control of Kokukuji Castle in Shizuoka province, with which he was able to guard the Imagawa clan's eastern borders. Some ten years later, when the neighbouring Izu province was also disrupted

by a succession crisis, Shinkurō invaded the region and claimed it for himself. Soon, Shinkurō used his control of Izu and Shizuoka to establish his independence as a ruling daimyō. In 1495, wanting to expand his power further, he took his army into the Uesugi-controlled Sagami province, laying siege to and then capturing Odawara Castle from the Omōri clan.

The capture of Odawara Castle significantly bolstered Shinkurō's ability to conquer Sagami province, which he fully controlled by 1560. Subsequent campaigns led to the fall of Kamakura, the former shōgunal capital, in 1512, followed by the capture of Arai Castle in 1518. This castle, on the Miura Peninsula, was controlled by Miura Yoshiatsu, whose son, Yoshimoto, believing defeat to be inevitable, killed himself by chopping off his own head. The siege of Arai was among the first steps taken by Shinkurō toward becoming one of the most powerful daimyō of the Sengoku period. Shinkurō would die in 1519, having established a powerful legacy as a brilliant commander – but not having fulfilled his ambition to be declared a shōgun. Once a *rōnin*, he would die the head of his own mighty clan, one which would continue its conquests and expansion following his death. His son, Ujitsuna, would give the clan a formidable new name, changing it from Ise to Hōjō. He also posthumously renamed his father Hōjō Soun, the first true Sengoku-daimyō.

However, at the same time as Shinkurō/Hōjō Soun was making his conquests in the east, several clans began contending for their own regional power in the west. By 1500, western Japan was ablaze with rivalries between clans, the two main powers being the Ōuchi and the Ōtomo, who had frequently come into conflict with one another following the end of the Ōnin War. The Ōuchi gained prominence from accumulating great wealth through trade with Korea and China, which funnelled through the important port of Yamaguchi, which they controlled, and which was often referred to as the Kyoto of the West. The Ōtomo, on the other hand, had amassed their power over hundreds of years, being the clan that primarily defended Kyūshū from

Below: Ise Shinkurō laying siege to Odawara Castle within view of sacred Mt. Fuji. Postcard published *c.*1930 in a series depicting legends of Japanese history. Ise Shinkurō, a lowly samurai, went to Kyoto to serve under Shōgun Ashikaga Yoshimasa, and later joined forces with Imagawa Yoshitada under the command of Kakari Azuma, wielding wits and ingenuity and devising deceptive strategies. He finally succeeded in conquering Odawara Castle and made it the family seat for almost 100 years.

the Mongol invasions of the late 1200s. They had also become major supporters of the Ashikaga Shōgunate following the overthrow of the Kamakura Shōgunate.

After some years of conflict between the two clans, peace broke out between them. This enabled the Ōuchi to join with the western branch of the Takeda clan and march on Kyoto, restoring Ashikaga Yoshitane as shōgun and winning the position of Shōgunal Deputy for Ōuchi Yoshiyoki. The Hosokawa clan, who supported the disposed shōgun Ashikaga Yoshizumi, would continue their fight against the Ōuchi for the next few years, forcing Yoshiyoki to remain in the capital instead of returning home. Ōuchi Yoshiyoki scored a victory over the Hosokawa at the Battle of Funa-Okayama in 1511. The following year, the Ōuchi-Hosokawa conflict ended when Ashikaga Yoshizumi suddenly died, breaking the Hosokawa will to fight. In the years after the end of the fighting with Hosokawa there would be some semblance of peace and stability in central Japan. However, in his absence, a new unchecked threat began to rise in the west.

The Amago Family was a daimyō clan based in the far west of Honshu in Chūgoku Region. In 1392 Amago Mochihisa became the deputy military governor of Izumo Province with his grandson Tsunehisa extending the families power into Aki and Bingo Provinces fighting against the Mōri and Ōuchi families. The power grew considerably during the Ōnin War thanks to Tsunehisa who also conquered Izumo Province and Oki Island in 1486. When Ōuchi Yoshioki marched upon Kyoto in 1508 in support of Ashikaga Yoshitane, Amago Tsunehisa took advantage of Yoshioki's distraction and secretly communicated with daimyō all over the Chūgoku region to counter the powerful Ōuchi clan. He finally succeeded in controlling 11 provinces by the 1520s. In 1515, Takeda Motoshige, a daimyō of Aki Province, returned to Aki after supporting Ōuchi Yoshioki in Kyoto, and changed his allegiance to the Amago clan. Motoshige then raided the Mōri clan's territory and surrounded Arita Castle with an army of over 5000. At this time the Mōri clan (a vassal of the Ōuchi), were neighbours of the Takeda in Aki.

The Amago family, a daimyō clan based in the far west of Honshu began their ascent to power in 1392 with Amago Mochihisa's appointment as deputy military governor of Izumo Province. His grandson,

Above: Ashikaga Yoshitane.

Tsunehisa, played a major role in expanding the clan's influence, extending their reach into Aki and Bingo Provinces through conflicts with the powerful Mōri and Ōuchi families. The Ōnin War (1467–77) proved to be a turning point, providing Tsunehisa with the opportunity to solidify his control over Izumo Province and conquer Oki Island in 1486. A key moment in their rise occurred in 1508 when Ōuchi Yoshioki marched on Kyoto in support of Shōgun Ashikaga Yoshitane. Tsunehisa took advantage of Yoshioki's absence, secretly communicating with various daimyō throughout the Chūgoku region to form a coalition against the dominant Ōuchi clan.

In 1515, Takeda Motoshige, a daimyō of Aki Province who had previously supported Ōuchi Yoshioki in Kyoto, shifted his allegiance to the Amago, subsequently launching a raid on the Mōri clan's territory and besieging Arita Castle with a force of over 5,000 soldiers. At this time, the Mōri clan were vassals of the Ōuchi and neighbours of the Takeda in Aki. In response, the leader of the Mōri clan Mōri Motonari met the stronger Takeda forces at the Battle of Arita-Nakaide in 1517. Even faced with an overwhelming enemy, Motonari held strong and engaged the Takeda vanguard until the main bulk of its forces arrived, led

Swords of the Samurai

Below: Two samurai from the late 19th century. The figure on the left is wearing Okegawa-Do-Gusoku armour with a *tachi* sword. The figure on the right wears tosei-gusoku armour and carries a *no-dachi* and a katana in his belt.

For Japan's ancient warriors and early samurai, the main weapon was the bow and arrow. Swords were simply considered to be just another extra weapon alongside several others.

By the 11th century, however, the practice of sword making had been elevated to an art form, with flexible, hardened and tempered laminated blades available in a variety of styles. The early samurai, clad in *ō-yoroi* armour and on horseback, wore a long sword called a *tachi*, with blade downward and its sheath fastened to their belt with two straps.

In the 13th and 14th centuries, the large two-handed *no-dachi* sword became popular. It could reach a length of 2m (6ft 6in). Such swords were usually used by *ashigaru*, who fought in light armour that did not restrict movement. They were carried on a warrior's back in a scabbard or on the shoulder.

However, as mounted warfare was replaced by firearms and supported infantry, it was realized that a shorter, more practical sword was necessary for hand-to-hand combat. To fight at close quarters with a sword needed skill; this, in turn, gave rise to the cult of the sword, which became the basis for the reverence of the sword, the violation of which could only be washed away by blood. Gradually, the sword became 'the soul of the samurai'.

This shorter sword, katana, was carried with the blade facing up and tucked into the belt. This method

Right: Daisho.

Right: A katana from the late 15th or early 16th century.

of carrying made it possible to strike at the same time as drawing the sword from the scabbard, which was vital in fast-paced samurai duels. A second shorter sword, the *wakizashi*, was customarily paired with the katana in the belt. Both weapons together were known as *daisho*. One of the main purposes of the shorter sword was its use in decapitating an opponent killed in battle. A third sword was sometimes carried. This was the *tanto*, the short-bladed knife-like weapon without a sword guard that was used in the samurai self-immolation ritual of *seppuku*.

From the end of the 16th century, the exclusive right to carry a katana, or the *daisho* pair, became a privilege of the samurai class. With the end of the civil wars, swords gradually lost their combat significance, but the tradition of carrying two swords continued to be a samurai class symbol. A samurai only parted with their swords when etiquette required, during an audience with the shōgun or the senior samurai, for example, when the weapons were handed over to servants. At home, a samurai's swords were placed on a special stand made of varnished wood in an alcove in the main room. In 1876, centuries of tradition came to an end when a law was passed that prohibited the wearing of swords, not just for the samurai but for all Japanese.

In terms of quality, it is believed that the best Japanese swords were those made around the Edo period (1603–1867).

by the western Takeda daimyō, Takeda Motoshige. They faced off on opposite banks of the Matauchi River, with the Takeda pressing the attacks against the much smaller Mōri army. Despite being outnumbered, Motonari initiated an aggressive assault. He divided his forces, sending half his army across the river while a smaller detachment executed a flanking manoeuvre against the Takeda position.

The Takeda army quickly pushed the Mōri samurai back to the river. In a turn of fortune, an overconfident Motoshige rode across the river to force his victory, only to be struck and killed by a Mōri arrow. This caused the Takeda army to panic, break and rout, resulting in a victory that paved the way for the rise of the Mōri clan. Motoshige's death led to the decline and destruction of the western Takeda clan. The Mōri would eventually become one of the most famous clans of the *Sengoku Jidai*. Coming from humble origins, Mōri Motonari would skilfully establish the Mōri clan as a rival power in the west.

Down in the far west, the Shimazu clan had ruled over the southern tip of Kyūshū for many years. By the mid-1400s, it was steadily expanding its supremacy, coming to dominate the provinces of Ōsumi and Hayuga in addition to the province of Satsuma. Its ultimate aim was to take over the complete control of Kyūshū. Once again, a succession dispute arose with the death of Shimazu Tatsuhisa in 1474. His son Shimazu Tadamasa assumed the role of clan head but could not unite the branches of the family. Great disarray ensued, spreading across all Shimazu-controlled territories in southern Kyūshū. In 1496, Tadamasa faced the rebellion of several of his vassals in Ōsumi, followed by the Kimotsuki clan in 1506 and the Ito clan taking Hayuga. With the Shimazu clan falling apart, Tadamasa committed *seppuku* in disgrace, the result of a combination of illness and his failure to suppress the Kimotsuki rebellion. This left the Shimazu with only Satsuma province.

Another clan that was now also beginning to fall apart was the once powerful Hosokawa. The first province it lost was Tosa on the island of Shikoku. There, the Ichijo clan, backed by the lesser Chosokobe and Motoyama clans, who were, in fact, also sometime rivals, removed all Hosokawa influence. This insurrection was followed by others and the Hosokawa continued to disintegrate.

Above: The Battle of Ōnin during the Ōnin War (1467–77) by Utagawa Yoshitora. Close, hand-to-hand fighting.

And so, the strong continued to fall to the lesser. At the beginning of the *Sengoku Jidai*, the Uesugi were ruling over Echigo, Kotsuke, Musashi and Sagami and were known to be one of the strongest allies of the Ashikaga Shōgunate. The clan was made up of several powerful branches, but following the Hōjō's triumph at Sagami, which brought to the fore the weakness of the clan, factions formed within the Uesugi and it splintered. However, the Uesugi would not wholly fade away. Instead, it evolved into three separate yet allied groups.

But not everything was falling apart during the civil wars. The economy flourished with the mass movement of troops being posted to distant areas, and the building of castles stimulated rather than hindered the circulation of goods. Moreover, as the military class became increasingly removed from actual involvement in local production, merchants and artisans were given new opportunities for commercial activity. Kyoto came to enjoy a faster pace of economic activity as it once again became the seat of government, and the samurai warrior class joined the nobility and the priesthood as members of a consuming elite.

The style of warfare changed over this period, through the introduction of units of *ashigaru,* which were lightly armed and lightly armoured foot soldiers. The employment of these troops had been notable during the street fighting in Kyoto. The *ashigaru* were deployed to attack the enemy's weak points or supply routes. They lacked entirely the samurai's pride in individual combat, were easily persuaded to change sides, and had no scruples about looting and burning temples and aristocratic houses. During the long and costly civil war, all armies relied largely on *ashigaru*, since military commanders were anxious to keep their main samurai forces intact. The foot soldier's weapons and armour were at first far from uniform. Although the *ashigaru* were initially recruited simply for wages, their connection with their employers became closer as time passed. They were incorporated into the daimyō's family forces as regular soldiers and would later be supplied with uniform weapons and armour.

By 1524, Hōjō Ujitsuna, having consolidated the move of the Hōjō capital to Odawara Castle and restructuring its defences and fortification, continued his expansion into the Kantō region. His interest at this time was on the fertile agricultural area dominated by Uesugi Tomooki, who ruled the area from Edo Castle in the centre of the Kantō plain. Having been prewarned of the threat from the Hōjō, Tomooki planned to meet his enemy's forces as they crossed the Takanawa River. Unfortunately, in these times, intelligence flowed easily both ways, and Ujitsuna was made aware of the Tomooki's plans. He circled his men around the Uesugi force and attacked it in the rear. The Uesugi was forced to fall back on Edo, but they discovered that the vassal charged with defending the castle, Ōta Suketada, had

changed sides and joined the Hōjō. This treacherous act forced Tomooki to continue his retreat into the Uesugi-held Mushashi province.

The continuing expansion of Hōjō conquests caused great concern within the region's clans and encouraged an ally of the Uesugi, the Satomi clan of the Awa province, to launch a retaliatory operation. A plan was concocted to hit the Hōjō where it was least expected and to cause maximum disarray by marching on Kamakura, the old capital of the shōgunate. Satomi Sanetaka, leading the Satomi forces, duly attacked the city, surprising the Hōjō and burning and looting freely. But this had little effect on Ujitsuna, who simply continued his invasion of the Kantō region.

The adjacent area to the west of the Kantō was Kai province. The Takeda clan had held it for some 300 years, and since 1507 it had been under the control of Takeda Nobutora. An ambitious daimyō, from the 1520s onwards he had engaged in periodic conflicts with the Hōjō and the Imagawa to the south and a few Shinano daimyō in the north. In 1531, a grouping of clans from Shinano formed an anti-Nobutora alliance that included the Suwa, the Imai and the Hiraga. It marched on the Takeda, but Nobutora was able to repel and defeat it.

A few years later, Kai province was attacked by another coalition, this time comprising two large and powerful clans, the Hōjō and the Imagawa. They formed a pact to invade the Takeda lands, which may have been successful had the Hōjō samurai not been forced to leave the fray and return to their own province to deal with Uesugi Tomooki, who had, in turn, invaded Hōjō lands when he noticed that its army was away. This then left the Takeda to fight the Imagawa in an inconclusive conflict that ended when the Imagawa broke off their invasion on the death of their daimyō, Imagawa Ujiteru, in 1535.

November 1536 saw Takeda Nobutura move again into Shinano province. On this occasion, he marched against Hiraga Genshin in Un-no-Kucchi Castle, taking with him his 15-year-old son, Takeda Harunobu. Nobutura was forced to retreat after a 34-day siege and the approach of winter, but Harunobu turned back with his rearguard troops and, taking the garrison by surprise, captured the castle.

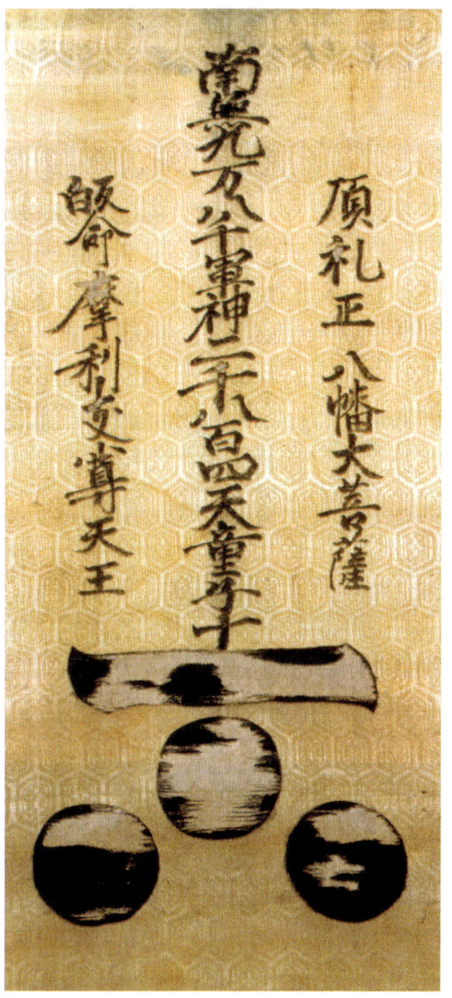

Left: The Battle Standard of Mōri Motonari.

Below: Modern re-enactors dressed as *ashigaru*.

This was the first major victory for Harunobu, who would later take the name Takeda Shingen and become one of the country's greatest daimyō.

The Hōjō clan was actively pursuing expansion, with Hōjō Ujitsuna increasing its power and maintaining its stability. A chance to strike at their enemy, the Uesugi, came when, in 1537, Uesugi Tomooki died. Taking advantage of the clan's weakened state, Ujitsuna attacked the Uesugi castle of Kawagoe. The castle quickly fell and Hōjō forces came to hold much of the power in Musashi province.

While the Hōjō clan was engaged in conflict with the Imagawa in 1538, Satomi Yoshitaka seized the opportunity to expand his clan's territory into Edo and Musashi province. Together with allies of the Ashikaga clan under Ashikaga Yoshiaki, the Satomi marched into the Musashi Plains. Being made aware of this action, Hōjō Ujitsuna quickly rounded up what troops he could from Izu and Sagami and marched from Odawara for Edo, leading an army of 20,000.

Above: Odawara Castle. A modern rebuild of the main keep.

Below: *Honmaru Goten*, the inner palace building of Kawagoe Castle and the only building to have survived to the modern day. The castle fell to Hōjō forces in 1537.

Yoshiaki was advised to attack the Hōjō before they crossed the Tonegawa River. However, he failed to take the advice and waited for them to approach him near Konodai Castle. As the battle was in full swing, a second wave of Ashikaga samurai under Ashikaga Motoyori, Yoshiaki's brother, and his son Yoshizumi, joined the battle along with the Satomi. The attack was a failure, and the Hōjō soon surrounded their enemies. The battle was hard fought. It destroyed the Ashikaga samurai and forced the Satomi to retreat. Angered by this failed attack, which resulted in the death of his son and his brother, Ashikaga Yoshiaki led a fierce counterattack that almost broke the Hōjō until an arrow pierced his chest armour, knocking him from his horse to the ground to be overwhelmed. With the Ashikaga beaten, Ujitsuna drove the Satomi forces back to Awa province to submit to Hōjō authority.

East-central Honshu was now in an almost constant state of war and major conflict as the larger clans continued to further their ambitions. The two branches of the Uesugi had come together in 1545 in the presence of the Hōjō menace, and a forceful coalition including the Imagawa and the Ashikaga of Koga had been formed to attack the Hōjō and regain Kawagoe Castle for the Uesugi. However, this group of allies hesitated in view of Odawara's might, which gave Ujitsuna time to prepare. When at length, they moved to the attack with 80,000 men and laid siege to the castle, Ujitsuna's son Ujiyasu, leading a relief force of 8,000 soldiers, slipped some samurai past the enemy lines and made use of ninjas to learn of his opponent's strategy and attitude. Using this intelligence, he led a night raid against the combined Uesugi forces, with his samurai instructed not to wear armour, travel light and not take trophy heads. The Uesugi were soundly beaten in one of the most notable examples of night fighting in samurai history. Hōjō Ujiyasu, at the head of a force a mere one-tenth that of the samurai of the Uesugi, inflicted a defeat which settled the supremacy of the Kantō.

Left: Hōjō Ujiyasu.

Ujitsuna had little time to contemplate on his victories and future plans when death overtook him in 1543. The headship of the family passed to Ujiyasu, who pushed west into Suruga, stood against the Kai in the north and threatened the Uesugi in the east. He was to become a still more extraordinary leader. The name of Hōjō Ujiyasu is enshrined in the hearts of the samurai. He combined, to an extraordinary degree, gentleness and bravery, magnanimity, resolution, learning and martial spirit. It was commonly said that from the age of 16 he had scarcely removed his armour, never once showed his back to a foe and had received nine wounds, all in the front. Before he died in 1570, he had the satisfaction of establishing a double link between the Hōjō and the house of the great samurai, Takeda Shingen, a son and a daughter from each family marrying a daughter and a son of the other.

The Taking of Heads

The severed heads of the defeated enemy, cleaned, combed and labelled with a name tag, are brought in front of the seated and victorious daimyō and presented as trophies of war....

This, like many other Japanese customs, was one that migrated from China in the earliest days of the Yamato Dynasty and came to the forefront with the samurai in the 10th century. In these early years, combat was seen as more of a noble and individual endeavour, where two samurai would single each other out on the battlefield and engage in a duel. To verify the defeat, the victor would exhibit the defeated foe's head to his lord.

An early record of this came in 939, when Taira Masakado led an attack on an outpost of the central government and captured the governor. He then continued his rebellion against the emperor, conquering further provinces and claiming to be the new emperor. The Kyoto government put a bounty on the rebel's head and when he was killed at the Battle of Kojima in 940 his head was taken and displayed to Emperor Suzaku in the capital.

And so it was that the taking of heads in battle was a way in which a samurai could distinguish himself and prove that he had done his duty. Once an enemy was defeated, he was decapitated. It was the responsibility of the samurai who took the head to

Below: Maeda Toshiie at the Battle of Okehazama collecting heads of his victims. He was to become one of Oda Nobunaga's leading generals.

Opposite: A formal head-viewing ceremony presided over by Hideyoshi, who is seated on a camp stool and surrounded by his retainers. A kneeling samurai holds each severed head up for inspection by Hideyoshi, who holds a fan in front of his face by custom so that the dead will not recognize him. The heads of slain enemy soldiers were collected by those who killed them so that they could claim recognition and reward. Prior to the ceremony, the heads were washed and made to look presentable; this was done by women of the samurai class. This was a once-common scene during the many wars fought in Japan prior to the Edo period.

ensure presentability and women trained in the art of arranging the heads were employed to clean, perfume and mount the head on a wooden or lacquered plate. When possible, the more notable heads were displayed while still housed in their *kabuto* helmets.

The samurai lord conducting the head viewing ceremony would inspect a selection of senior-ranked samurai heads and, on being satisfied of the identity of the enemy, would release the gruesome trophies to be either buried in the temples or returned to their families. Often captured enemy were made to identify the heads of their fallen comrades.

The taker of the head would be rewarded with gifts of wealth, praise or be given new rank, title, status and land within the daimyō's clan. Lower-ranked samurai heads would be displayed in bulk, tied by strings through the hair and around the head, and hung together on ropes and rails. Any bald heads, or those offering little to tie cords to, were pierced from just above the ear to the forehead, through which a string could be threaded for display.

The warriors of the Sengoku period at times announced their achievements in battle by raising high the heads of enemies they had defeated on the battlefield. Mounted samurai hung trophy heads from the left side of the saddle before bringing them back to the base camp.

A head-based reward system was open for exploitation. Some samurai would say the head of an *ashigaru* was a great hero and hope it was not recognized; others, after taking a valuable head, would abandon the battle, believing they had already taken their trophy. At times, the situation deteriorated and daimyō would even prohibit the taking of heads so that their men would focus on victory instead of reward.

CHAPTER 6

The Arrival of the Portuguese and Firearms

Due to its proximity with Korea, Japan had long been familiar with gunpowder weaponry invented in neighbouring China and introduced in the 13th century during the first Mongol invasion. These devices used flaming spears or arrows as projectiles but were not often used. Then, in 1543, the Portuguese trader and explorer Antonio Mota in his chartered Chinese Junk was hit by a severe storm, resulting in the ship making landfall on an unknown island. Portuguese traders would flood into Japan over the next few decades, bringing with them firearms and Christianity – leading to significant changes in both society and warfare. The regional daimyōs sought to exploit this new technology to their advantage, and continued their unceasing conflicts against their rivals.

This island was Tanagashima, off the southern coast of Kyūshū, and in arriving on it, Mota became the first European to set foot in Japan. It was part of the Shimazu clan's domain and its local daimyō, Tanagashima Tokitaka, was intrigued by the hand-held weapons carried by the Portuguese. Tokitaka requested a demonstration of their firearms and instantly recognized the potential of the matchlock arquebuses. He purchased two of them and put a swordsmith to work in copying the matchlock barrel and firing mechanism. They were an excellent improvement over earlier firearms, some of which had been developed in the Ryukyu Kingdom on Okinawa more than 50 years earlier.

These weapons were given the name 'Tanagashima', in recognition of where the Portuguese had landed. In time, they would spread throughout Japan. And as more armourers turned into gunsmiths, the name of these weapons gradually shifted from Tanagashima to 'Teppo'. Teppo began to appear on the battlefield, although it would be another 30 years before they were introduced in a manner that profoundly changed the face of warfare in Japan.

The Japanese arquebus was powered by a smouldering wick that ignited the gunpowder. The wick, a cotton cord impregnated with saltpetre, was attached to a serpentine, an S-shaped lever, in the curved shank of which the mainspring rested. When the shooter pressed the trigger, the smouldering wick was lowered to the ignition port, which was closed with a tight copper cover to prevent accidents. A spare fuse was carried wrapped around the arm or wrapped around the belt, since about 2m (6ft 6in) of wick was required to use the gun multiple times.

Thanks to the traditional Japanese talent of imitation and improvement, several innovations were made that increased the combat capabilities of the new weapons. For example, the Japanese introduced the idea of making lacquered cases that closed the bolt so that the guns would stay dry when not in use. One of the important improvements, made as early as the 17th century, was the waterproof shield for the ignition port. However, much more important were the changes the Japanese made to the cartridges. At that time, these were carried by both European musketeers and Moscow riflemen in a sling over their shoulders with a predetermined supply of gunpowder. The cartridge itself was a small wooden cylinder lined with leather for waterproofing, with a

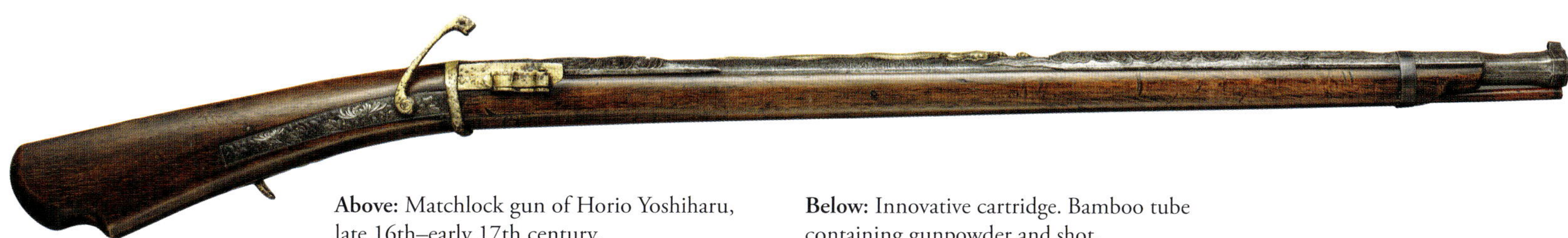

Above: Matchlock gun of Horio Yoshiharu, late 16th–early 17th century.

Below: Innovative cartridge. Bamboo tube containing gunpowder and shot.

tightly fitted hinged lid. The bullet and wad were in a separate bag, and the fine powder for the ignition hole was in a horn powder box. When loading, the powder was poured into the barrel from the cartridge, then the bullet and wad were taken out of the bag, all of which was sent to the barrel in turn.

The Japanese, however, were the first to produce the idea of combining powder and bullet in one cartridge, which certainly speaks of their amazing ingenuity. Outwardly, both the sling and the cartridges themselves looked like analogues of their European equivalents, but this is only at first glance. The fact is that the Japanese cartridge (or charger, as it was called by some) was drilled through, but its channel had the shape of a cone. Thanks to this, a bullet and then a wad were inserted into it from the wide upper end, which was closed with a lid, and then a wad, which advanced inside. Then, a charge of powder was poured into it, the lid was closed and the cartridge was ready for use.

Interestingly, the rate of fire of the large bow was significantly greater than that of any arquebus. In addition, the bow had another significant advantage: it did not require expensive gunpowder. Arrows for it could sometimes be used many times, but the main plus point was that they were produced in Japan, while good gunpowder had to be imported from Europe, usually England. But the penetrating power of firearms was much higher and made it possible to pierce any

Opposite: A 17th-century folding screen. In 1543 Portuguese sailors arrived in Tanegashima and introduced the arquebus.

Right: Exhibition of the Heki School Archery by Togo Shigemochi 1885. Illustates the laminated asymmetric long bow and the placing of the arrow on the right of the bow.

Above: Details of a Portuguese trader from a Namban screen. Known as the 'Southern Barbarians'.

enemy armour. Proof of this was given at the Battle of Nagashino in 1575, where the forces of two opposing daimyō lined up against each other. To counteract the devastating destructive power of his enemy Takeda Katsuyori's guns, the powerful warlord Oda Nobunaga lined up his archers and spearmen behind strong fortifications consisting of three rows of ditches, ramparts, and palisades.

But if Japan had 'discovered' Europeans and their weapons, Europe had now discovered Japan, and it was only a matter of time before the shores of Kyūshū would be visited by more 'southern barbarians', as the Japanese called them. Most of these incomers were Dutch, and they began arriving at ports such as Hirado and Nagasaki, increasing the local daimyōs' wealth through new trade and intensifying the destructiveness of war with the cannon they imported along with their arquebuses. Another import they brought with them was Christianity, introduced by the Spanish missionary Francis Xavier in 1549.

Yasuke: The African Samurai

In July 1579, the Portuguese priest Alessandro Valignano landed in Arima, on Kyūshū. He had previously been inspecting Jesuit missions in Goa, India, and arrived in Japan charged with the same task. Accompanying the prelate was his own personal bodyguard, an enslaved African named Yasuke.

It is not known from where Yasuke originated, or indeed if that was his proper name, but he had at some point in his life been sold by slave traders to a buyer in Goa. How Valignano came by him is also unclear, but he liked the young man and thought he would serve as a useful protector and valet in the strange new country they were visiting.

In Kyūshū, the arrival of the dark-skinned man together with the strangely clothed 'barbarians' caused great interest. At 1.9m (6ft 2in) tall, the muscular and striking Yasuke towered over most people in Japan, where the average height was around 1.6m (5ft 3in). Displaying his intelligence and a gift for language, over the next few months Yasuke quickly learned Japanese.

In March 1581, Yasuke accompanied Valignano on a trip from Kyūshū to the capital, Kyoto, where he was received by Oda Nobunaga. The powerful

daimyō was intrigued by the Japanese-speaking African and, when a short while later Valignano announced that he had to return to Goa, Nobunaga asked if he would leave his servant with him. The Jesuit, unwilling to insult his host, agreed. Yasuke was taken in by Nobunaga and given his freedom – and then appointed as the daimyō's weapon bearer and one of his bodyguards. This was a great honour and Yasuke worked hard to gain the trust of his new countrymen and learn samurai skills, while also becoming something of a permanent attraction at Nobunaga's court. In time he was gifted a *katana* sword and provided with a home in Azuchi castle and a stipend.

In March 1582, as a warrior in armour, Yasuke joined Nobunaga in combat, distinguishing himself at the Battle of Tenmokuzan against Takeda Katsuyori, the great rival of the Oda clan. Three months later, Yasuke once more joined Nobunaga on a campaign against the Mōri clan. While the main army marched off to fight, Nobunaga, Yasuke and 200 samurai and 29 trusted bodyguards based themselves at the Temple of Honno-Ji – the same place the two men had first met 15 months earlier. It was during this stopover that Akechi Mitsuhide, one of Nobunaga's generals, launched a rebellion. When he attacked the temple with an army of 13,000 men, setting it on fire and surrounding its perimeter, Nobunaga committed *seppuku.* Legend has it that his dying wish to Yasuke was that he prevent his enemy from taking his head.

In the aftermath of Nobunaga's death, Yasuke was captured after a fierce fight and made to stand before Akechi – who, perhaps surprisingly, spared his life and commanded that he be returned to the Jesuits. Yasuke disappears from history at this point, so his final fate is not known.

Historians argue that Yasuke was the first samurai of a non-Japanese heritage and he has been represented as such in modern fiction and video games. However, although he was recognized as an exceptional warrior, it is unlikely that he would have been accepted into the samurai class in such a short space of time. What is clear is that he was a valued and brave warrior who was much respected by Nobunaga and his peers.

Below: Japanese artwork illustrating the Portuguese visitors accompanied by their African servant, possibly Yasuke.

The Sengoku Daimyō

By the middle of the 16th century the provincial administrators and constables had been replaced by regional Sengoku-daimyō. A glance at their origins reveals that the majority of them had emerged from the lower levels of administrators or daimyō of smaller rural domains and had succeeded in replacing their former masters. No daimyō held more than a small fraction of the sum of domains within his province of assignment, and it cannot be thought that he held the province as a proprietary governor. On the contrary, the provinces controlled by the daimyō consisted of small scattered rural domains under the proprietorship of ji-samurai who regarded the land as their own and extracted dues from its cultivators.

Only in exceptional cases did family houses, such as the Ōuchi, transform themselves to Sengoku-daimyō status and they were the only daimyō of central Japan who survived the Ōnin War. This was because most inner circle daimyō, being constrained to reside in Kyoto and to rely on the bakufu for their authority, found themselves stranded after the Ōnin War when the shōgun's power declined. All other daimyō who successfully made the transition, such as the Shimazu and Ōtomo of Kyūshū, and the Imagawa and Takeda in the Kantō, were in peripheral areas and had not become involved in the politics of the bakufu.

Following the development of the Ōuchi beyond the Ōnin War illustrates how this family managed to hold on in Western Japan until it was forcibly removed by the Mōri. The family head, Ōuchi Norihiro,

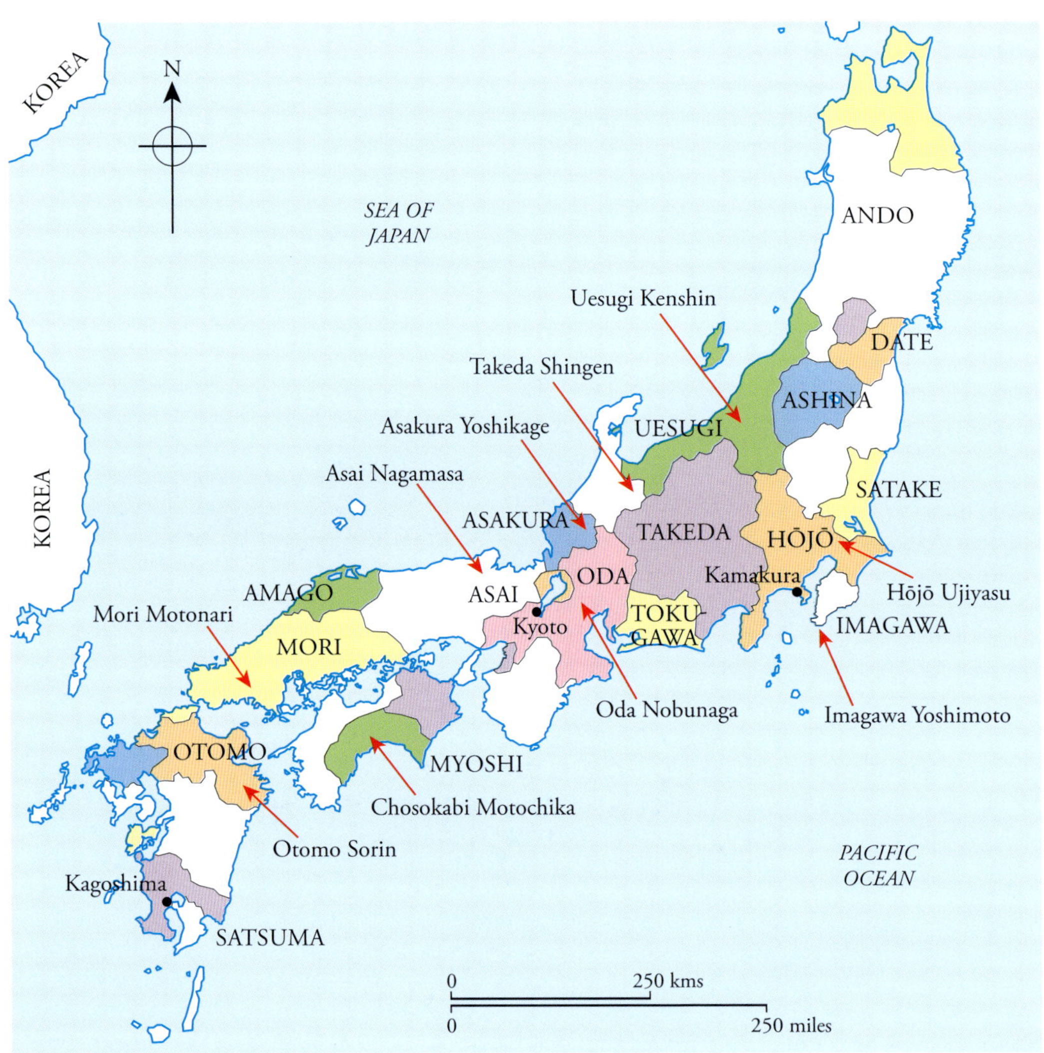

Left: Map illustrating the main Sengoku-daimyō territories and the key daimyō of the period.

frequently returned to his provincial base in Yamaguchi, with the approval of the shōgun, on the pretext of suppressing anti-bakufu rebellions in northern Kyūshū. He devoted his undivided attention to administering the Ōuchi territories, leaving his successor Masahiro a provincial structure that was already highly developed. This left Masahiro free to proceed to Kyoto after the outbreak of the Ōnin War and take leadership of the Western Army after the death of Yamana Mochitoyo.

In 1477, Masahiro finally returned to Yamaguchi, with regrets that he had stayed away so long. No sooner had Masahiro gone back to western Honshu than he launched a campaign to retake parts of northern Kyūshū, which had been seized while he was in Kyoto. By 1478 Masahiro's Kyūshū campaigns were bearing fruit. Lands confiscated from defeated daimyō or ji-samurai were granted to their supporters.

Although Masahiro temporarily neglected the Ōuchi's relations with the bakufu to concentrate on local administration, his successor Yoshioki actively participated in shōgunal affairs. Intervening on behalf of the deposed shōgun Ashikaga Yoshitane, he succeeded in regaining the position for him. In so doing Yoshioki gained for himself the position of deputy *kanrei*, and for the next 11 years he appeared as one of the central figures in Kyoto politics.

It was at this critical point that the Ōuchi's leadership faltered, when they were confronted with rebellious samurai in Aki and northern Kyūshū and peasant revolts within their own domains. Before Yoshioki could successfully pacify his territories, he was succeeded in 1528 by his son, Yoshitaka. Under Yoshitaka, the Ōuchi house pursued an aggressive military policy, fighting to retain control of its territories. But much of the fighting was left to the Ōuchi's vassals, while Yoshitaka himself occupied his time in cultural pursuits in Kyoto or Yamaguchi. As a result, Sue Harukata, an Ōuchi vassal who had done much of Yoshitaka's fighting, executed an insurrection in 1551 in which Yoshitaka was killed. The destruction of the Ōuchi house by the Sue plunged the former Ōuchi territories into a state of great uncertainty. But the Sue, having momentarily replaced the Ōuchi as masters of western Japan, were soon obliged to compete for this position with the Mōri of Aki.

Above: Takeda Harunobu (Shingen) – painted by Takeda Shingen's younger brother, Shoyoken Shinkanen who was a skilled painter.

The Takeda and the Uesugi

By 1540, three years before the arrival of the Portuguese, a major development would occur within the Takeda clan of Kai province. Takeda Harunobu took the field against his father, Takeda Nobutora, who had planned to disinherit him in favour of his younger brother. After his victory, Harunobu controlled the province of Kai, which had long been the seat of the Takeda family. He entered the priesthood in 1551, at which time he assumed the Buddhist name Shingen. Taking religious vows, however, in no way hampered his participation in worldly affairs. Takeda Shingen

Left: Nagao Kagetora (Uesugi Kenshin 1530–78). Here he is depicted on the eve of the Battle of Sado Island. Dressed in armour, he sits on a chair covered in deerskin and looks over his shoulder at a flock of birds in flight towards the horizon, towards the full moon.

would rank among the top six greatest warrior daimyō of the 16th century.

A further name on the top six list, Uesugi Kenshin, was not a member of the great Uesugi family which took such an important part in the affairs of the Kantō. He belonged instead to the Nagao clan. Kenshin, who was called in his youth Kagetora, found himself engaged in his twenty-first year in a contest with his elder brother, whom he killed. By way of penance, he took religious orders under the name of Kenshin and would have retired from the world had not his general insisted on his remaining in command. It was at this time that Kenshin became a member of the Uesugi clan.

Uesugi Kenshin had managed to gather for adversaries the two great daimyō of highest renown in his era, Hōjō Ujimasa and Takeda Shingen. Their feud had far-reaching effects, for Kenshin's ambition was to become master of the whole Kantō region. He attempted to achieve this under the pretence of re-establishing the original Uesugi, but his expansion southward from Echigo province was barred by Shingen in Shinano and Kai, while his expansion eastward was blocked by the Hōjō in Sagami and Musashi.

The site of the struggle between Shingen and Kenshin was Kawanakajima. There, the two Sengoku-daimyō, recognized as the two greatest strategists of their time, met five times between 1553 and 1561 in fierce and violent conflict. The two daimyō used similar battlefield tactical structures; the head of the army, consisting of arquebusiers, artillerymen and archers, was followed by companies of infantry armed with long spears. Then came the cavalry, and after them the main body, attached to which were drummers and conch-blowers. The whole army was divided into right and left wings, with a body of samurai kept in reserve. At the opening of the battle, the samurai horsemen dismounted and advanced on foot.

Victory was never claimed by either participant's banners. Peace was at length restored for a brief time in 1558. Kenshin had a desire to take back control of the Kantō region from the Hōjō. In 1560 he was able to go forward. Mustering an army said to have been 110,000 strong, he attacked the Hōjō in Odawara. The Uesugi breached the defences and burned the castle town. But Ujiyasu would not be tempted into the open and Kenshin had to withdraw after two months due to dwindling supplies and the imminent threat posed by Takeda Shingen's resurgence.

In September 1561, Kenshin left Kasugayama Castle with 13,000 warriors, determined to destroy Shingen. He left some of his forces at the Zenkoji Temple in Nagano province and took up a position on a mountain to the west of, and looking down upon, Shingen's Kaizu Castle (now Matsushiro Castle). Unbeknownst to Kenshin, the castle garrisoned a mere 150 samurai and their retainers, leaving them utterly unprepared for the Uesugi onslaught. However, the samurai general in command of the castle, Kosaka Masanobu, through a system of signal fires informed Takeda Shingen in his

fortified residence 130 km (80 miles) away in Kofu of Kenshin's moves.

Shingen left Kofu with 16,000 men, acquiring 4,000 more as he travelled through Shinano province, approaching Kawanakajima on the west bank of the Chikuma river and keeping the river between him and the hills. Shingen then camped on the west bank of the river near the Amenomiya ford. Kenshin's 13,000 troops camped on Mount Saijo, hoping to be able to fall on his enemy upon the latter's arrival. But with the river between them a stalemate ensued. To achieve victory, one side had to disrupt the other's plans through surprise tactics, throwing their opponent off balance.

Takeda Shingen moved first, quickly crossing the river beneath Kenshin's positions and moving his entire force – increased by reinforcements to 20,000 – into Kaizu Castle. Shingen's general, Yamamoto Kansuke, devised a plan to go around Mount Saigo, using 8,000 samurai under Kosaka Masanobu, and ambush the Uesugi army in camp, driving the remaining Uesugi samurai down onto the plain. However, Uesugi spies discovered movements in the Takeda castle at night and Uesugi Kenshin's samurai moved down the mountain to the plain, quietly using cloth covers on their horses' hooves to deaden the noise. Before dawn, the remaining Takeda samurai had moved from the castle and had taken positions on the Hachiman plain with Shingen's headquarters in the centre of the plain. As the sun rose and the morning mist dispersed, Shingen's men were surprised to find Kenshin's army ready to attack them. The Uesugi had successfully crossed the river, leaving a rearguard of 3,000 to protect the crossing, then charged the Takeda in waves. Kenshin's leading units were mounted samurai led by Kakizaki Kageie and they clashed with Takeda Nobushige's unit, resulting in the death of Nobushige. The Takeda main body held firm,

Below: Battle of Kawanakajima.

but the fierce rotating attacks by the Uesugi were taking their toll.

Seeing that his cunning plan had failed, Yamamoto Kansuke accepted responsibility for the disaster in true samurai fashion and charged into the enemy ranks. After a legendary fight, sustaining many wounds, he retired to a quite area and committed *seppuku*.

The Uesugi forces eventually breached the Takeda command post, setting the stage for one of history's most legendary duels. A lone mounted samurai crashing through the maku curtains of the Takeda headquarters, presented Takeda Shingen with a dire threat: Uesugi Kenshin himself. Caught off guard and unable to draw his sword, Shingen's only option was to defend himself with his heavy wooden war fan. He skilfully parried Kenshin's mounted sword attacks, managing to protect himself as best he could. Despite his efforts, Shingen's armour was cut three times, and his war fan suffered seven blows. The timely intervention of a bodyguard, whose spear struck Kenshin's horse, provided a crucial respite. The rearing horse, combined with the arrival of more of Shingen's guards, ultimately drove Kenshin away, saving Shingen from further harm. Just as Kenshin seemed poised for victory, a sudden and fierce counterattack threatened his rear, turning the tide of battle.

The Takeda samurai who had ascended Mount Saijo followed the Uesugi down to the plain and managed to drive through their rearguard at the river crossing, catching the retreating Uesugi samurai. Shingen's army, exhausted from the battle, did not attempt to pursue Kenshin's retreat. This action at Kawanakajima had been costly for both sides. Kenshin had lost roughly 13,000 men; Shingen around 12,400. It was one of the largest battles ever fought in Japanese history. There followed another indecisive battle at Kawanakajima, and thereafter Kenshin renewed attacks upon the Hōjō, but the results were always unclear. Peace was concluded between the Takeda and the Hōjō, and Kenshin turned his full strength against his perennial foe, Shingen. But at this stage the situation was changed by the appearance of Oda Nobunaga, a figure who would become one of the most important people in Japanese history (see below).

The Hōjō and the Satomi

In 1564, the Satomi clan staged a remarkable comeback, reclaiming Konodai Castle with a force of 8,000 samurai while the Hōjō were engaged elsewhere. The Hōjō,

Below: Incident at Kawanakajima. The Uesugi samurai broke through the Takeda defences enabling Kenshin to attack Shingen, who saved the sword blow with his battle fan.

under Ujiyasu, swiftly assembled a 20,000-strong army in response. Anticipating a siege, the Satomi adopted a defensive posture. However, when the Hōjō advanced the Satomi unexpectedly launched a counterattack, luring the enemy into a trap. Feigning retreat, they drew the Hōjō forces toward the castle. Ujiyasu, recognizing the Satomi's ploy, orchestrated a tactical withdrawal, leading the Satomi to believe they had achieved a decisive victory. Sake barrels were brought out and the Satomi samurai partied, drinking well into the night. At dawn, the Hōjō forces attacked the castle from all sides, surprising the hungover Satomi and leaving them surrounded and soundly beaten. Satomi Yoshihiro barely escaped with his life, and his young son, likely fighting in his first battle, was killed in the retreat. Masaki Nobushige, the highest retainer in the Satomi army, died in action. The Satomi would never challenge the Hōjō in battle again.

Above: Oda Nobunaga's son, Oda Nobukatsu, married the daughter of Kitabatake Tomonori as a peace settlement.

The Imagawa, Kitabatake, Saitō and Oda Clans

The Imagawa had formed a barrier in Suruga province for many generations. In the middle of the 16th century the head of the family was Yoshimoto. His influence extended over the three Owari Bay coastal provinces of Suruga, Totomi and Mikawa, which formed the eastern side of the Izu promontory. On the western side of Owari Bay lay Ise province, the site of the principal Shinto shrine and the original domain of the Taira family, and where the remnants of the Southern Court had their home. Ise's hereditary daimyō was a member of the Kitabatake family. In 1560, discord among the clan's chief retainers provided an excuse for the armed intervention of Oda Nobunaga, the local daimyō who was just embarking on a plan to extend his power base as far across Japan as possible. As a peace settlement, Nobunaga's son, Nobukatsu, married a daughter of the daimyō Kitabatake Tomonori. In 1561, the Doki clan of Mino on the northern border of Owari Bay destroyed its rival Saitō clan, who were in turn crushed by the Oda from their base in Owari. Having thus gained control of the northern and western Owari Bay region through marriage and conquest, the Oda then took Mikawa, the final, eastern area by shattering the Imagawa clan in power there. From this position, the Oda was able to sweep further west into Ise province.

In 1576, Nobunaga and Nobukatsu solidified their control over Ise Province through the assassination of much of the Kitabatake leadership. Emboldened by this success, Nobukatsu aimed to expand his territory into the neighbouring Iga Province. In October 1579, he led an army of 8,000 men through Nagano Pass, only to be met with a devastating ambush. The Iga warriors, utilizing their intimate knowledge of the terrain and employing effective guerrilla tactics, inflicted heavy casualties and forced Nobukatsu into a disorganized retreat. This defeat was a major setback, compounded by the fact that Nobukatsu had launched the campaign without consulting Nobunaga. Driven in part by a desire to prove his worth, Nobukatsu instead incurred his father's wrath, facing threats of disownment. To restore his own authority and rectify his son's mistake, Nobunaga launched a massive retaliatory invasion of Iga in September 1581. At the height of his power, controlling most of central Japan,

Nobunaga commanded a force of approximately 42,000 men, attacking Iga from all directions. Faced with such overwhelming odds, organized resistance quickly collapsed. These two campaigns are collectively known as the Tenshō Iga War.

The Asakura, Asai, Rokkaku and Hatakeyama Clans

The province of Omi, which surrounded Lake Biwa, had special importance since it commanded the approaches to Kyoto from the east. Hence it became the scene of much change and fighting, in which the Hosokawa, Kyogoku, Rokkaku and Asai families all took part. Finally, in the middle of the 16th century, the Asai gained the ascendancy by obtaining the assistance of the Asakura of Echizen. Echizen shared a common border with the north of Omi and had originally been under the control of the Shiba clan. The Asakura subsequently obtained the position of high constable and acquired a great deal of power during the *Ikkō-ikki* revolt by driving the turbulent priests from the province. At that era, or a little later, the provinces of Kii, Kawachi, Izumi and Yamato were all the scenes of fierce fighting between ambitious clans which had little to contribute to the overall situation in the country.

The Mōri and the Amako Clans

The Ōuchi clan was very powerfully situated and its Sengoku-daimyō, Ōuchi Yoshioki (1477–1528), controlled the Iwami, Aki, Suwa and Nagato provinces at the western end of Honshu, as well as the northern Chikuzen and Buzen provinces of Kyūshū.

Yoshioki was the samurai lord who marched to Kyoto in 1508 at the head of a great army to restore Ashikaga Yoshitane as shōgun. Eleven years later, on his return to the west, he was followed by many nobles from Kyoto and his chief provincial town, Yamaguchi, on the Shimonoseki Strait, prospered well. His son, Yoshitaka, proved to be a weakling and after being defeated by his senior retainer, Sue Harukata, committed *seppuku* having convinced his ally the ambitious clan leader Mōri Motonari to avenge him.

Having obtained a shōgunal mandate from Kyoto, Motonari took to the field in 1555 against the Sue, and with only 3,000 samurai succeeded in shattering Harukata's force of 20,000 at the Battle of Oshikibata. Having completed the wish of Yoshitaka, Mōri Motonari made no attempt to restore the Ōuchi clan. He continued the campaign against Sue Harukata,

Left: Ōuchi Yoshioki, the powerful daimyō of the Ōuchi clan. His successors proved much weaker and were unable to prevent its extinction later in the century.

who had secured control of the Ōuchi by making the adopted son of Yoshitaka, Ōuchi Yoshinaga, the head of the clan. Mōri Motonari defeated the Sue in the decisive Battle of Miyajima in October 1555, thereby acquiring the entire Ōuchi legacy. Thereafter, the Ōuchi clan became extinct and Motonari succeeded to all its domains on the suicide of Yoshinaga in May 1557.

Motonari's province of Iwami shared its eastern border with the Izumo province under the control of the Sengoku-daimyō Amako Tsunehisa (1458–1540), who had gained power and lands after the fall of the Yamana clan. This daimyō, and his grandson Amako Yoshihisa (1545–1610), were great rivals of the Ōuchi family and on their downfall came into collision with Mōri Motonari. The feud ended with the extinction of the Amako clan and the absorption of its domains by the Mōri when Gassantoda Castle, a large mountain castle in Izumo Province, fell to the Mōri in 1566.

The Mōri owed their rapid growth to a series of successful alliances with the lower daimyō of Aki and Bingo. After the victory at Miyajima, the Mōri tightened military discipline to unify their control over the various groups of ji-samurai. In this way, the Mōri had succeeded in uniting the 13 provinces covering the entire westernmost part of Honshu under their rule and constructed a fully independent Sengoku-daimyō power base by the time Motonari died in 1571.

Above: The Great Battle at Miyajima, 1555. The only battle ever fought on the sacred island of Miyajima. Between the forces of Sue Harukata and Mōri Motonari with the Mōri winning a decisive victory. Print by Yoshitoshi.

Below: Statue of Chōsokabe Motochika located in the Hachiman Shrine of Kochi, Shikoku. Motochika, one of the Sengoku Daimyō, conquered all Shikoku Island. He prayed his victory at the Hachiman Shrine. This statue was built in 1999 for the 400th anniversary after his death.

The Miyoshi, Ichijo, Kono and Chōsokabe Clans

In the middle of the 15th century, nearly the whole of the island of Shikoku and its four provinces were under the control of Hosokawa Katsumoto with his senior vassals the Miyoshi, Ichijo, Kono and Chōsokabe clans. Motochika, a retainer of the Ichijo, was able to gain power in the Tosa province while remaining loyal and then marched on the Aki clan in Awa province to the east of Tosa. With 7,000 samurai, he defeated Aki Kunitora at the Battle of Yanagare in 1569, then went on to take Aki Castle. Later, Motochika was to receive orders from Oda Nobunaga to conquer the other three provinces of Shikoku in the interests of Nobunaga's son, Nobutada. This he dutifully would do and, on the death of the Odas, became the lord of Shikoku.

The Daimyō in Kyūshū

The southern island of Kyūshū was to have a significant role with the arrival of the 'southern barbarians' from the West and their weapons. The area consisted of nine provinces and the two offshore islands of Iki and Tsushima. The families connected to Kyūshū were the Shimazu, Ōtomo, Ryuzoji, Kikuchi and Shoni.

In Kyūshū, the Ōtomo clan supported the cause of the Northern Court, and made themselves masters of Buzen, Bungo, Chikuzen, Chikugo, Hizen and Higo. Ōtomo Sōrin (1530–87), previously known as Yoshishige, was one of the few daimyō to convert to Christianity. In 1559, Ōtomo Sōrin came into conflict with the Mōri for control of Kyūshū. This was temporarily resolved two years later with a peace treaty, but relations soon became violent again when Sōrin's efforts to put down unrest in some of his provinces prompted the interference of the Mōri.

In 1569, Tachibana Dosetsu, a senior retainer of the Ōtomo, was attacked by the Mōri. He was defeated and lost his castle. When Sorin heard of this, he threatened the Mōri foothold in Buzen province and, at the Battle of Tatarahama that year, forced the Mōri to retreat and retook Tachibana Castle. By this time, the Ōtomo had a controlling influence over seven of the nine provinces on Kyūshū. Sorin's final years were consumed by a fruitless struggle against the formidable power of the Shimazu, Ryuzoji and Akizuki clans.

The Shimazu clan exerted control over the Satsuma, Osumi and Hyuga provinces in Japan and were in constant conflict with the Ōtomo and other daimyō on the island. The clan emerged victorious from all their campaigns and Shimazu Yoshihisa in 1586 succeeded in unifying and controlling the entire Kyūshū region. He retired in 1587.

Right: Statue of Ōtomo Sorin, Jingujiura Park, Oita City, Oita Prefecture, Eastern Kyūshū.

Above: Date Masamune statue in Sendai City Park, North-East Honshu.

The Tohoku Region

The northeastern region of Honshu was home to many clans who fought among themselves for supremacy. Of these, the most influential were the Mogami of Yamagata, the Date of Yonezawa and the Ashina of Aizu. The Date clan attained its greatest distinction in the time of the Sengoku-daimyō Date Masamune (1566–1636), known colloquially as the 'One-eyed-Dragon of Oshu', having lost his right eye as a child due to an infection. The Date clan was fortunate in being able to stand aloof from some of the destructive strife of the 16th century. However, the region was decimated during the Age of the Warring States, as was the rest of the country, and the Date overwhelmed the power of the Nikaido, the Ashina and the Tamura, and fought less decisively against the Satake of Hitachi. The Mogami clan, a branch of the Ashikaga family in the Dewa province, were confronted by the Uesugi of Echigo. Further north, the Tsugaru and the Nambu came into conflict.

Right: Set of *gomai-do gusoku* type armour owned by Date Masamune. It shows Masamune's distinct taste for beauty in the combination of a black body consisting of five iron plates, a Suji-kabuto helmet constructed from 62 iron plates, and a gold-leaf covered ornament, or *Maedate*, designed with an asymmetrically-shaped crescent moon motif. The Gomai-do (five-panel body) style, also known as *Sendai-do*, was handed down through successive lords and vassals.

Firearms of the Samurai

Although Japan was aware of gunpowder and firearms in use in China for many years, they saw that it was crude and inefficient and did not import the equipment and technology. That changed quickly when the Portuguese arrived.

However, a chance discovery aboard a ship, made to seek safe anchorage in a storm in 1543 on the Island of Tanegashima, of several matchlock arquebuses in the possession of two Portuguese traders sparked an interest that initiated the military revolution that was to come. Shogūn Ashikaga Yoshiharu ordered blacksmiths in the town of Kunitomo to replicate them. In this way Kunitomo became Japan's centre of firearms manufacture.

This was later followed by a trader landing a supply of the weapons in Kyūshū. Originally the gun was called a Tanegashima after the first location they were encountered, but were later known as *teppo*. With Japanese ingenuity and skills, it was believed that over 250,000 were produced and used extensively within ten years.

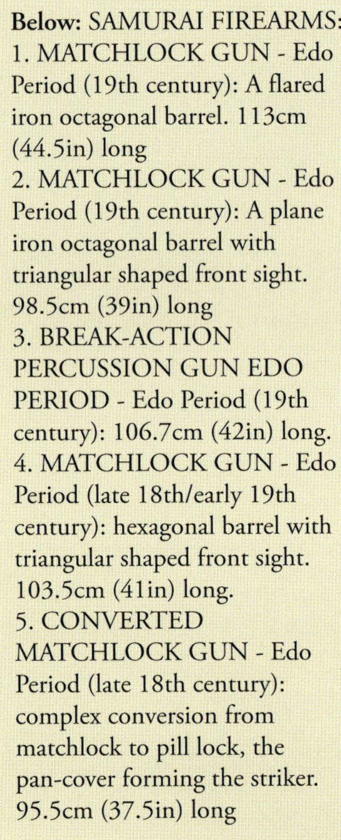

Below: SAMURAI FIREARMS:
1. MATCHLOCK GUN - Edo Period (19th century): A flared iron octagonal barrel. 113cm (44.5in) long
2. MATCHLOCK GUN - Edo Period (19th century): A plane iron octagonal barrel with triangular shaped front sight. 98.5cm (39in) long
3. BREAK-ACTION PERCUSSION GUN EDO PERIOD - Edo Period (19th century): 106.7cm (42in) long.
4. MATCHLOCK GUN - Edo Period (late 18th/early 19th century): hexagonal barrel with triangular shaped front sight. 103.5cm (41in) long.
5. CONVERTED MATCHLOCK GUN - Edo Period (late 18th century): complex conversion from matchlock to pill lock, the pan-cover forming the striker. 95.5cm (37.5in) long

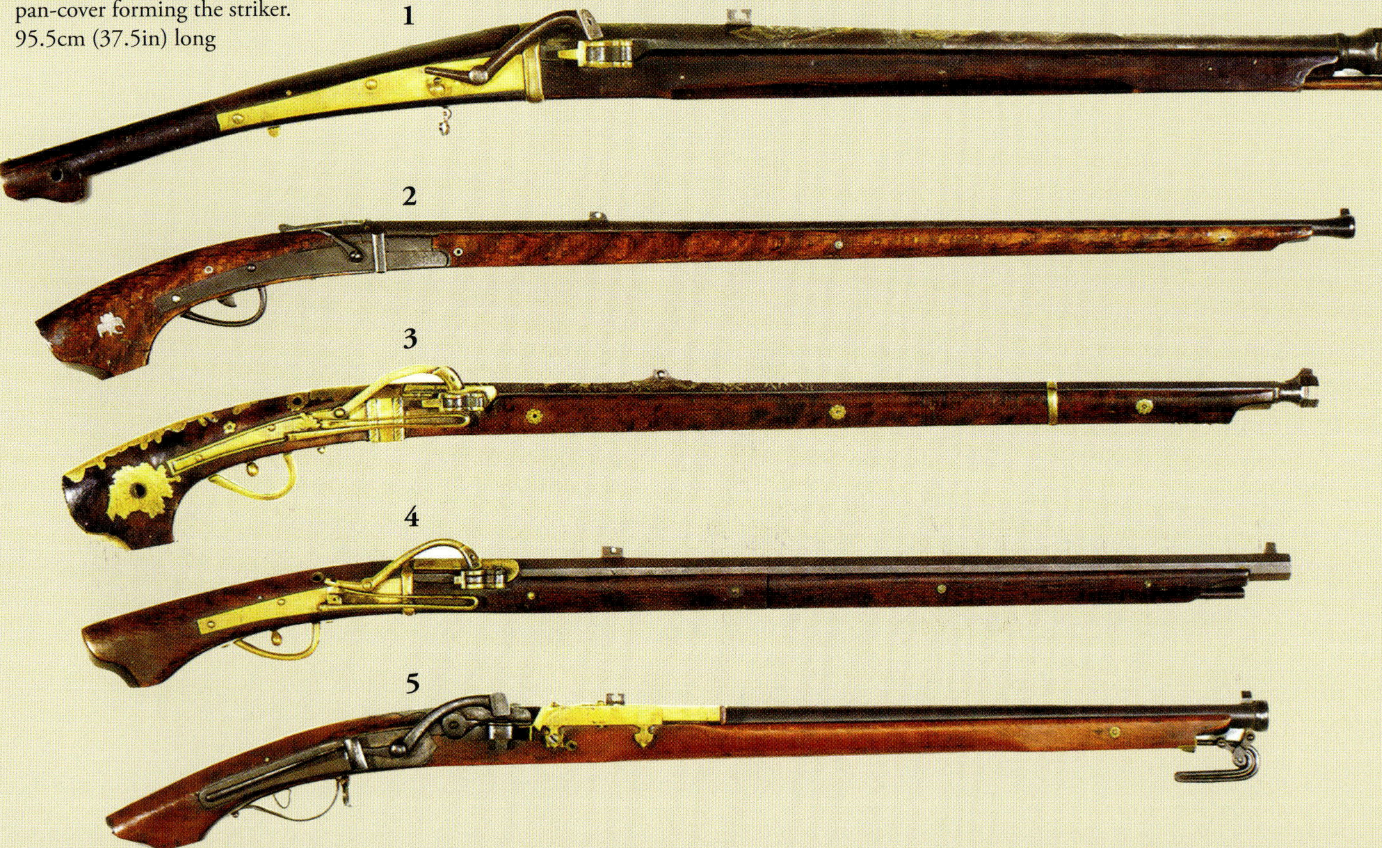

Left: Large calibre arquebus matchlocks.

Of course, the arquebus as a weapon had many disadvantages. It was rather primitive and awkward to handle and the reloading process could take well over a minute – during which time an archer could loose eight arrows. It was also not at accurate as a bow. After several volleys from guns using black powder, battlefield visibility was reduced.

The samurai soon worked on improving their *teppo*. Larger calibre weapons were introduced, such as the 3m-long (9ft 8in) wall-gun used in sieges, and techniques were developed for firing in the rain or at night. An added advantage was that unskilled peasants could be trained to fire an arquebus in just a couple of days; to become an archer took several years.

In 1549, Oda Nobunaga ordered 500 matchlocks from Kunitomo for his troops and used them effectively in battle, developing a staggered firing pattern. Four years later, Takeda Shingen ordered 300 *teppo* matchlocks, although he was unable to deploy them effectively on the battlefield.

An arquebusier's equipment included two powder pots, a larger one for the powder poured into the barrel and a smaller one for fine seed powder used in the firing pan. These were produced in a wide variety of designs and material. Attached to the belt was a box or pouch for bullets (lead balls), a powder flask and a coil of rope wick soaked in saltpetre.

Another innovation created in Japan was the bamboo tube cartridge containing pre-measured charges of gun powder, a bullet and wadding. This enabled the gunner to quickly load the weapon. As these initial guns were primarily used by the *ashigaru*, they were of low quality. As the samurai became fascinated with the pieces and began to use them, the quality, decoration and cost increased.

By the start of the 19th century, the *teppo* was outdated and began to be replaced by muskets and then breach-loading guns. By the end of the Satsuma Rebellion in 1877, the use of black powder weapons had ended.

Below: Illustrations on the use of *teppo* from *Geijutsu Hiden Tokai* by Omori Genmasatomi, 1855. Left: Firing using the saddle as a rest; centre: firing from horseback; right: using rope to provide inclination accuracy.

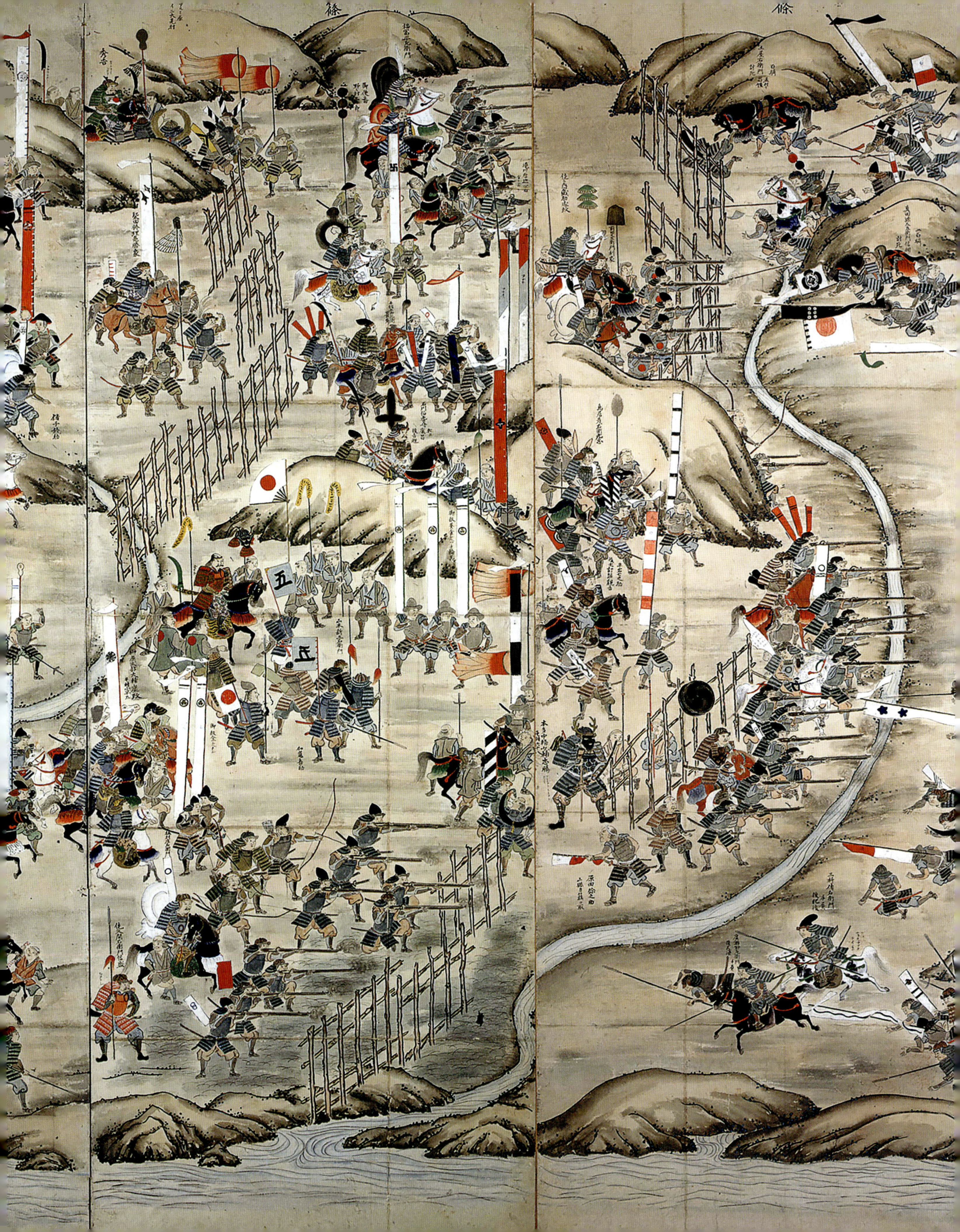

CHAPTER 7

The Unifiers of Japan

By the mid-16th century, the movement toward the decentralization of feudal power had pushed about as far as it could go without the country descending into total anarchy and fragmentation. After decades of continuous fighting, 1560 was to prove a turning point in the Age of the Warring States. For almost 100 years, the country had been enmeshed in a series of expanding civil wars that had seen a few important daimyō emerge in the provinces who could provide a focus for regional unity. Among the contending daimyō were some who dreamed of crushing their rivals and conquering and reuniting the country. The age of senseless violence was coming to an end. Now began the first steps towards unification – and the glory days of the Oda clan.

Ever since the outbreak of the Ōnin War in 1467, the military governors from across the country had risen due to the weakness of the Ashikaga Shōgunate and the central government. Several religious orders owned large areas of land with their temples, and often engaged in violent disputes with one another. They kept private armies enlisted from warrior monks, local samurai, temple cleaners, artisans and farmers and the local daimyō usually did not intervene when the temples sent their forces into battle. However, as the larger daimyōs were following a gradual process of consolidating their power in ever-larger regional blocks, the temples would eventually learn that their formerly unquestioned right to exercise their influence would one day be swept away.

The family's original and most influential leader was Oda Nobunaga (1534–1582). His roots were in the fertile and strategically located Owari province, in central Honshu, where his family had only been minor warrior retainers serving the Shiba clan, a branch of the Ashikaga clan. The Shiba rotated the deputy shōgun position with the Hosokawa and the Hatekeyama and, like them, the Shiba were weakened from internal family disputes of the sort that characterized the Ōnin War and were unable to control warriors in their provincial lands. The Oda, who carried out mundane functions in the province on behalf of the absentee Shiba daimyō, took advantage of this weakness and overthrew the Shiba and assumed control of the province. After his father's death in 1551, Nobunaga slowly eliminated rival military figures in the area, consolidating his leadership of the entire province by 1559.

Left: Oda Nobunaga. The first unifier of Japan.

The Battle of Okehazama

Right: Imagawa Yoshimoto from the series 'Heroic Taiheiki Tales'. A fierce general who relied on the governors of Suruga and Totomi provinces.

In June 1560, Imagawa Yoshimoto crossed the border into Owari province. His objective was to enter Kyoto and seize control of the shōgunate from the weak Ashikaga shōgun. Yoshimoto was a powerful Sengoku-daimyō who controlled the Suruga, Totomi and Mikawa provinces. He also had a strong influence over the Matsudaira clan of Mikawa province. He was a politician with little aptitude as a warrior and leader and for some years had become reliant on his uncle Imagawa Sessai for military command and strategy. This ended with Sessai's death in 1557. However, Yoshimoto's negotiating skills did lead to an alliance between his family and the Hōjō and Takeda Shingen.

With a secure treaty in force, these three allies were able to each devote their full attention and efforts to accomplishing their own objectives without worrying about the other two. Hōjō Ujiyasu could continue dominating the Kanto region, Takada Shingen could focus on his war against Uesugi Kenshin, and Imagawa Yoshimoto could concentrate on his campaign to claim Kyoto.

By Yoshimoto's side as he headed out toward Kyoto was 17-year-old Matsudaira Motoyasu of Mikawa, a young general at the head of a force of 25,000–40,000 samurai. In time, Motoyasu, would change his name to Tokugawa Ieyasu when he became the third of the country's great unifiers. The clans that stood between Yoshimoto and Kyoto were not as strong as the Imagawa. All Yoshimoto needed to do was push aside any opposition along the way and his victory could be achieved.

The initial stages of the invasion of Owari went well for the Imagawa-Matsudaira samurai, easily overwhelming and destroying the castles along the Oda frontier. Marune Castle, a frontier fortress in the possession of Oda Nobunaga, was personally captured by Motoyasu, after a short siege in which he used concentrated arquebus fire, with one shot killing the castle commander, Sakuma Mōrishige.

With the Oda unable to stop the advance and on the verge of collapse, Yoshimoto, with victory in his sight, needed to regroup his forces before staging an attack on the Oda clan base of Kiyosu Castle. Many of his troops were spread out along the route, having to garrison and safeguard the fortresses already captured. Nobunaga was unwilling to wait at Kiyosu for the larger forces of the Imagawa to attack and lay siege. Desiring to meet his enemy in the field, Nobunaga overruled his advisers and set out with around 2,000 samurai. Arriving at Narumi Castle, which had been in Imagawa hands for some time, Nobunaga debriefed his scouts who filled him on the enemy's position. With a brilliant *ruse-de-guerre*, Nobunaga ordered his samurai to place their banners opposite Narumi in order to trick the Imagawa into believing that was where the main body of Oda troops were stationed.

The Imagawa were camped in a forested area known as Okehazama and Yoshimoto was sufficiently confident to briefly pause for a head-viewing ceremony of his Oda adversaries. Under cover of a dark night and a thunderstorm with heavy rain, Nobunaga moved

his force around and above the sleeping Imagawa using mountain roads. The Imagawa lookouts did not see the Oda samurai coming and, as the rain began to cease near dawn, Nobunaga launched a surprise attack on Yoshimoto's camp. Even though the Oda were outnumbered, they caught the Imagawa completely unawares, with many of them still asleep, unarmed, or drunk from the previous night's victory celebrations. As Yoshimoto emerged from his tent to meet the attackers he was ambushed, cut down and decapitated.

Nobunaga's troops marked their victory by collecting about 3,000 enemy heads, while the remnants of the invading Imagawa army fled home. No attempt was made to pursue the fugitives into Mikawa and Motoyasu returned home confident that his clan could finally break free from the grips of his now weakened masters. The Oda had won the brief yet important engagement at Okehazama and Nobunaga was now viewed in a new light by his peers – and by himself. A short time later, he and Matsudaira Motoyasu established a formal alliance in order to secure his eastern border.

Above: The Battle of Okehazama in 1560 between the forces of Oda Nobunaga and Imagawa Yoshimoto by Chikanobu. Nobunaga's surprise attack on Imagawa's encampment proved victorious.

Also serving with Nobunaga at this time as his sandal-bearer was a former *ashigaru* called Kinoshita Tokichiro. Nobunaga saw that he was smart and cunning and, eventually would appoint him to a number of leadership positions. In time, as he became a successful military commander, Kinoshita Tokichiro would change his name to Toyotomi Hideyoshi and establish himself – along with Nobunaga and Tokugawa Ieyasu – as one of Japan's three great unifiers. So it was that all three of the country's most iconic leaders were present and on the same side at this famous engagement.

Oda Nobunaga

Oda Nobunaga (1534–1582), who began life as a small-scale daimyō, rose to prominence both for his ability as a military tactician and for his foresight in recognizing how technological developments were affecting the way that battles were fought and won.

Samurai tactics on the battlefield had been changing gradually in the century or so before Nobunaga's time. Polearms, pikes and lances became favoured over swords and increased remarkably in length, while long swords fell from favour. The shortened *katana* became a rare sight on the battlefield and evolved into more of a weapon for personal protection. Bows remained the dominant projectile weapon, although the arquebus matchlock, which had been introduced around 1543, gradually gained favour and use. By 1550 guns and improved cannon influenced the organization of military units and techniques of fortification, as stone castles gained favour over wooden and earthwork structures. Mountain castles remained important through the mid-1500s, but it was not until the final three decades of the century that extensive castles, occupying large plains with substantial stone walls, would be constructed.

From early on, Nobunaga realized the importance of firearms for success on the battlefield. Using the new matchlock gun, Nobunaga formed permanent, lower level armed units that possessed the ability to fight in battles and sieges for prolonged periods since they were free from the need to engage in farming and land activities. He set up the first of these units in 1549, supplying it with 500 matchlocks purchased from gunsmiths in nearby Kunitomi, in Omi province. More units followed, made up of highly mobile samurai and *ashigaru* armed with matchlock guns and these became the foundation of Nobunaga's army.

As his power grew, Nobunaga brought the port city of Sakai under his direct control. Sakai was an entry-point for foreign trade and a key manufacturing centre, and Nobunaga arranged for many of his swords and other weapons to be made there.

Below: An arquebus firearms unit, from an antique scroll.

Below: Saitō Tatsuoki in a print by Utagawa Kuniyoshi. He was killed at Tonezaka when the Oda invaded Echizen in 1573.

With an eye on taking ever more territory, when in 1561 his old enemy in neighbouring Mino province died and left the leadership of his clan to the teenaged Saitō Tatsuoki, Nobunaga led his samurai into the territory and won two quick victories that handed him the advantage. Mino's teenage leader, with far fewer troops than his rival, fought back and for the next couple of years the Oda and Saitō remained at war. In 1563, Nobunaga moved his power base up to the newly constructed Komakiyama Castle to better manage his forces.

In 1567, Oda Nobunaga launched an attack on Mino province from Sunomata Castle, leading his forces across the Kiso River and attracting the support of many disaffected former Saitō retainers along the way. The objective was to capture the last Saitō stronghold, Inabayama Castle. Despite the demoralizing sight of Saitō banners among their attackers, the defenders maintained a strong defensive position within the impregnable mountaintop castle.

Above: The reconstructed Inabayama Castle (also known as Gifu Castle).

Left: Hideyoshi Toyotomi leads an assault group to enter Inabayama Castle by Tsukioka Yoshitoshi.

After two weeks of siege, Nobunaga's old sandal-bearer-turned-military-commander Toyotomi Hideyoshi suggested a plan to quickly secure Inabayama from its stubborn defenders. Leading a small group of samurai, Hideyoshi scaled the steep cliffs of Mount Inaba and attacked the garrison from inside. In the chaos this caused, he was able to open the castle's gates for the main Oda assault, signalling to the men below that they should attack by having his men wave their water gourds on the top of their spears. With the fall of Inabayama, the Saitō were truly defeated and Mino was in the hands of Nobunaga, who made the captured castle his new base of operations. In recognition of his achievements in battle, Hideoshi was promoted to the rank of full samurai.

Following his success in Mino, Nobunaga received a private message of congratulation from Emperor Omigachi, who also asked the warlord to come to Kyoto and restore order in the capital. While not refusing this command, Nobunaga saw in it a pathway

to achieving his aim of uniting and then controlling the country under his military rule. At that time there was no effective shōgunal central authority in Kyoto, and for ambitious Sengoku-daimyō like Nobunaga the shōgunate remained a potential source of legitimacy against rival clans. This became even more of a fact when the deposed shōgun Ashikaga Yoshiaki came to Nobunaga and asked for his help in regaining the shōgunate. If Nobunaga did this, he knew he could install Ashikaga Yoshiaki and then use him to advance his own agenda. Yoshiaki, for his part, needed Nobunaga's military backing and offered him several important and powerful political positions, which he declined. Instead, Nobunaga requested that he be officially recognized as the controller of the critical merchant city and firearms manufacturing centre of Sakai. By 1568, Nobunaga was in a strong enough position to march on Kyoto with a force of 60,000 men and reinstate the Ashikaga Shōgunate. He also intended to use Kyoto as a base from which to win control of Honshu's Kansai region and so complete his takeover of the entire west and central area of Japan's largest and most important island.

Above: Suzuki Saemon Shigeyuki aiming his Pistol from Ambush at Nobunaga.

Nobunaga's march to power was not uncontested and he met with stiff resistance, particularly from rival daimyō such as the Azai, the Asakura and, later, the Takeda clans. In 1570, for example, two incidents reminded Nobunaga that he was not going to have everything his own way. The first event came when a rival daimyō attempted to have Nobunaga assassinated by a matchlock marksman as he made his way to Gifu Castle. Two shots were fired but failed to injure Nobunaga and the perpetrator was captured and killed. If one or more of the assassin's bullets had found their mark Japan's history would have turned out very differently. Then, in July that same year, Nobunaga defeated the allied forces of Asakura and Asai at the Battle of Anegawa, but only narrowly. It would be another three years before Nobunaga would decisively defeat the Asai and Asakura clans.

In addition to the Asakura and Asai, Nobunaga was also concerned about the devout Enryaku-ji warrior monks, or *sohei*. This was a group which, from its vast temple base on Mount Hiei, had amassed significant amounts of power and privilege that made them a regional rival to Nobunaga. Eager to eliminate them as a threat, Nobunaga went on the attack.

On a fateful September night in 1571, Oda Nobunaga unleashed a force of 30,000 men on the great temple site. Under the command of Nobunaga's

Left: A 19th-century photograph of a man wearing the costume of a warrior monk, armed with a *naginata* and *tachi*, common weapons used by the *sōhei* warrior monks.

trusted lieutenants Sakuma Nobumōri, Ikeda Tsuneoki and Akechi Mitsuhide, the Oda burned down or destroyed every temple, monastery, statue, shrine and living quarters they encountered. Around 300 buildings were levelled and, it is estimated, between 2,000–5,000 monks, men, women and children were massacred – both at the site and in and around the mountain as they tried to escape. While the survivors were eventually permitted to rebuild Enryaku-ji, the temple would never regain its former glory or influence. The era of meddling warrior monks had definitively been ended.

Nobunaga faced a much more prolonged and difficult campaign, however, against the temple-fortress of Honganji, the headquarters of the Shin branch of Buddhism, which resisted his authority in Ōsaka and in Echizen province. It took him a full decade, from 1570–1580, before he successfully suppressed the militant sectarians. In so doing, he forever eliminated Buddhism as an institution of rule. For more than 500 years, Japan's major temples had enjoyed patronage from the imperial household and Kyoto's aristocracy. After Nobunaga's campaign, temples no longer maintained armies nor possessed the wealth they once did.

Another source of conflict for Nobunaga came from his rival Sengoku-daimyō, Takeda Shingen. While marching from Kai to Kyoto in 1572, his army passed into Mikawa, which was the domain of Nobunaga's ally Tokugawa Ieyasu. There, his troops were confronted by 8,000 of Ieyasu's men

Right: Enryaku-ji Temple on Mt. Hiei. Present day photo of the reconstructed complex.

and Nobunaga's 3,000 reinforcements at the Battle of Mikatagahara. The Takeda army heavily outnumbered its enemy and soon the Tokugawa-Oda alliance found itself encircled. Many of Tokugawa Ieyasu's retainers perished in the battle and Ieyasu himself was only just dissuaded from embarking on what would probably have been a disastrous charge to personally rescue his trapped general, Mizuno Tadashige. Instead, the Tokugawa forces were compelled to retreat, which they were only able to do without being completely routed when one of Ieyasu's retainers, Natsume Yoshinobu, led a heroic suicide charge against the advancing Takeda forces.

Ieyasu, accompanied by only five men, retreated to Hamamatsu Castle, leaving the gates open and lighting braziers to guide the rest of his men on their retreat. The Tokugawa commander Sakai Tadatsugu beat a large war drum to encourage the retreating forces to enter the castle. The Takeda vanguard, led by Baba Nobuharu and Yamagata Masakage, mistakenly believed this to be a trap and halted their advance and then decided to withdraw.

Above: The Battle of Mikatagahara by Chikanobu. Takeda Shingen is in the centre of the picture leading his cavalry in a charge against the Oda-Tokugawa samurai.

The Battle of Mikatagahara was one of Takeda Shingen's most famous military victories and one of the most notable demonstrations of cavalry tactics of the Sengoku period. The battle was also Tokugawa Ieyasu's most decisive defeat. The Tokugawa army was effectively annihilated, with around 1,000 dead and Ieyasu himself only narrowly escaping death through a bluff and perilous night attack. For Shingen, however, there would be no follow up. In February 1573 he was injured at the Siege of Noda Castle and died three months later. Some historians say that he was shot by one of Ieyasu's samurai snipers, others that he was hit by a stray bullet. Many believe that he simply died of illness.

Nobunaga now took action to discredit Ashikaga Yoshiaki to make way for his own succession to the position of shōgun. Yoshiaki became aware of Nobunaga's accusations that he had been neglecting

Above: Ashikaga Yoshiaki escaping, painted by Utagawa Toyonobu.

his duties and was indulging in corruption and became openly hostile and took up arms. Nobunaga tried to placate the shōgun and sent Hideyoshi to try to persuade him to return to Kyoto from Kawachi, where he had fled. But Yoshiaki refused to back down and placed himself under the protection of the Mōri family. Even so, by removing himself from the capital Yoshiaki had effectively handed supreme political power to Nobunaga. Yoshiaki would hold onto the shōgunate until 1588, but from 1573 he no longer held any authority.

With Ashikaga Yoshiaki driven into exile, the imperial court bowed to the inevitable and began to cultivate Nobunaga. He returned the compliment by offering financial support to the emperor and the aristocracy. In this way, Nobunaga acquired the political and social legitimacy to add to the power that he had seized by military means. None of this made his position unassailable, though. All across the country there were many great Sengoku-daimyō with the ability to put into the field armies much larger than those of the Oda and its allies.

The Castle of Azuchi

Even though there was continual warfare in the provinces of clan against clan, the character of the fighting and of the bows, arrows, swords and other weapons conventionally used was such that there was little need for the forces at war to build elaborate defences. There was nothing that anyone in the West would regard as a castle, for example. There were forts, but these were little more than systems of outlying defences, trenches, earthen walls, and wooden palisades. No more than that was needed so long as fighting was either hand-to-hand or conducted with missiles no more penetrating than arrows. But when firearms were introduced from Europe, stone castles began to be built.

The first of these new fortresses was built at Azuchi, in Omi province, between 1576–79 and designed by Niwa Nagahide, one of Nobunaga's generals. In its centre rose a tower 30m (98ft) high, standing

Below: A contemporary illustration of Azuchi Castle showing the construction on the mountain top.

Above: The layout of Azuchi Castle.

on a massive stone basement 22m (72ft) in height. Together, the whole edifice formed a structure absolutely without precedent in Japan. The interior space was divided into four round courtyards. The central tower consisted of seven floors; in addition to storage rooms and an arsenal, it housed luxurious residential apartments and reception halls. The tower was of wood and had, therefore, no capacity for resisting cannon but the presence of embrasures in the walls indicate the attention Nobunaga paid to firearms. The cost of constructing this colossal edifice was very heavy, and funds had to be collected from the whole of the 11 provinces then under Nobunaga's control.

Nobunaga was not the only one of the Sengoku-daimyō to build castles; he was, however, the first to realize the political uses of monumental castle architecture as well as the first to build a castle town.

Azuchi Castle was constructed not just as a military stronghold but also as Nobunaga's residence and court. The castle complex became the site for public spectacles, including sumo tournaments, tea ceremonies and sound-and-light shows. To build up Azuchi as a thriving town, Nobunaga ordered his retainers to reside at the base of the castle and offered numerous incentives to attract merchants and artisans to take up residence there.

Kyūshū and Shikoku

For some time, the western islands of Kyūshū and Shikoku had been relatively conflict-free and stable, enjoying their status as centres of trade and culture. That was about to change by the early 1570s, however, as both the Shimazu and Chōsokabe families began growing in ambition.

In 1566, Shimazu Yoshihisa inherited leadership of the Shimazu clan and the position of daimyō of Satsuma Province from his father. Soon after, he embarked on an ambitious campaign to bring all of Kyūshū under Shimazu control, working closely with his three brothers. This campaign began in earnest in 1572 with a significant victory against the Itō clan at the Battle of Kizaki, setting the stage for further conquests.

At the Battle of Kizaki in 1572, Itō Yotasuke's 3,000 samurai advanced on the heavily outnumbered Shimazu forces, led by Yoshihisa's brother, Yoshihiro. Despite being outnumbered ten to one, Yoshihiro cleverly employed a ruse, using banners and strategic positioning to mislead the Itō's Sagara allies into believing the Shimazu army was much larger. This deception prompted the Sagara to retreat to Higo, freeing the Shimazu to return to their besieged Kakuto Castle. As the Itō army attempted to follow the Sagara, Yoshihiro launched a surprise rear attack with just 300 samurai, completely scattering and destroying the Itō forces.

Following his 1578 victory over the Ōtomo at Mimigawa, Shimazu Yoshihisa rapidly expanded his clan's territory. He captured Minamata Castle in Higo Province in 1581 with a large force of 115,000 men. Victories at Okitanawate against the Ryūzōji clan and the defeat of the Aso clan by early 1584 solidified the Shimazu's dominance. By mid-1585, they controlled most of Kyūshū, with only the Ōtomo's holdings remaining outside their grasp. Unification of Kyūshū seemed imminent. However, this ambition was thwarted by Toyotomi Hideyoshi's overwhelming force of over 200,000 samurai, which

Left: Shimazu Yoshihiro by Yoshitora.

compelled the Shimazu to surrender. Yoshihisa subsequently retired as a Buddhist priest and devoted himself to poetry. He remains recognized as one of the greatest leaders of his time.

The Ito clan had also exerted their authority for many years over the province of Tosa on the island of Shikoku, ruling over smaller clans there, such as the Chōsokabe, Motoyama and Aki. With the Ito's loss of control, these retainer families gained increased independence. Of these, the Chōsokabe clan would prosper the most. Then, by forming alliances with local families, Chōsokabe Motochika was able to build his power base. Seven years later, he defeated the Aki clan with a force of 7,000 samurai and took Aki Castle while still appearing loyal to his masters, the Ichijō family.

By 1573, with the slow decline of the overall rulers of Tosa, the Ichijō clan, Motochika seized their power base of Nakamura. This, however, sparked a war that dragged on for another two years. It ended with the Battle of Shimantogawa in which the Ichijō were utterly defeated and Tosa fell entirely to the Chōsokabe. Just like the Shimazu in Kyūshū, this put Motoshika in a perfect spot to begin a campaign of conquest over the island of Shikoku.

Samurai Castles

Japan today boasts over 300 castles, many meticulously restored to their former glory. These imposing structures, often surrounded by deep moats and sturdy stone walls, served as the power centres of feudal Japan.

For centuries, castles were the epicentres of political and military control, housing the samurai elite and governing vast domains. Their significance in shaping Japan's medieval history cannot be undervalued.

Many of Japan's castles were built in the 15th and 16th centuries when the country was in a state of constant conflict and warfare, a period known as the Sengoku Period. Castle architecture developed rapidly during this era in response to the new techniques in warfare and evolving technology, including the arrival of firearms from Europe, which gave rise to the need for thick stone walls, seen at their massive best at Ōsaka and Nagoya castles. Other essential features could include defensive moats, shooting holes for arrows and guns, stone-dropping openings, and a complex inner pathway layout designed to confuse intruders. Apart from the stone walls, Japanese castle buildings were built of wood, making them particularly prone to fire. White plaster applied over mud walls was the primary fireproofing measure.

The colour of Japanese castle walls offers intriguing insights into their history. Fortresses built in the early 16th century, like Matsumoto and Okayama, typically featured black, lacquered wooden exteriors. However, a shift toward white plaster-covered walls emerged with later castles, such as Hikone and Himeji, built in the early Edo period between 1600 and 1640, offered superior fire protection. While some theories link these colour variations to the rivalries between Toyotomi Hideyoshi and Tokugawa Ieyasu, aesthetic preferences often played a more significant role in the final design.

The samurai's castles were strategically positioned to safeguard the significant provincial capitals and thoroughfares, such as the Tokaido and Nakasendo roads and other transportation routes. Being in such

critical positions, it is easy to see how the castles shaped the nation's urban development. The towns that grew up around the fortresses in the Edo period were peopled with merchants, artisans and entertainers who serviced the feudal lord and his samurai community living behind the strong defences of the castle walls. Once thriving centres of power, these fortresses have evolved into diverse communities, with some flourishing into modern cities while others retain a historic charm.

Japan's Original Castles

Japan boasts 12 remarkably well-preserved castles, each a testament to the nation's rich history. These architectural marvels include Bitchu-Matsuyama, Hikone, Himeji, Hirosaki, Inuyama, Iyo Matsuyama, Kochi, Marugame, Maruoka, Matsue, Matsumoto, and Uwajima Castles. These fortresses are symbols of feudal power and offer invaluable insights into Japan's past.

Matsue

Maruoka

Inuyama

Hirosaki

N

SEA OF JAPAN

KOREA

Sendai

Niigate

Tokyo

Yokohama

Nagoya

Kyoto

Himeji

Ōsaka

Hiroshima

Fukuoka

Kumamoto

Nagasaki

Kagoshima

PACIFIC OCEAN

0 250 kms

0 250 miles

Matsumoto

Bitchu Matsuyama

Hikone

Marugame

Himeji

Kochi

Iyo Matsuyama

Uwajima

Takeda Katsuyori and Nagashino

Campaigns, conspiracies, alliances and battles continuously alternated in those years. It was clear that soon the new leader of the Takeda clan, Takeda Katsuyori, would attempt another advance on Kyoto. The Oda territory covered a significant portion of the important Tokaido road, which led to Kyoto, a highway that Katsuyori would need to march his armies through to get to the capital. However, Katsuyori still needed to deal with the same problem his father had before him: the Tokugawa clan. For a while, it had been a matter of debate how the Takeda should deal with the Tokugawa and the Oda. In 1574, they captured the Tokugawa stronghold of Takatenjin Castle in Totomi province and began pressing on the Oda again, capturing the clan's Akichi Castle in Mino. Tokugawa Ieyasu was one of Nobunaga's most important allies, being a key player on the borderlands of the eastern provinces.

In 1575, Takeda Katsuyori set out at the head of an army of 15,000 to take Tokugawa Ieyasu's capital city at Okazaki. A traitor in Ieyasu's camp had offered to open the citadel's gates to let Katsuyoti in. The plot was discovered and dealt with at the last moment, so Katsuyori decided to lay siege to Yoshida Castle instead. Once he arrived however, he found that Ieyasu had reinforced the stronghold with an extra 6,000 samurai and Katsuyori's siege plans petered out. An attempt to take the smaller Nagashino Castle ended in similarly indecisive fashion when he was faced with stronger than expected resistance. Worse still, when he had been camped outside the castle's walls for two weeks Katsuyori received the unwelcome news that Nobunaga and Ieyasu were heading his way at the head of an army of 38,000 men.

Katsuyori held a meeting with his top retainers, who each urged him to withdraw to Kai province, knowing that the combined might of Nobunaga and Ieyasu could not be defeated. However, a number of Katsuyori's younger commanders such as Atube Katsusuke argued

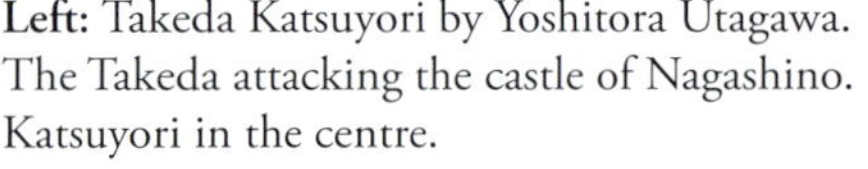

Left: Takeda Katsuyori by Yoshitora Utagawa. The Takeda attacking the castle of Nagashino. Katsuyori in the centre.

that it would be cowardly to retreat and that the Takeda had a long history of always achieving victory. This swayed Katsuyori and he emerged from his meeting determined to stand his ground and face the Oda–Tokugawa force in the open, where the famed Takeda cavalry could prove decisive. Meanwhile, the Oda–Tokugawa army marched to Shitaragahara, where it made camp and erected fortifications, including a 2km long (1.24 mile) defensive palisade. Fearing an attack

Above: A six-panel screen depicting the Battle of Nagashino. The combined forces of Oda Nobunaga and Tokugawa Ieyasu systematically employed a large number of matchlock rifles to defeat the army of Takeda Katsuyori.

Below: Battle of Nagashino by Yoshitoshi. Showing the rolling fusillade cutting down the Takeda.

from the rear, Takeda Katsuyori lifted the siege of Nagashino Castle and positioned his army so that it was facing the enemy's defences.

Along with their regular weapons and armour, each of the Oda samurai carried with them a long, wooden pole. Fifteen hundred of them also carried matchlock guns. The firearm had quickly been introduced and accepted by the samurai, but never on such a scale. Although it was a powerful weapon, Oda Nobunaga realized that the gun had a major shortcoming in that it was a single-shot weapon that took at least 30 seconds to prime and reload after firing. This was not ideal in a full battle situation. To counter this, Nobunaga organized his gunners into three ranks along the barricade he built. This meant a volley of gunfire could be released every 10 seconds.

On the morning of 21 May 1575, in position behind their fortifications, the Oda–Tokugawa troops armed with bows, matchlock guns and long spears awaited the attack of the Takeda. Katsuyori knew his opponents carried firearms, but he hadn't anticipated that Nobunaga had arranged his men in three banks and that they were therefore able to shoot down advancing Takeda fighters three times faster than expected. The first wave of Katsuyori's attackers, consisting of samurai whose task was to break through the palisade, was simply swept away by the volleys of arquebus fire. It had rained the night before the battle, making the ground wet, soggy and unsuitable for cavalry, so Katsuyori had to abandon his plan to send in the mounted samurai. Instead, he ordered more infantry to attack the Oda–Tokugawa defences – and they were shot to pieces as they attempted to scale the wooden palisade and cross the ditch beyond it.

When Katsuyori finally gave the order to retreat after eight hours of bloody fighting, around 10,000 Takeda and 6,000 Oda-Tokugawa troops lay dead. Defeated, Takeda Katsuyori quickly fled the scene, escaping to the Suganuma clan's Busetsu Castle, about 20km (12.4 miles) away. Oda Nobunaga, by contrast, emerged from the Battle of Nagashino-Shitaragahara with both his reputation and his power increased. Japan's history was about to head in a new direction.

Betrayal and Death

In 1577, Nobunaga appointed Hideyoshi to enter the Chugoku region, which was under the influence of the Mōri clan, to subjugate the western part of Honshu. Hideyoshi set off with high hopes, promising his leader that, once he had fulfilled his mission, he would completely conquer Kyūshū and then move on to Korea. In the event, even with 10,000 fully equipped and highly trained samurai behind him, it took Hideyoshi five years to slowly crush the Mōri coalition in the southwest.

In April 1582, Hideyoshi and 30,000 troops, including 10,000 Ukita clan troops, began the siege of Takamatsu Castle in Bitch province, which was defended by Shimizu Muneharu, a retainer of the Mōri, with a force of 3,000. The castle stood in a marshy plain and the attackers dug ditches 1.5km (one mile) long to

Above: The siege and submergence of Takamatsu Castle.

Left: The Honnō-ji Incident, the assassination of Oda Nobunaga.

Above: Death in Battle of Takeda Katsuyori on Mount Tenmoku-Kunitsuna.

divert a nearby river and flood the valley. The water rose, flooding the castle while those inside it were fired on by arquebusiers standing on towers installed on barges. On hearing of the siege, the daimyō Mōri Terumoto sent around 40,000 troops to help the defenders. Hideyoshi had no option but to request additional forces from Nobunaga, who amassed a large army under his six most loyal commanders. He sent them off to the southwest, ordering Hideyoshi to finish attacking before he arrived at Takamatsu Castle. Nobunaga expected to soon follow the dispatched troops together with his personal guard.

Before that, though, he stopped at the Honnō-ji Temple in Kyoto, a location he had used many times as his headquarters. While there, he suddenly found himself besieged on 21 June 1582 by Akechi Mitsuhide, one of the commanders he had dispatched to provide relief to Hideyoshi. It is not clear why Mitsuhide rebelled against Nobunaga, but his plan worked. Trapped with just 100 samurai of his personal guard. Nobunaga had no chance of surviving the attack. He and his men fought valiantly and it was only when a gunshot shattered Nobunaga's arm that he realized his end had come. He set fire to the temple and committed *seppuku*. As for Akechi Mitsuhide, he did not try to assume power himself and was hunted down and killed by Hideyoshi's forces around two weeks after the death of Nobunaga.

Nobunaga had conquered about a third of Japan, established policies to encourage trade, and amassed a sizable army. He was by any measure a hugely successful warlord. The question now was who would succeed him. His remaining son, Nobutaka, was far from Kyoto when news arrived that his father and older brother had been killed. He was not considered a strong enough candidate to lead the country and was forced aside in favour of Hideyoshi. He proved to be a very able commander and skilfully set about consolidating his predecessor's territories, ousting rival claimants to his power and significantly expanding his personal domain. Assuming control of the Oda clan's military operations, he embarked on a campaign to unify Japan – a monumental task he achieved within eight years, in 1590. Denied the title of shōgun due to his humble origins, Hideyoshi accepted the position of regent (*kampaku*) instead, adopting the surname Toyotomi bestowed by the imperial court.

The 1582 battle of Tenmokuzan was the final attempt by Takeda Katsuyori to resist the combined forces of Tokugawa Ieyasu and Oda Nobunaga. In his bid to hide from his pursuers, Katsuyori burned his castle at Shinpu and fled into the mountains to another stronghold, Iwadono Castle. This was held by Oyamada Nobushige who, however, denied entry to Katsuyori, who was then forced to commit *seppuku*. His army, in an attempt to resist enemy attacks, was completely destroyed.

Seppuku – Ritual Death for the Samurai

Above: A *tanto* prepared for ritual use.

The harsh realities of warfare, coupled with the stringent demands of the samurai code, often led to *seppuku*, a ritualized form of suicide. This practice, originating in the 12th century, served as a means to restore honour after committing a grave error or when facing certain defeat. It was also something a person was obliged to do if commanded to by their lord. Initially reserved for samurai, *seppuku* also extended to high-ranking court officials. By choosing this path, individuals sought to preserve their family's honour rather than endure a dishonourable execution or capture.

Seppuku also served as a poignant expression of loyalty. Upon the death of their lord in battle, samurai retainers often followed him in death to uphold his and their honour. Failure to do so resulted in the stigmatized status of a *rōnin*, a masterless samurai. These outcast warriors roamed the land, compelled to seek new employment or resort to banditry.

Seppuku was a highly ritualized act designed to demonstrate courage and resolve in the face of death. While often performed with meticulous ceremony, the realities of battlefield conditions frequently necessitated a more hurried and less formal approach. The ideal of a graceful, self-inflicted death contrasted sharply with the often-desperate circumstances in which *seppuku* was carried out. The practice involved a ritualistic disembowelment using a short sword (*tanto*), typically drawing the blade across the abdomen from left to right. In some cases, a vertical incision was made to hasten death. To alleviate suffering and maintain dignity, a trusted companion known as a *kaishakunin* would often be present to decapitate the individual immediately following the initial incision.

Women of the samurai class were expected to adhere to a similar code of honour as their male counterparts. *Jigai,* the female equivalent of *seppuku*, involved severing the jugular vein with a knife. This act was seen as a way to maintain honour and avoid the potential dishonour of falling into enemy hands.

The Sengoku period, a time of intense warfare, witnessed the emergence of a new form of leadership sacrifice. To preserve the lives of his retainers, a defeated commander might choose to die alone. Shimizu Muneharu's tragic fate exemplifies this. Cornered in Takamatsu Castle by Toyotomi Hideyoshi's forces in 1582, Muneharu secured the safety of his men by committing *seppuku* after the castle was flooded. This act solidified the idea of a leader's ultimate sacrifice for his retainers.

Below: Scene of seppuku in the 1893 work *Tokugawa bakufu keiji zufu* (*An Illustrated Guide to the Punishments of the Tokugawa Shogunate*). White cloth covers tatami, and a sword is placed on a wooden stand in front. To the right, an assistant prepares to perform kaishaku.

豊臣太閤秀吉公
黒田長政
福島正則
橋宗重
加藤主計頭清正
出版兼編輯
前田正三郎

CHAPTER 8

The Rise of Toyotomi Hideyoshi

With the death of Oda Nobunaga, a new power vacuum emerged. Yet it was a short-lived one as his right-hand man, Toyotomi Hideyoshi, soon emerged as Japan's most powerful man. It was an astonishing rise for a man who was born as a peasant – but his rise did not come unopposed. He established an uneasy peace among the warring daimyōs, but one of Nobunaga's former retainers – Tokugawa Ieyasu – was not so willing to accept this new regime.

The news of Nobunaga's death was kept secret. Hideyoshi quickly offered the Mōri clan a truce on favourable terms and returned to Kyoto with his troops and hosted Nobunaga's funeral rites. Hideyoshi's path to power was not straightforward. After dealing with Akechi Mitsuhide, the rebel who provoked Nobunaga's suicide, he quickly proclaimed the fallen warlord's one-year-old grandson as his heir.

Some senior figures in the Oda clan opposed this and Nobunaga's third son, Nobutaka, was put forward as an alternative candidate for new leader. One of his chief backers was a senior daimyō, Shibata Katsuie, and in 1583 his army clashed with that of Hideyoshi's at Shizugatake near Lake Biwa. When Hideyoshi emerged victorious from that encounter, Shibata Katsuie committed *seppuku*, followed soon after by Oda Nobutaka. In the aftermath of the battle, the claims to authority of Nobunaga's baby grandson were quietly forgotten. All of Nobunaga's senior retainers and generals accepted the authority of Hideyoshi – except Tokugawa Ieyasu.

In 1583, Hideyoshi began constructing his own castle at the site of the former Ishiyama Hongan-ji temple in Ōsaka, the old headquarters of the *Ikkō-ikki*. The basic plan was for it to be modelled on Azuchi Castle, but surpassing it in every way. Hideyoshi invited merchants from Kyoto and Sakai to settle there and created a great city. The Castle of Ōsaka is a colossal fortress, the dimensions of which are still a wonder, though only a portion of the building survives. Materials for the work were requisitioned from 30 provinces, their principal components being immense granite rocks, many of which measured 4.26m (14ft) in length and breadth, and some were 12.2m (40ft) long and 3m (10ft) wide. Hideyoshi was consolidating his position in power.

Two years had elapsed since the Honnō-ji Incident of 1582, which saw Oda Nobunaga's downfall. Toyotomi Hideyoshi, having defeated Akechi Mitsuhide, believed he held a strategic advantage. However, Tokugawa Ieyasu was also rapidly gaining power, setting the stage for a confrontation. Both men, expecting trouble, began to recruit allies. For Hideyoshi, these were the Mōri and Uesugi clans. For Tokugawa Ieyasu, it was the Hōjō clan, which had not been finished off by Nobunaga, and the clans of Shikoku Island. Hideyoshi had to solve his problem with the Tokugawa.

Fortunately for Ieyasu, he found an ally in Oda Nobunaga's second son, Nobukatsu, who objected to Hideyoshi's dominance within the clan. The simmering hostility

Left: Toyotomi Hideyoshi.

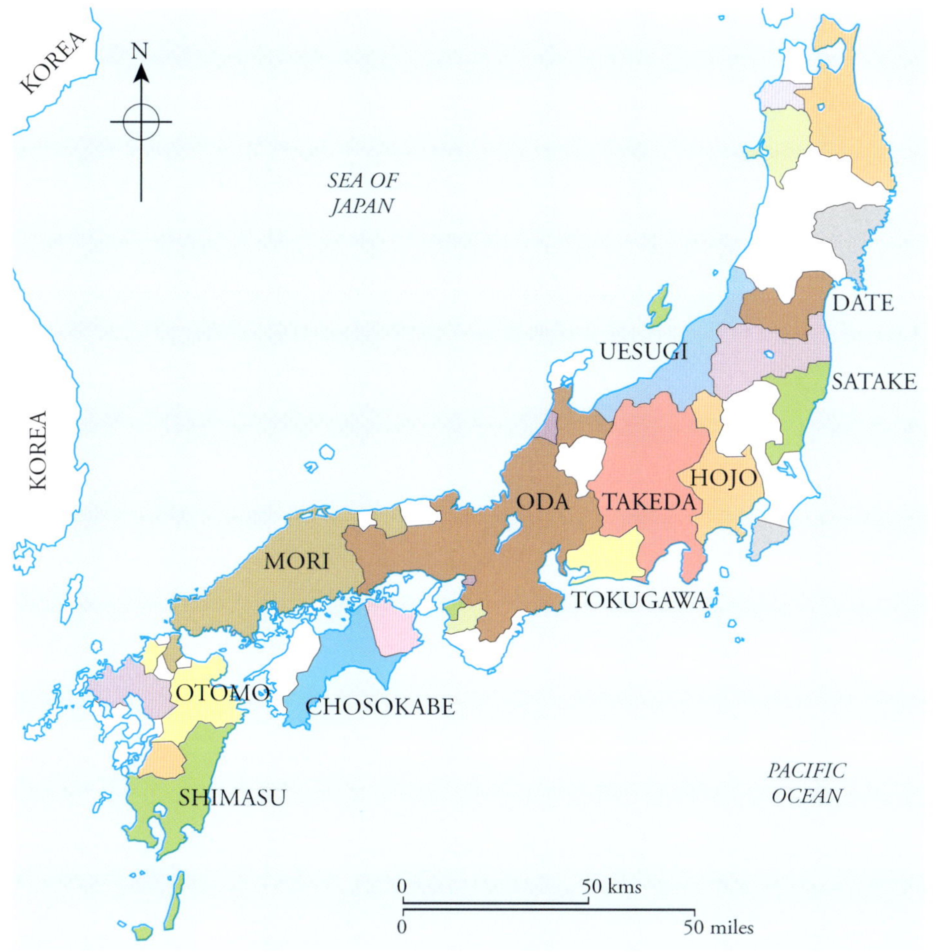

between the two men boiled over when Nobukatsu accused three senior Oda family retainers of spying on him on behalf of Hideyoshi and had them executed. Hideyoshi took this as a declaration of violence against himself and sent troops to take Nobukatsu. This was the excuse Ieyasu needed to attack his rival and increase his own power base and he willingly offered Nobukatsu his help against Hideyoshi. Although on paper Hideyoshi's army of 100,000 men was three times larger than Ieyasu's, it was thinly spread out across the country fighting local rebellions. This allowed Ieyasu to arrive in Oda-controlled territory in March 1584 with 15,000 samurai and take Komakiyama Castle, which he fortified with moats and trenches and made his base of operations.

The first person to take on Ieyasu was Hideyoshi's ally, Mōri

Above: Map of Japan, *c.* 1580.

Right: Ōsaka Castle.

Left: Replica of Hideyoshi's armour.

Nagayoshi, who on 27 April that year arrived at Komakiyama Castle with 3,000 samurai but almost immediately retreated following a surprise attack on his camp by 5,000 Tokugawa warriors. Meanwhile, Hideyoshi took possession of Inuyama Castle about 10km (6.2 miles) away and set up his headquarters there. Over the next nine months, the forces of two of the three great unifiers of Japan fought and skirmished across the region, meeting most memorably at the Battle of Nagakute later that year. Here, Ieyasu claimed victory when his samurai took the heads of 2,800 enemy troops, who were led on the day by Hideyoshi's ally, Mōri Nagayoshi, in return for the loss of just 600 of his own men.

The conflict dragged on for a few more months after this, with neither side willing to engage in all-out battle. Eventually, Hideyoshi and Oda Nobukatsu agreed peace terms, in which they were soon joined by Ieyasu. Hideyoshi was eager to launch a planned invasion of Korea, so this conflict was an annoying distraction for him. Ieyasu, for his part, recognized that it was in his

Below: Battle of Komaki and Nagakute six-panel screen. In the centre of the third panel from the left you can see Ii Naomasa's firearms unit.

Above: Kyūshū prior to the Kyūshū campaign.

interest to ally himself to Hideyoshi's plan for national unification and agreed to become his former rival's subject.

With one set of enemies brought on side, Hideyoshi was free now to focus on bringing under his control those parts of Japan that still resisted him. This meant the islands of Shikoku and Kyūshū and, on the island of Honshu, the areas controlled by the Hōjō and Date clans. His first stop was Shikoku, which he invaded in 1585 with a fleet of 600 ships and more than 100 boats. The landings involved three separate armies totalling 113,000 men. The first army, led by Hashiba Hidenaga and Toyotomi Hidetsugu, targeted the Awa and Tosa provinces, landing on Akashi Island. The second army, under Ukita Hideie, advanced toward Sanuki province. The third army, commanded by Mōri Terumoto, Kobayakawa Takakage and Kikkawa Motonaga, landed in Iyo province.

Despite the overwhelming odds and ignoring the advice of his advisors, Chōsokabe Motochika, the ruler of Shikoku, chose to defend his territories. The conflict culminated in a 26-day siege of Ichinomiya Castle. Motochika made a brief attempt to break the siege but then negotiated a surrender with Hideyoshi. As part of the agreement, Motochika retained control of Tosa province, while the rest of Shikoku was divided among Hideyoshi's generals.

With his eye still on invading Korea, Hideyoshi then turned his attention to the southernmost of the main Japanese islands, Kyūshū. Early in 1587, he successfully organized a campaign by some 250,000 troops against its dominant Shimazu clan. Although a powerful family, the Shimazu's military resources were spread throughout the island, where they were engaged in conflict with other clans, particularly the Ōtomo to the north.

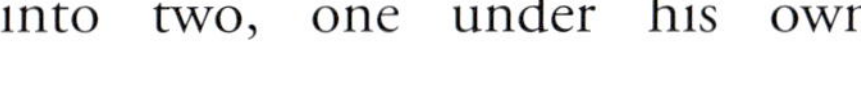

Hideyoshi's forces were divided into two, one under his own command and the other commanded by his brother Hashiba Hidenaga. With Hidenaga's army landing and moving in from the northeast of the island and Hideyoshi and his samurai attacking from the west coast, the two groups made their way south, defeating the Shimazu in one battle after the next. The plan was to meet up in Satsuma province and attack the Shimazu's home castle in Kagoshima from land and from the sea. The two-pronged attack of this so-called Imperial Expeditionary Force left the Shimazu clan in a hopeless situation. Shimazu Yoshihisa, head of the Satsuma clan met with Hideyoshi and agreed terms of surrender whereby he agreed to shave his head as a monk and be sent to Kyoto as a hostage. The government of Satsuma, Osumi and half of the Hyuga province, meanwhile, would pass to his brother Yoshihiro. The rest of the Shimazu's possessions were passed to Hideyoshi's three senior retainers, Kato Kiyomasa, Konishi Yukinaga and Kuroda Nagamasa.

In the north of Honshu, controlled by the Hōjō family, the clan leader Hōjō Ujimasa proved to be much less of an effective politician and military tactician than

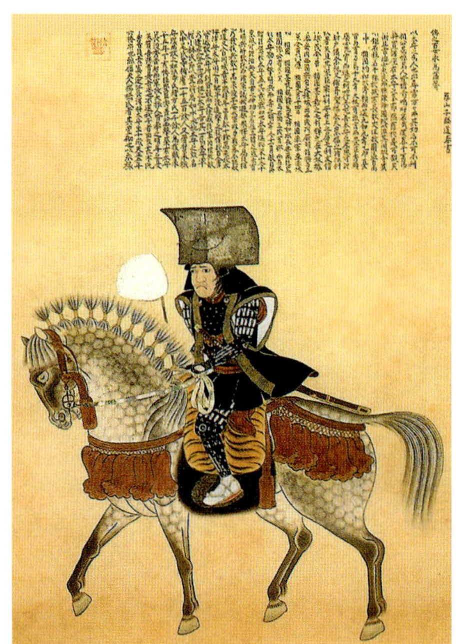

Above: (From left to right): Kato Kiyomasa, Konishi Yukinaga and Kuroda Nagamasa.

Below: Hideyoshi with his tactician Kuroda Kanbe Yoshitaka.

his illustrious great-grandfather, Hōjō Soun. After a five-month siege of his capital at Odawara, Ujimasa committed *seppuku* and his domain passed to Tokugawa Ieyasu.

Having witnessed the provinces around him fall one by one, Date Masamune, the last independent northern Sengoku-daimyō, decided to submit himself to Hideyoshi. Thus, by 1590 the low-born Toyotomi Hideyoshi had pacified and unified all of Japan, marking the end of more than 130 years of conflict. Although he could have become shōgun, Hideyoshi instead only accepted the title of Regent (*kampaku*) from the emperor, perhaps in recognition of his peasant origins.

Through alliance building, adept negotiation and the generous treatment of defeated enemies, he was able to reduce opposition to his rule. In this way, Hideyoshi introduced the idea of association, which meant that the daimyō could continue to rule their domains if they recognized him as their overlord. Hideyoshi also sought to bring stability to the land through social

reform. First, he tried to disarm peasant villagers, knowing that local people posed a significant threat to his conquests through the leagues of farmers, merchants, mercenaries, militant monks and other 'non-warriors' they sometimes created to oppose their rulers. He sought to do this by carrying out his famous 'sword hunt' of 1588, collecting all manner of weapons for the ostensible purpose of melting them down to build a Great Buddha statue.

Next, he ordered that land use surveys be undertaken across the country so that he could discover its productivity – and its taxable value. The Great Buddha was one of many building projects initiated by Hideyoshi through which he exercised his authority over the daimyō, who were charged with contributing to their construction. He also made the daimyō help fund the construction of various castles, including his retirement castle at Fushimi, south of Kyoto, his lavish mansion in Uchino, Kyoto, and even a stone and earthen wall around the city.

Campaigning in Kyūshū, he became alarmed at the influence of the Christian missionaries and the conversion of senior samurai and their families as well as the common people. Not that converting to the Western religion was necessarily a barrier to progress. Konishi Yukinaga and Sou Yoshitoshi, both daimyō of southern territories, were Christian and they led the initial attack against Korea. A more notable Christian samurai was Takayama Ukon ('Blessed Dom Justo').

In 1587, Hideyoshi banned missionary activity in Japan – but, desirous of continued trade with the Europeans, did not enforce it. His suspicions became more pronounced in 1597, when a Spanish ship, the *San Felipe*, was shipwrecked. The captain of the ship attempted to recover his confiscated cargo and insinuated that the missionaries were in Japan preparing for an invasion. In response, Hideyoshi ordered that 26 Christians (three Japanese lay Jesuit brothers, 17 Japanese laymen, five Europeans and one Mexican Franciscan missionary) be put to death by crucifixion, in Nagasaki. Thus, he became the first Japanese ruler to prosecute Christianity.

Above: Takayama Ukon ('Blessed Dom Justo'). He converted to Christianity in 1564 and continued to practise his faith until forced to leave Japan in 1614.

Below: Hideyoshi's order to ban the activities of the Christian missionaries, 24 July 1587.

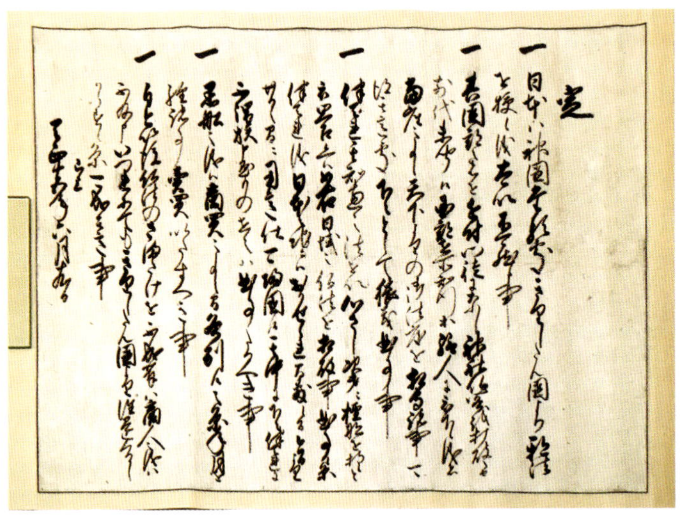

The Invasion of Korea

Not long after Hideyoshi unified Japan, he sent messengers to the Korean kingdom of Choson, asking to be allowed access to the Korean peninsula so that his armies could pass through to conquer China. The Koreans raised doubts and objections but, despite the determination of its diplomats, Hideyoshi ordered daimyōs, mostly from the south, to lead their samurai forces to Korea.

No country was worse prepared to withstand the military might of Japan than Korea in 1594. It was a society consisting of only two classes: the aristocracy and the slaves. The former led a life much like the pampered nobility of the Heian period, only without the samurai to protect them from aggressors since the rest of the population hardly bothered them.

The Korean army was poorly staffed, poorly organized and lacked modern weapons. It was no match for the well-trained samurai force. What Korea lacked in military ability, though, it made up for in geography. Korea has a mountainous, rugged landscape with many hidden gorges and valleys. Japan's advancing troops found themselves short of provisions, especially as the local peasantry adopted a scorched earth policy whenever the enemy approached a village or farmstead. Any supplies and resupplies the Japanese needed had to come from overseas, with all the hazards that held.

In 1591, Hideyoshi established a base on the northwest coast of the island of Kyūshū in a newly constructed castle, Nagoya, located in Hizen province facing Tsushima Island. This was so that he could prepare an invasion fleet. Some of Hideyoshi's closest allies sent troops for the invasion force, while other daimyō less loyal to him, including the Tokugawa and Date, did not. Hideyoshi remained in Nagoya Castle rather than directing the invasion from Korea. The first

Below: Takenouchi no Sukune at the fore of a large ship bound for Korea.

Left: Japan's invasion of Korea, 1592.

wave of troops was to concentrate on Tsushima island and then strike for Korea, capturing the entire country. The second wave was to land later, link up with the first wave and, Hideyoshi hoped, launch an offensive against China.

The organization and financing were entrusted to his daimyō, who proved to be remarkably effective. The expedition was launched in May 1592, and a force of some 160,000 personnel landed at Busan on the southeastern coast of Korea. Approximately a third of the force was armed fighting units, samurai, their attendants and *ashigaru*, while the other two-thirds filled a support and logistics role. The overall commander of the first division of the army was Konishi Yukinaga, with unit commanders Kato Kiyomasa, Kuroda Nagamasa, Kobayakawa Takakage and Mōri Terumoto. The composition of a daimyō's military force can be illustrated by the example of Gotō Sumiharu, a smaller domain lord. His army consisted of 705 individuals, including 27 horsemen. Of these, 220 were frontline combatants, while the remaining 485 provided support functions.

The Korean forces were no match for samurai and *ashigaru* hardened by a lifetime of internal wars. Seoul soon fell to Konishi Yukinaga's force, and in July the Japanese reached and took Pyongyang. Kato Kiyomasa's force pushed northeast, taking Wonsan and moving toward the Tumen River and the Manchurian border. In the meantime, Konishi Yukinaga stayed in the west, awaiting reinforcements which would enable

Right: Battle of Bukgwan 1592–93. During Kato Kiyomasa's North-eastern campaign. A newly formed force of Koreans caused significant problems for the Japanese, resulting in Kiyomasa's army retreating having lost almost half of his 20,00 troops.

Left: The siege of Pyongyang, 1593.

The invading force was severely short of supplies and the local population was in the grip of an epidemic and hunger. A stalemate ensued and Hideyoshi agreed to a ceasefire. While negotiations were carried out, some 70,000 Japanese troops and labourers remained in Korea, stationed in the south part of the peninsula. High-ranking samurai and daimyō passed their time in tea ceremony gatherings and other leisure pursuits, while lower-ranking *ashigaru* practised agriculture. The samurai held small areas in the south throughout the peace negotiations. They stayed until 1596, when the campaign petered out.

Despite strong opposition from the Korean leaders, the Ming court and the Hideyoshi regime tried to negotiate a peaceful end to the war. But when negotiations broke down, Hideyoshi ordered a resumption of the invasion in 1597, this time arming his ships with cannon. The land forces were to be commanded by the daimyō

the expedition to advance the last 120km (75 miles) to the Yalu River and into China.

Under intense pressure from Japan, the Korean king requested military assistance from the Ming Emperor in China and in 1593 a Chinese army of 43,000 troops attacked the Japanese forces at Pyongyang, forcing them to retreat. Although Korea's army was inferior to Japan's, its navy was far more advanced technically and tactically. The Korean Admiral Yi Sun-sin enjoyed considerable success against Hideyoshi's fleet, deploying his special armoured 'turtle' warships against it. Hideyoshi's navy was little more than transport ships. What warships he had were oared and square sailed and not easy to manoeuvre. The only seaborne force that could have rivalled that of Korea was that of the region's pirates – but Hideyoshi had cleared the sea of them. With his command of the sea, Admiral Yi Sun-sin was able to cut off the expeditionary force both from its expected reinforcements and from resupply.

Right: Replica of a Korean turtle ship (*geobukseon*).

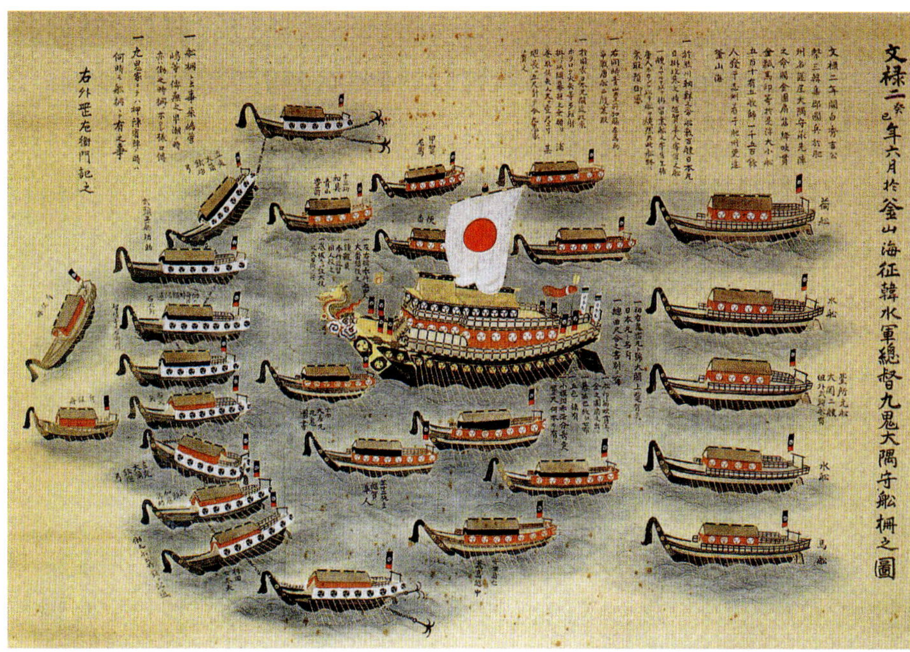

Right: Battle of Busan between the Korean Navy and Japanese Navy in June 1593.

Katō Kiyomasa and he was put in charge of 149,000 samurai and *ashigaru*. The Korean fleet was now a different force, as Yi Sun-sin had been removed from command and replaced by a political appointment. Hideyoshi's fleet quickly defeated him, sinking 160 ships. But the second campaign met with little success after this since, recognizing his mistake, the king reappointed Yi Sun-sin, who led a naval force of iron-clad turtle ships to devastate the significantly larger Hideyoshi fleet. Admiral Yi Sun-sin was killed in one of the last sea fights before the end of the war.

While conflict dragged on, Hideyoshi fell ill and died at Fushimi Castle in September 1598. His five-year-old son Toyotomi Hideyori succeeded him as head of the Toyotomi clan. While Hideyoshi was on his deathbed, he appointed five of his trusted Sengoku-daimyō to act as guardians in a 'Council of Five Regents' until Hideyori came of age. To avoid causing any instability, Hideyoshi's death was kept secret. Soon after, the Council ordered the invasion force to withdraw and concluded the war. The whole expeditionary force was back in Japan by the end of the year.

The twin campaigns in Korea ended in defeat for Hideyoshi's invaders and resulted in the forced removal to Japan of 50,000–60,000 Koreans. The conflict, known as the Imjin War, had been brutal and savage, with atrocities committed on the population and fighting forces by troops of all three nations involved: Japan, Korea and China. The casualties far exceeded those that occurred anywhere else in the world during the 16th and 17th centuries. It took a devastated Korea 200 years to recover its pre-war prosperity.

Contrary to Hideyoshi's intentions, the Japanese invasions of Korea significantly weakened the Toyotomi clan's power in Japan. The aftermath of the war involved the collapse of the regime and socially transformed the entire region. The losses suffered by the many daimyō during the campaign were a contributing factor to the imbalance of power after the war. During the war, many daimyō had found reason to quarrel with one another, leaving ominous rifts among the Toyotomi vassals. As the western-based daimyō of Kyūshū and western Honshu clans contributed most of the forces used during the Korean conflict, it left the pro-Hideyoshi alliance weakened for the eventual struggle with the mostly eastern-backed forces of Tokugawa Ieyasu, who had not contributed any troops to the expeditionary forces.

Left: Statue of Admiral Yi Sun-sin in Seoul.

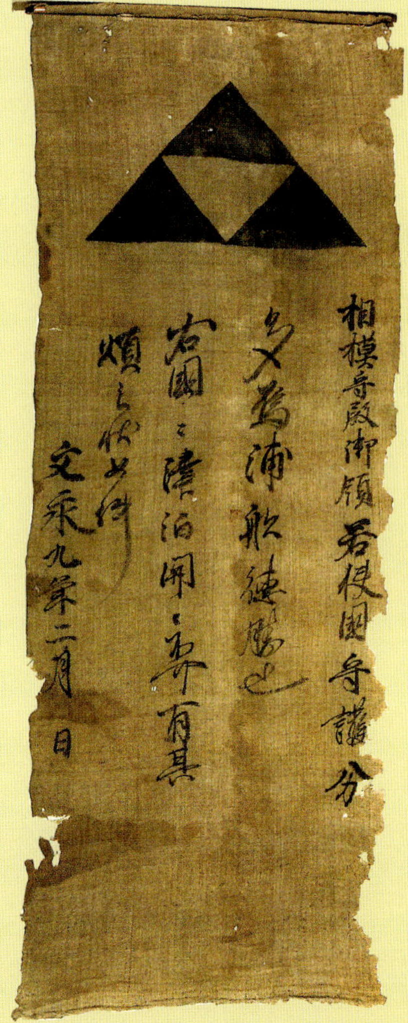

Above: Hōjō clan banner from 1272.

Samurai Banners and Flags

Samurai banners and heraldry underwent a gradual evolution. Initially, simple flags emblazoned with family crests served as a means of identification during battle.

The Gempei War of the 12th century witnessed the use of red and white banners by the Taira and Minamoto clans respectively. While individual flags existed, a foolproof system was yet to emerge. The extent to which these flags assimilated recognizable family crests remains uncertain, as some might have featured solely red or white colours. These early military banners were typically long poles with a horizontal bar supporting a hanging streamer (*hata-jirushi*) and often bore written prayers to the war god, Hachiman. This practice persisted alongside the later adoption of family crest flags.

This simple system sufficed during periods of two-sided conflicts and with a centralized government. However, as warfare became more complex, individual banners emerged as a means of identification. In contemporary woodcut depictions of the late 13th-century Mongol invasions, the use of coloured banners adorned with family crests are clearly seen. These banners served as a visual identifier for individual lords, aiding in post-battle recognition and reward claims. While these banners and flags initially functioned more like regimental standards, they played a crucial role in distinguishing units under different commanders.

The decline of the Ashikaga Shōgunate and the ensuing civil war in the mid-15th century created a new landscape of conflict. Combatants in the field faced the urgent need for effective identification. With

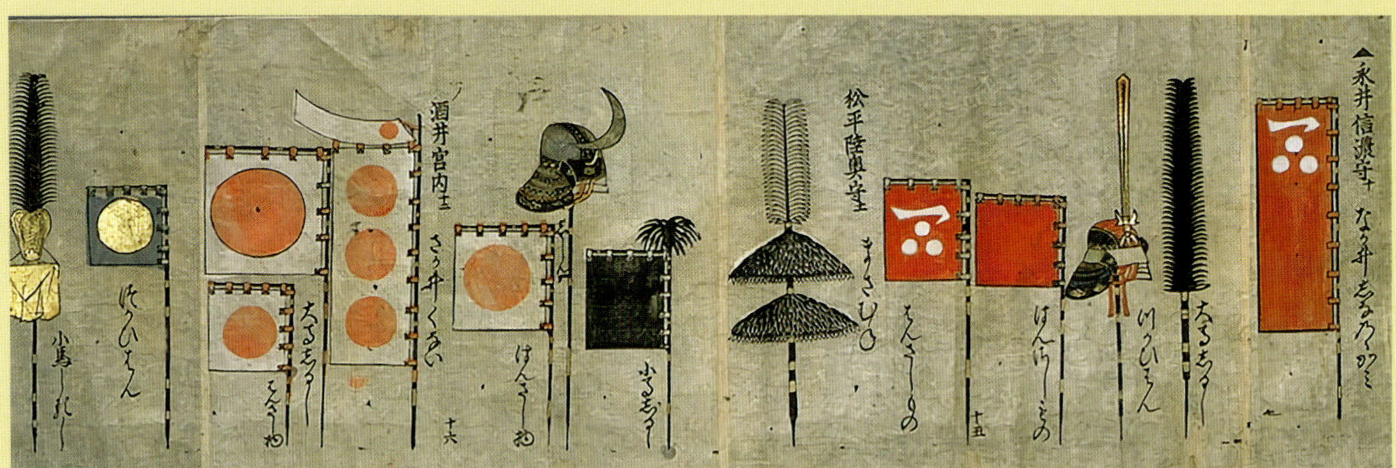

Below: A page from the 15th-century book, *O Uma Jirushi*, by *Kyūan* depicting different types of *Uma-jirushi* (heraldic banners and flags used in medieval Japanese warfare).

regional administrators asserting their independence as daimyō, the political landscape had become increasingly complex, involving multiple factions and alliances. In this context, heraldry emerged as a crucial tool for distinguishing between opposing forces.

The evolving nature of warfare necessitated the introduction of new types of devices. Large units and sections began carrying tall banners (*nobori*) to aid in identification. Daimyō and their commanders adopted distinctive flags (*uma jirushi*) for easy recognition amid the chaos of battle. Even individual foot samurai and *ashigaru* were equipped with banners (*sashimono*) fitted to their back, facilitating identification within the increasingly complex armies of the period.

The increased use of peasant recruits into the armies of the daimyō during the Sengoku period heightened the challenge of battlefield identification. As an illustration, Uesugi Kenshin's army in 1572 comprised around 6,800 individuals, of which 6,200 were infantry, including a significant 400 standard bearers. This highlights the crucial role of banners and flags in maintaining order and distinguishing units. To manage the complexities of banner placement, a specialized position of flag commissioner (*hata bugyo*) was established.

In the 16th century, new types of banners appeared. With the early *hata-jirushi*, only the top edge of the banner was attached to the pole, making it a flowing flag (*nagarebata*). Later, taking into consideration the effects of wind, flags with a strip of cloth fastening the top edge and one side to the pole became sturdier. These new military banners were known as *nobori,* identifying larger units. Some *nobori* were so large that the standard bearer had to carry it secured on his back, and two or even four *ashigaru* walking next to him held it by tied ropes. *Nobori* were the banners of individual units, but for personal identification a flag of a similar design but smaller in size, called a *sashimono*, was used, which was attached to the back

Left: A banner worn on the back for identification (*sashimono*), 18th century.

of the samurai in a wooden tube and possibly with two cords to the rings on the front of the cuirass. Generally, the *sashimono* depicted the daimyō's family crest (*mon*) for whom the samurai served, while the units themselves were distinguished by their colours.

The daimyō or unit commanders used a large square flag (*uma-jirushi*) developed from the tall narrow banners with their clan insignia clearly visible. Not satisfied with simple squares of coloured material, daimyō and senior commanders wanted to stand out more and resorted to different shapes and materials (*o-uma-jirushi*). Often unique ones became famous for a daimyō, such as Toyotomi Hideyoshi's golden gourd banner, or Tokugawa Ieyasu's golden folding fan banner. While these three-dimensional designs were popular, other famous examples were written text on a large *nobori* style flag, such as the pious Katō Kiyomasa's banner that featured a mantra of the Nichiren Buddhist sect.

In addition to the *o-uma-jirushi* themselves, there were also *sashimono* in the form of three-dimensional figures, sometimes of the most fantastic appearance. Sometimes, the role of the *sashimono* was played by a human skull mounted on a pole, a fur ball or balls of black or white fur, peacock feathers or wooden prayer tablets attached to the same poles as the *sashimono.* Another rather common version was to wear between two and five smaller poles with thin strips of cloth attached to them.

Thanks to such memorable and clearly visible emblems, we can easily recognize certain figures of that era in artwork of the time. The six-part painted screen of the late 16th century depicting the Battle of Nagashino while illustrating the intensity of the battle identifies key participants. Tokugawa Ieyasu is easily recognized by his standard of a golden fan; Takeda Katsuyori, with his white banner, leads the reserve into battle and it is also easy to recognize Toyotomi Hideyoshi.

CHAPTER 9

The Rise of the Tokugawa

The death of Hideyoshi threatened to undermine the peace he had created through his own force of personality. His son, Hideyori, was only five years old when he died. He appointed a Council of Regents of five of the most powerful daimyōs to rule in his son's stead – but this group worried that one among them might have ambitions to claim power for themselves. One of these five, Tokugawa Ieyasu, seized power after the Battle of Sekigahara in 1600 – and established a new regime that lasted for more than two-and-a-half centuries.

Above: Daimyō Tokugawa Ieyasu (1543–1616) by Utagawa Yoshitora.

The Council of Regents that Hideyoshi appointed on his deathbed was supposed to guide and advise his son Hideyori until he came of age. It comprised five experienced and wealthy daimyō generals whose differences, Hideyoshi believed, would balance out harmoniously while they moulded his son into an ideal ruler. These statesmen were Tokugawa Ieyasu, Maeda Toshiie, Ukita Hideie, Uesugi Kagekatsu and Mōri Terumoto – and as soon as Hideyoshi put his child's welfare in their hands they began to fall out. As the most powerful daimyō, Ieyasu was the designated Senior Regent. This did not sit well with his colleagues, who, quite rightly, were worried by Ieyasu's ambition. They feared that the leader of the Tokugawa clan wanted the shōgunate for himself. Trouble lay ahead.

For his part, Ieyasu saw it as perfectly reasonable that he should dominate the regency. He was, after all, by far the richest man among them and therefore had a greater stake in the country. Wealth in Japan at that time was not always easy to calculate. The most common measurement used was to calculate a person's assets in *koku.* This was a quantity of rice equivalent to 150kg (331lb) and valued at around 18 grams (0.6oz) of gold. One *koku* was theoretically sufficient to feed one person for one year. The empire was at this time composed of 214 feudal domains, each of which would have had a minimum value of 10,000 *koku* and a good samurai could expect to be paid 100 *koku* annually. These estates yielded to their daimyō holders a total income of 19 million *koku*, and of that total the domains of the five regents constituted one-third, with Ieyasu's estates providing him with 2,557,000 *koku* – an income of around £2.5 billion in today's money, a staggering amount.

After Hideyoshi's death, Ieyasu briefly relocated to Fushimi Castle, Hideyoshi's magnificent new palace in Kyoto, and approved several political marriages to cement alliances between his clan and those of his neighbours. Both the other regents and several senior daimyō councillors were troubled by these moves,

Below: The Council of Five Elders. Appointed by Hideyoshi and tasked to make sure that his son, Hideyori, would succeed him as taikō. From left to right: Tokugawa Ieyasu, Ukita Hideie, Maeda Toshiie, Uesugi Kagekatsu, Mōri Terumoto.

Above: Fushimi Castle, Kyoto. Constructed from 1592 to 1594 by Toyotomi Hideyoshi at the end of the Sengoku period as his retirement residence.

alleging that he was deliberately breaking his vow to Hideyoshi by arranging marriages for political ends and seeking to supplant the young Toyotomi heir. When Ieyasu had paid his complimentary visit to Hideyori, the ministers Masuda and Nagatsuka pressed him to remain there by arguing that his separation from Hideyori would lead to suspicion and discord. On the pretext of being Hideyori's resident guardian, Ieyasu moved his headquarters to Ōsaka Castle, Hideyoshi's stronghold, not to Fushimi which Hideyoshi had allocated to him.

However, a coalition of senior daimyō councillors had formed in addition to – and in some respects against – the Council of Regents, to assert the authority of the Toyotomi clan. Among them was Ishida Mitsunari, who even went as far as to order an assassination attempt on Ieyasu. When that failed, Ieyasu declined to execute him and instead sent Mitsunari to his own stronghold at Hikone, in Omi province, with orders to refrain from any further rebellious actions. It is clear that Ishida Mitsunari wished to ensure that Hideyori became shōgun as the rightful heir and, in turn, called on his supporters to revolt against Tokugawa Ieyasu, whom he accused of having a desire to become shōgun himself.

Both adversaries sent out numerous messengers with letters to enlist the support of the daimyō in various parts

of the country, but it was impossible to say for sure who would wholeheartedly support one side or the other and who would eventually turn out to be traitors. Ieyasu had expected a plot against him to develop and had secretly begun to mobilize his forces. However, there was one impatient daimyō who lacked patience and provoked a general uprising. His name was Mitsunari, a supporter of Uesugi Kagekatsu, one of the five regents. He began to gather supporters and *rōnin* around him and bought weapons, food, ammunition and other supplies in open preparation for war. On 22 August 1600, Mitsunari and his coalition formally denounced Ieyasu for his actions and other transgressions. Ieyasu responded with a declaration of war.

The following week, Mitsunari, in support of Toyotomi Hideyori, made his own move by attacking Fushimi Castle near Kyoto with some 35,000 samurai. The castle, commanded by Torii Motonada with a garrison of 2,000, needed to withstand the onslaught to enable the Tokugawa troops to regroup and prevent Ishida reaching Kyoto. The Torii force gave fierce resistance, knowing they were in a fight to the death. After eight days, all that remained of the garrison was 200 samurai and they continued to fight wave after wave of assault troops for a further two days. The Siege of Fushimi Castle had cost the invading Hideyoshi army 3,000 men, and, more importantly, ten days that they couldn't afford to waste. The capture of Fushimi meant reinforcements for Mitsunari's army could arrive and now he received samurai from the Shimazu clan. Tokugawa Ieyasu arrived shortly after with a combined army of 90,000 warriors to meet the Western Army of Toyotomi Hideyoshi at the Battle of Sekigahara.

The loyalists who sought to preserve the Toyotomi legacy and

Right: The Nimai-Dō Gusoku armour of Ishida Mitsunari.

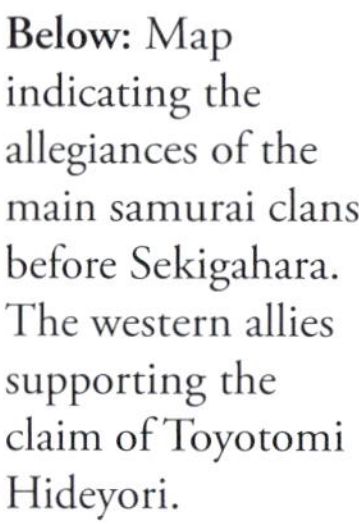

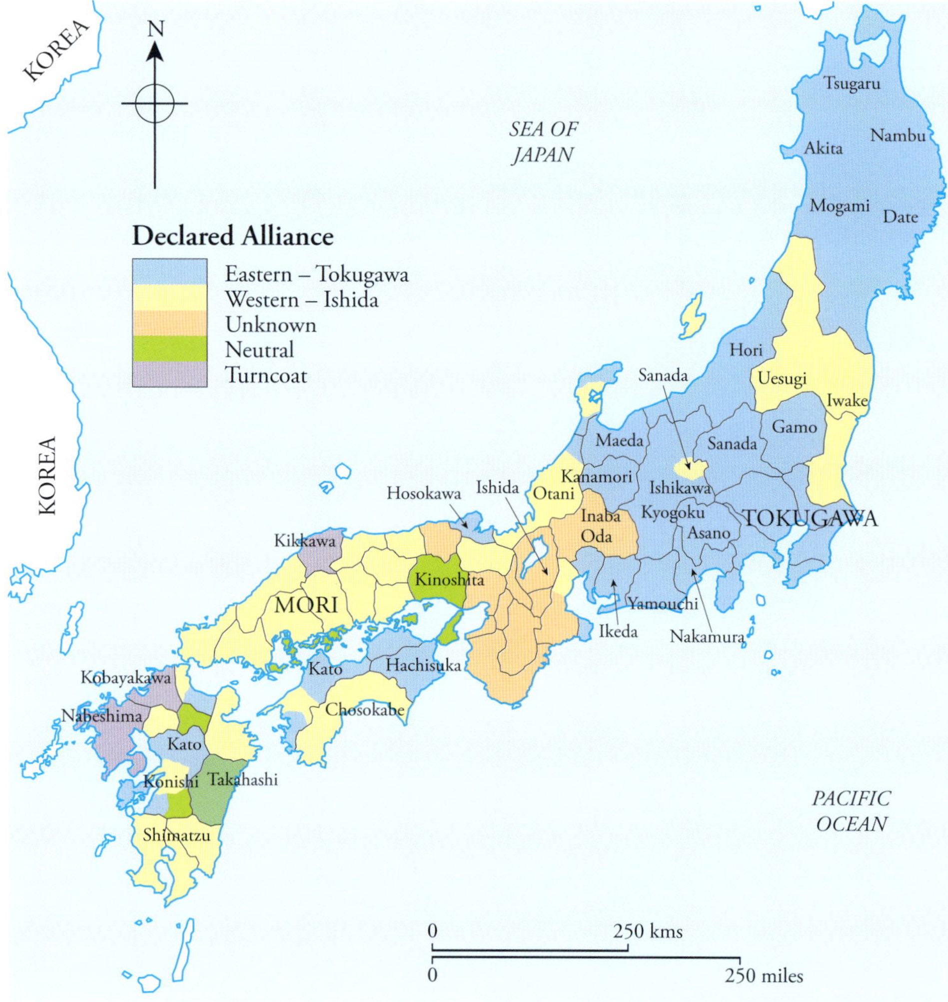

Below: Map indicating the allegiances of the main samurai clans before Sekigahara. The western allies supporting the claim of Toyotomi Hideyori.

halt Ieyasu's rise to power were based mostly in western Japan and they were to clash with the eastern daimyō supporting Tokugawa Ieyasu.

Ieyasu's fear of treachery among his own coalition kept him at the Tokugawa base in Edo, which he was reluctant to leave until battle commitment was shown. His allies, Ikeda Terumasa and Fukushima Masanori, former Hideyoshi commanders with 31,000 troops, had assembled at Kiyosu Castle, situated about halfway between Ōsaka and Edo. On hearing of Ieyasu's doubt, they attacked Oda Hidenobu, a Toyotomi supporter and grandson of Nobunaga, in Gifu Castle and defeated him. With this castle secured, Ieyasu formed his troops and marched toward Ōsaka, where Mitsunari's main force was located.

The Tokugawa army was divided into two parts, one commanded by Ieyasu, comprising 30,000 troops, and the other of 36,000, commanded by his son, Hidetada, although his advance was delayed because of skirmishes with Mitsunari's retainers. When Ieyasu left his base his intention was for his armies to regroup in Mino province. However, once he was on the move Ieyasu was persuaded to continue his advance by his advisers.

Above: Torii Mototada. He was a close personal friend and vassal of Tokugawa Ieyasu. Defended Fushi Castle to the bitter end.

Below: Map of Central Japan showing the movement routes of the opposing armies.

The Battle of Sekigahara

This battle was to be one of the most significant – perhaps *the* most significant – conflicts in the history of the samurai. It was to signal the end of the Sengoku Period and initiate momentous changes throughout Japan.

On the evening of 20 October 1600, the opposing armies arrived near the small village of Sekigahara, situated on an intersection of the east-west Nakasendo road, one of the country's main transport arteries. October had been a cold month in central Honshu, with heavy rainfall turning what roads there were to mud. The troops on both the opposing sides were cold, wet, and exhausted.

Ishida Mitsunari, a skilled strategist but a less renowned warrior, had put together a coalition of almost 82,000 men loyal to Hideyori that boasted renowned samurai clans like the Mōri, Kobayakawa, Kikkawa, Ukita and Shimazu. Most were from the west of Japan, which is why the force was known as the Western Army. Arriving first at Sekigahara, Mitsunari deployed his forces strategically. Ukita Hideie commanded the central position, flanked by Shimazu Yoshihiro to the north and Otani Yoshitsugu to the south. Kobayakawa Hideaki occupied the Matsuo mountainside, while Mōri Hidemoto and Chōsokabe Mōrichika held the Nangu mountain to the southwest, facing Ieyasu's rear.

Ieyasu had also been successful in gaining the alliance of notable daimyō families such as the Kato, the Hosokawa and the Kuroda, as well as some able senior daimyō and generals who had already fought alongside him on numerous campaigns. Their strong powerbase in eastern Honshu meant that the Tokugawa force was referred to as the Army of the East. Its 74,000 samurai troops entered the valley from Nakasendo in the east, with Fukushima Masanori at the vanguard and Ii Naomasa commanding a key section of around 30 rapid deployment elite samurai.

On the morning of 21 October, a thick fog blanketed the valley. As it lifted, Naomasa's shock force pre-empted Ieyasu's orders and charged the forces of Ukita Hideie, joined by Fukushima Masanori's eastern army advance guard crashing into the centre of the Western Army's defence line. Ieyasu moved his left flank forward to support Naomasa and Masanori and pushed his right wing against Mitsunari. The fighting was intense, and many samurai became bogged down in terrain made a quagmire by the overnight rain. Masanori's attack made some progress, but as he advanced his flank became opposed by Otani Yoshitsugu's battle-hardened samurai, who held their position. By 10 am there was action over a wide area, with close combat and melee hampered by the amount of gun smoke and reduced visibility. The

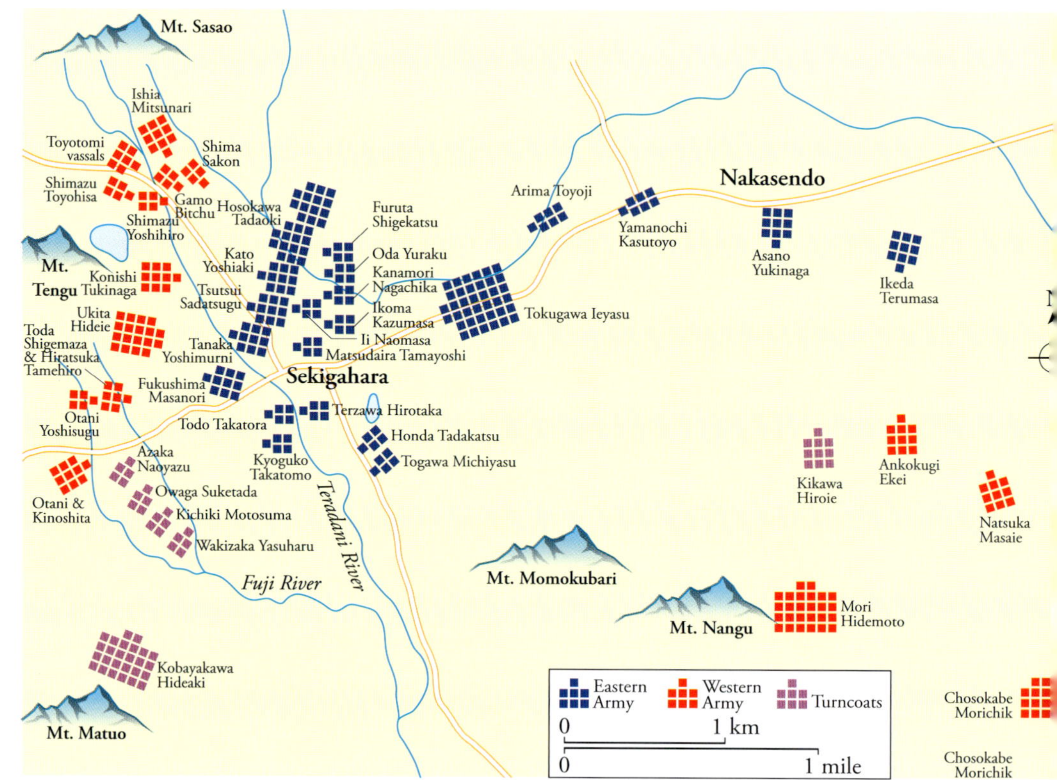

Right: Sekigahara Battlefield as the opposing troops move into position on 21 October 1600.

battle was favouring the Western Army, but it needed reinforcements. Shimazu Yoshihiro had been ordered to advance but refused to commit his 2,000 samurai. Another important general who was conspicuously inactive during the early battle was Kobayakawa Hideaki on Mount Matsuo just south of the Otani forces. Hideaki had about 15,600 men. Unknown to Mitsunari, Kobayakawa Hideaki had secretly pledged allegiance to Ieyasu. At noon, Hideaki dramatically betrayed the Western Army, charging down Mount Matsuo into the heart of the Otani forces. This unexpected attack, coupled with the subsequent defection of four other Western clans, shattered the Western Army's morale. Desperate, Otani Yoshitsugu committed *seppuku* to avoid capture, while Ukita Hideie fled the battlefield as the Kobayakawa overwhelmed his forces. Meanwhile, Ii Naomasa engaged the Shimazu in a fierce battle.

By 1.30 pm, the situation was hopeless for Mitsunari.

Above: Sekigahara Battle Screen.

Right: Otani Yoshitsugu was very loyal to Ishida Mitsunari and although ill joined the western force. He was carried into battle and commanded from a simple open palanquin. Although mostly blind and his body crippled with leprosy, his mind remained sharp. When the Kobayakawa army turned traitor at the height of the battle and struck at the Otani samurai, Yoshitsugu, realizing the end was close and committed *seppuku*. He was the only daimyō to have committed seppuku on the battlefield at Sekigahara. His head remains hidden somewhere on the mountain.

Above: The statue of Ii Naomasa was erected in front of the train station of Hikone.

He fled, leaving Yoshihiro to fight a brave rearguard action before forcing his way through Ieyasu's lines and escaping. As Yoshihiro and his last 200 samurai began to leave the battlefield, they provided a volley of arquebus fire to cover their retreat. One of their musket balls managed to wound Ii Naomasa in the arm, knocking him from his horse and forcing him to stop giving pursuit.

With his right flank collapsing, Mitsunari ordered Mōri Hidemoto into action. The 28,000 Western Army forces on Mount Nangu, despite their strength, numbers and ideal position in Ieyasu's rear, had done nothing the whole battle. Indeed, Kikkawa Hiroie, leading the advance of the Mōri, had been a turncoat all along and had promised Ieyasu not to fight the Army of the East in an attempt to secure a more favourable position for the Mōri clan in the new Tokugawa-dominated Japan. Seeing that the battle was over, the Mōri also took their leave of the battlefield.

At 2.00 pm, after six hours of fighting, Tokugawa Ieyasu declared his army victorious and 30 minutes later conducted the head-viewing ceremony. It had been a costly battle with about 30,000 dead. Mitsunari was caught three days after the battle on Mount Ibuki and executed with other captured leaders of the Western Army on the riverbed at Kyoto.

Aftermath

The Battle of Sekigahara marked the decisive conclusion of the Age of the Warring States. Ishida Mitsunari's Western Army was decisively defeated, allowing Ieyasu to swiftly capture Sawayama and Ōsaka castles. Mitsunari was executed within a month. In the aftermath, Ieyasu realigned the political landscape by confiscating lands from defeated daimyō and bestowing them upon loyal allies such as Kobayakawa Hideaki and Kikkawa Hiroie. As a strategic move, he installed Toyotomi Hideyori in Ōsaka Castle to appease the remnants of the Western Army. Finally, in 1603, Ieyasu was granted the title of shōgun by Emperor Go-Yozei, establishing the Tokugawa Shōgunate, which would govern Japan in peace for over two centuries.

On 22 October, the survivors of the battle of Sekigahara began to drift in through the gates of Ōsaka Castle with the wildest and most exaggerated tales of disaster. Following them one after the other, came the unbeaten units of Nabeshima, of Chōsokabe and of Mōri Hidemoto. The more courageous among these, notably Mōri Hidemoto and the Tachibana, were strongly in favour of continuing the struggle. Ōsaka had a huge store of provisions and around 75,000 troops. It would be impregnable to all the forces that Ieyasu could bring against it while awaiting reinforcements from the west. However, despite this, Mōri Terumoto, Hidemoto's cousin and leader of the Mōri clan, was by no means eager to prolong the contest with Ieyasu. If he could come off with no territorial loss, he would be more than content to surrender Ōsaka and all that it contained and quietly withdraw to his capital of Hiroshima. Therefore, Terumoto was easily persuaded to hand over the castle to Ieyasu, who entered it on 1 November. With the castle surrendered without conflict and safely in Tokugawa hands, Ieyasu declared that it was the duty of a warrior to fight, especially the supposed 'commander of the army', so Mōri Terumoto's lands were reduced and transferred to others as rewards.

Tokugawa Ieyasu's authority in Japan was now unchallenged. However, Toyotomi Hideyori was still considered a potential ruler of Japan, and his family

was still one of the richest and most influential in the country. Hideyori was young and most senior daimyō believed that a shōgunate headed by Ieyasu would only be temporary. Ieyasu was 60 years old in 1603, an advanced age in that period, and years of campaigning would have taken their toll on him.

To ensure that his authority was quickly accepted throughout the country, Tokugawa Ieyasu had to develop an effective and well organized system of government. His first step was to reward the daimyōs who had fought for him and to punish those who had resisted. Ieyasu confiscated 90 of the 214 feudal domains and severely reduced a further four – those of the Mōri, Satake, Uesugi and Akita. The greater part of the wealth generated by the domains was retained by the Tokugawa, as were rights in forests, mines, harbours and important commercial centres. At the same time, he rewarded daimyōs who had fought on his side with fiefs in his own former domains, where it was important for him to have reliable adherents. Here and elsewhere throughout the country they were established as independent daimyōs and constituted the bulwark of the house of Tokugawa. They numbered about 60.

Even though Ieyasu was the undisputed ruler, his next problem was to give constitutional form to his control. For that purpose, he decided to restore the bakufu, with himself as shōgun. Nobunaga and Hideyoshi were not descendants of Minamoto family and so could not legally claim the title of 'Shōgun'. However, Ieyasu was related to the first shōgun and so could take the title. The emperor officially appointed Ieyasu shōgun in 1603, but then he took no advantage of the office for some time. He was careful to avoid the impression that he intended to displace Hideyori, since there were still senior daimyō in or near Ōsaka who would rise to protect him and would have been joined by daimyōs hostile to the Tokugawa, especially those in the west.

Ieyasu had decided soon after entering Ōsaka in 1600 to make his capital at Edo, the stronghold of his own great domains in the Kanto. Here was to be the centre of his military power, and within the next few years he took steps to strengthen Edo Castle and to protect it by a screen of fortresses at key points in the

Below: Sekigahara Sengoku Armour Museum. Types of armour worn at the Battle of Sekigahara.

Left: Detail of Edo Castle, from a 17th-century folding screen.

surrounding country. At the same time, he developed foreign trade links with the Dutch, Spanish and English and promoted a programme of shipbuilding. Ieyasu left his eldest son, Hidetada, in charge of Edo Castle while he resided elsewhere, concentrating on strengthening his own position for the future. At that time, the nation was divided evenly into two factors: one obedient to the Tokugawa, the other prepared to await Hideyori's coming of age and the restoration of the Toyotomi.

To Ieyasu's great frustration, his son Hidetada orchestrated a marriage between his beloved granddaughter Sen and Toyotomi Hideyori, who was living in seclusion at Ōsaka Castle with his mother. This attempted diplomatic overture failed to pacify Hideyori's ambitions and was to lead to conflict.

After being officially recognized as shōgun, Ieyasu's influence increased rapidly, while Toyotomi Hideyoshi's son, Hideyori, and Ieyasu's only real rival for rulership of Japan, found his position was weakened by the deaths of such faithful supporters as Asano Nagamasa, Kato Kiyomasa and Maeda Toshinaga. While after 1603, Japan is more or less unified, it certainly is not without conflict. Tokugawa Ieyasu is embroiled in a campaign to suppress Hideyori, Toyotomi Hideyoshi's son, and Ieyasu's only real rival for rulership of Japan. To prevent future shōgunal succession squabbles, Ieyasu abdicated in 1605 in favour of Hidetada, who assumed a role as formal head of the bakufu bureaucracy. (Ieyasu, though retired, retained significant power and influence until his death in 1616).

Ieyasu's long-awaited move against Hideyori finally came in 1614, after the passing of Hideyoshi's remaining senior loyalist daimyō. Using a pretext involving an inscription on a restored bell at Hōkō-ji Temple, which Ieyasu regarded as an insult, he initiated an attack on Ōsaka Castle. Although deserted by the other great feudal lords, Hideyori found support among the numerous *rōnin*, masterless warriors displaced by the Tokugawa's rise. He assembled a considerable force of over 90,000 of these warriors. Even though the Tokugawa army possessed a significant numerical advantage, the imposing defences of Ōsaka Castle proved impenetrable, successfully repelling the initial Tokugawa assault.

The Ōsaka Campaign

Ieyasu looked for a reason he could challenge Hideyori. A rumour was generated that Ōsaka Castle was being strengthened by more fortifications and the recruiting of additional troops to swell its defences while increasing food and armament reserves. Initially, there was little truth in this – and Hideyori even turned down the opportunity to buy a batch of premium English gunpowder from European traders (which was, of course, immediately purchased by Ieyasu). But by October 1614, Hideyori finally accepted the counsel of his advisors that he should protect himself against the Tokugawa threat.

In preparation for a future siege, Hideyori surrounding his castle with additional moats, behind which was a wall with loopholes for archers and musketeers. Hideyori also tried to form alliances with the major daimyō, but they were all either on the side of the Tokugawa or preferred to remain neutral. The samurai who did come to Ōsaka were mostly *rōnin*, masterless and displaced retainers of dispossesed daimyō who had chosen the wrong side at Sekigahara such as Ono Harunaga and his brother Harafusa, Kimura Shigenari, Oda Kabunaga's brother Oda Yuraku, Tosokabe Mōrishige and, finally, an important player in the forthcoming conflict, Sanada Yukimura. However, even with the difficulties in front of him, Hideyori had gathered an impressive army of over 90,000 men. The castle defenders had good artillery purchased by Hideyori from the Dutch, and there were catapult incendiary devices placed at 100m (328ft) intervals along the walls. This made Ōsaka Castle the most imposing fortress in the country.

Not surprisingly, since the religion had emerged from Kyūshū in the west, there were many Christians among the castle's defenders. Several of the daimyō were Christians, like Gotō Mototsugu and Kimura Shigenari. There had been intermittent persecutions of Japanese Christians during this period, including some martyrdoms of converts and missionary priests. Tokugawa Hidetada, Ieyasu's heir, would not tolerate the religion. With so many Christians supporting the Toyotomi, this only intensified the bad feeling against the faith on the opposing side.

In early November 1614, Ieyasu ordered Hidetada to mobilize all of his troops in Edo and asked his senior retainers do the same. The 50,000-strong Army of the East soon left Edo with Hidetada at its head, followed by Tokugawa Yoshinao with a further 15,000 and men

Below: Siege of Ōsaka Castle, 1614.

Sakakibara Yasumasa – Warrior and General

Sakakibara Yasumasa (1548–1606) was a daimyō of the late Sengoku–early Edo period who served the Tokugawa clan as an important samurai and military commander. He was considered one of the four *Shitenno*, the so-called 'Four Guardian Kings' that the Tokugawa heavily relied on for support, the other three being Ii Naomasa, Honda Tadakatsu and Sakai Tadatsugu. In 1590, after distinguishing himself in numerous military campaigns, Yasumasa was made lord of Tatebayashi Castle in Kosuke province and given an income of 100,000 *koku*, a vast sum.

In 1566, aged 19, Yasumasa passed his rite of passage to adulthood and was soon after made *hatamoto* ('Guardian of the Banner', a high-ranking samurai), along with Honda Tadakatsu. Both men were given 50 horsemen and appointed commanders of Tokugawa Ieyasu's hatamoto unit. With, on average, three infantry soldiers attached to each horse-mounted samurai, Yasumasa must have overseen around 200 men.

Yasumasa fought at Anegawa in 1570, at Mikata-Ga-Hara in 1573 and at the battle of Nagashino in 1575. He participated in Ieyasu's many battles and was given excellent reports. It was said that Ieyasu would never be defeated with Yasumasa at his side, whether at a castle siege or a field battle.

Although young, he was put in charge of increasingly large forces, such was his proficiency as a warrior and a leader. He particularly excelled himself at the Battle of Komaki and Nagakute in 1584 – which was in a fact not one engagement but a series of fights in and around Mount Komaki and Inayuma Castle.

The first of these battles was fought around Mount Komaki and gave rise to the name 'Battle of Komaki.' The rest of the battles took place around Nagakute. Forces called to support Inuyama Castle, north of Nagoya, arrived in the area near the castle. Ieyasu, however,

Left: In this portrait, Sakakibara Yasumasa sits in armour cross-legged style, in light yellowish green undergarments. The armour cuirass has a crawling dragon motif and the *kusazuri* (a protective skirt that hangs from the bottom of the cuirass) with a *tatsunami* (wave crest) pattern. The *kabuto* (helmet) has a standing front decoration of a *sankoken* (sword shape). In the portrait Yasumasa wears a tachi-type sword, its scabbard lavishly clad with *fukurin* (gilt edging), and a rather long *wakizashi* (short sword). His right hand, wearing a tanned-leather glove, holds a *saihai* (command baton) for directing the troops.

Above: Sakakibara Yasumasa and Toyotomi Hideyoshi on Mt. Komaki – displaying an episode from the Battle of Komaki in 1584 with Sakakibara Yasumasa and Toyotomi Hideyoshi. Yasumasa charges down a slope chasing Hideyoshi. with his personal standard flying from his back and holding his spear with both hands. Illustrates details of the armour and weapons, the saddle and stirrups.

had already known of these plans and had Sakakibara Yasumasa and Sakai Tadatsugu move 5,000 troops to the area that same evening. In this battle in 1584, Yasumasa quickly defeated Hideyoshi's detachment. As a result, Toyotomi Hidetsugu, Hideyoshi's nephew, lost most of his army. Ikeda Tsuneoki and Mori Nagayoshi were defeated. Although Yasumasa was one of the 'Four Guardians', his remaining image is somewhat less than the others. However, Yasumasa Sakakibara's success in the Tokugawa army was as good as Honda Tadakatsu and Ii Naomasa. He took charge of almost all the battles in which he participated until Ii Naomasa came to power. He supported Tokugawa Ieyasu in an era when he was forced to fight harshly, and significantly paved the way for him to become Shōgun.

On 11 May 1606 he died in Tatebayashi due to illness. He was 59 years old.

A SAMURAI WARRIOR'S ARMOUR

This is the armour worn by Sakakibara Yasumasa (1548–1606), The body cuirass is a two-piece type with black-lacquered iron panels tied with X-shaped stitches, hinges on the left side and seven five-tiered *kusazuri* (a protective panel that hangs from the bottom of the cuirass). A design of a crawling dragon is depicted in gold lacquer on the cuirass and a wave pattern is depicted on the bottom two tiers of the *kusazuri*. The *kabuto* (helmet), the most expensive part of the armour, is made from 62 vertical panels and has a *maetate* (a decoration on the front of a helmet) of copper-plated *sankoken* (a sword) at the front. Although originally black leather strips were used to tie the panels to the cuirass, the current *shikoro* (neck protection) of the helmet and the *kusazuri* are tentatively bound with purple thread. There are ornamental metal fittings with the family crest of the Sakakibara family, on the breast and hand and wrist protector.

such as Date Masamune with 10,000, Uesugi Kagekatsu with 5,000 and Satake Yoshinobu with 1,500. When it arrived at Ōsaka Castle in early December, Ieyasu's army numbered around 180,000, double that of the defenders.

Hidetada wished to carry out a general assault against the fortifications, but Ieyasu was satisfied to bring forward the artillery and order a barrage. Even though the garrison was heavily outnumbered, their defences held firm. In one incident, Ii Naotaka's Red Devils (an elite force of shock samurai so named for their blood-red armour) managed to scale the outer wall and displace the defenders – but once inside they were met with volley after volley of matchlock fire and were forced to retreat with heavy losses.

Eventually, Ieyasu proposed a peace deal with Hideyori. Despite his castle being incredibly well fortified and stocked with enough supplies to hold out for several years, Hideyori did not want to prolong the conflict and, on 22 January 1615, he signed a peace treaty with Ieyasu. As part of the armistice Hideyori swore a solemn oath that he would not rebel against Ieyasu or Hidetada, and that he would consult with the Tokugawa on any important decisions he needed to make while still being allowed to rule in Ōsaka. The Tokugawa forces ended what was known as the 'Winter siege' and withdrew. With the conflict over, Ieyasu ordered two of his commanders, Honda Tadamasa and Honda Masayuri, to dismantle Ōsaka Castle's exterior defences, which they did by demolishing the outer walls and filling in the moats. When Hideyori complained this had not been agreed in the peace treaty, Ieyasu gave him the unanswerable reply that, since the agreement they made had been one of eternal peace, the defences were not necessary.

Below: Kimura Shigenari overcoming attackers.

Left: Artillery team in action from an antique book.

That eternal peace, however, lasted just six months. When rumours began to circulate that he was recruiting *rōnin* and re-fortifying Ōsaka Castle, Hideyori knew that Ieyasu was planning to move against him once and for all. He decided to prove the rumours were true and embarked on a *rōnin* recruitment drive, building an army of 100,000 men. As before, there were many Christians among them, along with several foreign priests who based themselves in Ōsaka Castle – from whose walls hung six large banners displaying the crucifix. But rather than wait for his partially dismantled fortress to be besieged, Hideyori decided that attack was the best form of defence and embarked on what was known as his Summer Campaign to meet the Tokugawa in the field.

By the end of May, Gotō Mototsugu and his advance force of around 3,000 samurai were at Dōmyōji Temple, 20km (12.4 miles) southeast of Ōsaka Castle, ready to prevent the Tokugawa from entering the Ōsaka plain. But, when planned reinforcements failed to arrive on time, Hideyori's forces were routed and Mototsugu,

Right: Detail from a folding screen showing the siege of Ōsaka in 1615. Honda Tadatomo leads an attack on the Ōsaka defenders.

having been shot and wounded, committed *seppuku*. By the time the main Ōsaka army of 12,000 men under Sanada Yukimura did turn up, it struggled to make any headway against its far more numerous enemy and decided to retreat to the relative safety of the partially dismantled Ōsaka Castle. Another Ōsaka force of 10,000 made up of the Chōsokabe and Kimura samurai held up the Tokugawa advance for six hours, but it was not enough. On the evening of 2 June, an Ōsaka council of war met and agreed that its army would face the Tokugawa forces about 4km (2.5 miles) south of the castle on open ground. At around noon the following day, Hideyori's army of approximately 54,000 was crushed by a Tokugawa force of 150,000. With Hideyori dealt with, the Tokugawa attacked his castle and stormed it.

According to an account by an employee of the Dutch East India Company in Hirado, several of the Toyotomi senior daimyō, anticipating defeat, committed *seppuku* and several more senior retainers set the castle on fire and attempted to defect to Ieyasu. Hideyori had them thrown off the castle walls, but could not extinguish the fire. The account also stated that about 10,000 people perished in the resulting blaze and countless commoners and castle staff were killed as they attempted to flee the violence enveloping their city. Hideyori and his wife and mother committed *seppuku* in the burning fortress.

Above: Battle of Dōmyōji. On 3 June 1615 the Eastern Army of Tokugawa Ieyasu and the Ōsaka Army of Toyotomi Hideyori clashed at Dōmyōji, Ōsaka. This battle was one of Japan's major historical battles between samurai forces.

The last of the Toyotomi clan, Hideyori's eight-year-old son, was beheaded to prevent him posing a threat in the future. A considerable number of *rōnin* were also executed and their heads were displayed along the road from Kyoto to Fushimi. In contrast to the drawn out winter campaign six months earlier, this summer assault had succeeded in destroying the Toyotomi clan in less than 24 hours.

Following the fall of Ōsaka, the shōgunate implemented strict building regulations, limiting each province to a single castle and mandating that a daimyō could only own one fortress. Henceforth, constructing or repairing a castle required explicit shōgunate approval. This policy led to the demolition of numerous castles.

Ieyasu's victory came at a high personal cost. He had sustained several wounds during the Ōsaka campaign and his health declined precipitously. On 1 June 1616, the final architect of a unified Japan passed away, leaving the Tokugawa Shōgunate to his descendants. This dynasty would govern Japan for an uninterrupted period of more than 250 years in what was known as the Edo Period.

Pax Tokugawa

In September 1615, following the fall of Ōsaka Castle, Ieyasu and Hidetada summoned all the provincial daimyō to Edo and drew up a set of laws to regulate their behaviour. They were known as the 'Laws for the Military Houses'. One of these laws, on military training and sport, ran as follows:

The arts of peace and war, including archery and horsemanship, should be pursued single mindedly. From of old the rule has been to practice the 'arts of peace on the left hand and the arts of war on the right'; both must be mastered. Archery and horsemanship are indispensable to military men. Though arms are called instruments of evil, there are times when they must be resorted to. In peacetime we should not be oblivious to the danger of war. Should we not then prepare ourselves for it?

This was also the time that the cult of the 'Way of the Warrior' (later known as Bushidō) was formalized and strengthened by the injection of Confucian notions, emphasizing loyalty and honour and the proper reverence for superiors, along with total dedication to the service of one's lord (see pages 42–45). Although the fighting warrior had adhered to a code or spirit over time, this was the birth of that particular code of morals and behaviour that gives the samurai a chivalrous place in history.

In support of these laws, the bakufu despatched Provincial Censors to estates where there may have been opportunities for conflict, such as those where the daimyō were ill or too young to exert their authority, and where they remained for extended periods. Additionally, the Tokugawa sent out inspectors, initially on a loose basis, but formalized in 1633. These inspectors were tasked with enquiring into the application of laws and the spread of Christian religion, while also reporting on the state of commerce, population, standards of living and similar matters.

The essential feature of government by the Tokugawa shōguns was a determination to keep the peace. The basis of Ieyasu's civil policy was to distribute fiefs in such a way that his most trusted daimyō and retainers occupied domains from which they could keep watch on daimyō whose allegiance was doubtful. Having won a clear-cut victory on a national scale, Ieyasu was able to reward or punish every daimyō in the realm. The dependable daimyō were known as 'Hereditary Lords of the house of Tokugawa' (*Fudai*); on the opposite side of this were the 'Outside Lords' (*Tozama*), who were those who had hereditary ties to the Tokugawa or who had been on the wrong side at the Battle of Sekigahara. These daimyō maintained a hostile attitude throughout the Edo period and some of them were to rebel. By setting up these systems, the bakufu provided an efficient nationwide espionage system and performed the function of unifying or supervising all daimyō. This was the height of feudalism.

SAMURAI EDUCATION AND TRAINING

'*Die when it is right to die, strike when to strike is right.*'

The upbringing of future samurai took place within the framework of an unwritten code, passed on in stories and legend, implying rules and standards that are characteristic of a true samurai. The cornerstone of samurai education was the development of strong moral character based on the principles of Buddhism and Confucianism. The preparation took place in stages, first, the student had to learn the basics of swimming, riding and jiu-jitsu. Then followed the mastery of archery, swordsmanship and the use of polearms (Naginata and Yari). Practising with weapons, the students learned to develop instant reaction, flexibility and dexterity whilst constantly developing physically. Alongside the physical training was Zen meditation, calligraphy, ikebana, the tea ceremony, literature and poetry (such as the death poem written before battles).

On a boy's 7th birthday, he would be given a *wakizashi* short sword, to wear with pride, and then be presented to the head of the samurai school he would attend for the next nine years. At the age of 13, the student would be expected to accompany his father into battle and on coming of age at 16, would be presented with the Daisho pair of swords.

Above: Utagawa Kuniyoshi, *The 47 Loyal Retainers Achieve Their Goal.*

The Forty-Seven Akō Rōnin

One of the best and revered tales of the samurai which serves to illustrate the 'Bushidō' concepts of loyalty and honour is that of the retainers of the daimyō of the Akō domain.

Early in 1701, Asano Naganori, the young and recently named daimyō of the Akō domain, while serving the shogūn in Edo, was appointed to receive and feast an envoy from the Imperial Court. A high shogūnal official, named Kira Yoshinaga was allocated to teach him the proper ceremonies to be observed for the occasion. Kira, a greedy official, was dissatisfied with the gifts that Naganori brought to him in return for his instruction and taught wrongly some protocols which then caused humiliation and further public embarrassment. Naganori could not hold his temper and later ambushed Kira wounding him in the face with his *wakizashi* short sword. Naganori was arrested, disarmed and confined in one of the apartments of the palace. The shōgunal law on such matters was clear, drawing a weapon within the confines of the shōgun's castle was a capital offence, whatever the motivation behind it. Accordingly, Naganori was ordered to commit *seppuku*, and his domain confiscated. His retainers so becoming masterless and without fiefs were declared *rōnin*, some of them then took service with other daimyōs, and others became merchants.

Now amongst these retainers was his principal *hatamoto*, a man called Oishi Kuranosuke, who, with forty-six other faithful retainers, formed a league to avenge their master's death by subsequently killing Kira Yoshinaga. In order to allay the suspicions of a retaliation, by either the Kira house

or the shōgunate, the Akō samurai agreed to scatter and lay low for some time, reassembling nearly two years later, after Kira Yoshinaka had long since relaxed his guard.

In December 1702 during a heavy fall of snow and bitter cold, the *rōnin* determined that no more favourable opportunity could occur for carrying out their purpose. Oishi Kuranosuke sent a messenger to the neighbouring houses, bearing the following message:

'We, the rōnin who were formerly in the service of Asano Naganori, are this night about to break into the residence of Kira Yoshinaga, to avenge our lord. As we are neither night robbers nor ruffians, no hurt will be done to the neighbouring houses. We pray you to set your minds at rest.'

Since Kira was hated by his neighbours for his greed and officiousness, they did not unite their forces to assist him. The 47 samurai then attacked Kira's Edo residence, which was still defenders by some twenty Kira samurai. In the fierce fighting that followed the attack all of the defenders were killed and Kira was captured. Oishi Kuranosuke went down on his knees, and addressing the old man very respectfully, said:

'My lord, we are the retainers of Asano Naganori. last year your lordship and our master quarrelled in the palace, and our master was sentenced to seppuku, and his family was ruined. We have come tonight to avenge him, as is the duty of faithful and loyal men. I pray your lordship to acknowledge the justice of our purpose. And now, my lord, we beseech you to perform seppuku. I myself shall have the honour to act as your second, and when, with all humility, I shall have received your lordship's head, it is my intention to lay it as an offering upon the grave of Asano Naganori.'

When the job was done, they then surrendered themselves to shogūnal authorities for judgement. After a lengthy debate, they were ordered to commit suicide. They met their death nobly; and their corpses were carried to Sengakuji, and buried in front of the tomb of their master, Asano Naganori. And when the story of this incident became known, the people flocked to pray at the graves of the faithful men.

In the decade following Sekigahara, powerful daimyō such as the Kato, Asano, Kuroda, Ikeda, Nabeshima, Hosokawa and Shimazu were subjected to stringent control measures. They were compelled to provide labour and resources for the construction of strategic castles. A compulsory system of alternate attendance in Edo was imposed, requiring daimyō to spend every other year at the shōgun's court. As a further control mechanism, daimyō were forced to leave family members as hostages in the capital. Rigorous checkpoints were established to monitor the movement of people and goods, with particular attention paid to firearms and the departure of women as potential indicators of rebellion.

In 1549, Christianity arrived in Kyūshū, together with trade goods and firearms. All would soon spread throughout the country. The daimyō who ruled Nagasaki, Omura Sumitada, converted to Christianity with all his retainers in 1563. By 1582 there were 200 churches in Kyūshū.

Below: St Francis Xavier Statue, Hirado, Nagasaki.

At first, Hideyoshi appeared sympathetic to Christianity and he favourably compared the Jesuits to Buddhist monks. However, he moved against Christianity immediately upon completing his conquest of Kyūshū. This was followed by a decree that the Jesuit missionaries must leave Japan. Then, in 1612, Ieyasu declared Christianity an 'evil faith' and issued a number of anti-Christian directives. Two years later he ordered the destruction of all churches and summoned all priests to Nagasaki. This situation was caused by disagreements between Christians in Japan, with Portuguese and Spanish Catholics on one side and Dutch and English protestants on the other.

The west of Kyūshū had always been a poor part of Japan, having a hot climate and suffering from tropical storms. There had been a greater than usual drought from 1634, finally resulting in a disastrous crop failure in 1637. It would have been usual in these circumstances for the daimyō to forego the collection of taxes. However, the recently appointed local daimyō, Matsukura Shigehara and Terazawa Hiroyaka, were

Right: A Maria Kannon statue, used for Christian worship in secret, as the Virgin Maria is disguised as the Buddhist figure Kannon.

Below: The Great Martyrdom. Catholic priests and converts in Nagasaki.

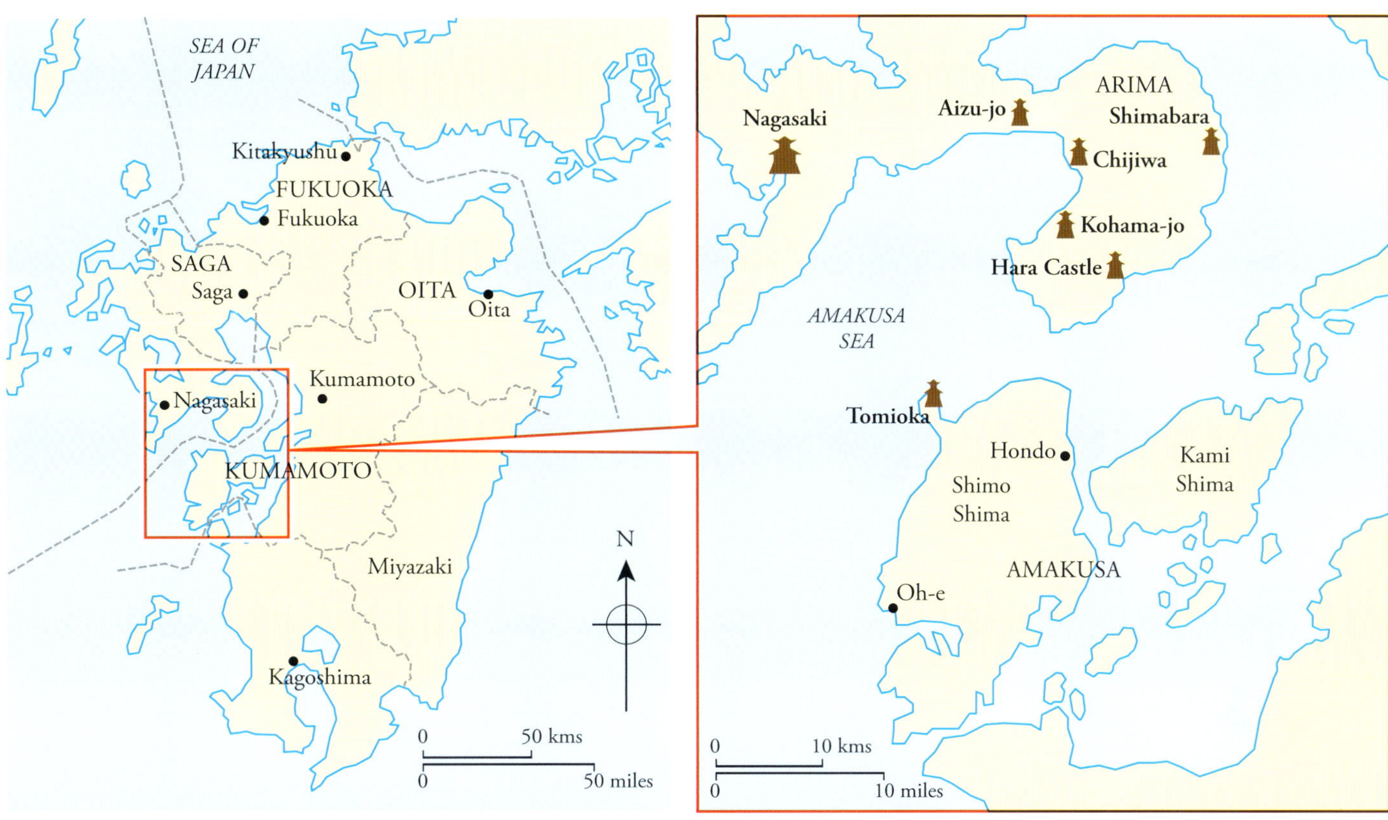

Above: Map of Kyūshū and the rebellious areas, 1637–38.

tyrannical persecutors and regarded the collection of taxes as necessary for them to pay their own dues to their superiors. Persecutions and punishments imposed upon wives or daughters of tax-defaulters included plunging them into icy water and their being suspended upside-down and naked. Frequently, women were seized and kept as hostages until they died or, as the authorities hoped, their families found the tax payments they owed.

The Shimabara Rebellion ignited in October 1637, when a local magistrate was slain while attempting to disrupt a Christian service. This incident escalated when 16 farmers were arrested and executed for their Christian faith. The ensuing outrage sparked a full-scale revolt. Enraged peasants attacked and killed the magistrate responsible, setting off a wider insurrection against the shōgunate. Rebel forces besieged Shimabara Castle, razing the town and seizing weapons. It's important to remember at this point that, while the discontent was sparked by Christian persecution, there were underlying economic and social grievances too. The Shimabara Rebellion was not purely a religious revolt.

Left: This flag was used during the Shimabara-Amakusa Uprising. It depicts a chalice and communion bread in the centre and two angels on either side, as well as retaining bloodstains and arrow marks.

Once news of the uprising spread through the peninsular and the islands, many other oppressed inhabitants joined in. Towns and villages became scenes of conflict. The powerful daimyō in the neighbouring provinces could only stand by and watch the revolt develop.

In November 1637, Matsukura Shigeharu set out for the court at Edo to request assistance in putting down the revolt. At this time, Edo could be reached in 16 days in a hurry: six by boat and ten over land. Usually, though, it took far longer than this. The rebels took advantage of this fact, knowing that it could be weeks before reinforcements against them were sent. Many village headmen and farmers had been samurai under the previous daimyō and were classed as *rōnin*. As skilled fighters they were able to repel a 3,000-strong Terazawa force sent against them. To save on guns and bullets the rebels collected large stones that could be fired at the enemy with catapult devices.

Above: Battle map of Hara Castle during the Shimabara Rebellion.

Left: Amakusa Shiro, based on a 17th-century painting.

The shōgunate had little idea that the revolt of a small band of oppressed peasants in the latter months of 1637 in Kyūshū, mostly Christians and displaced *rōnin*, would have such an effect on the ability of the bakufu to maintain the unopposed rule of feudal law throughout the provinces. The revolt culminated in the siege of a fortification on the site of the abandoned Hara Castle on the Shimabara Peninsula that had been hastily prepared to await a punitive force of samurai. Among the occupants of the castle were some 200 *rōnin* who were former samurai. They provided the peasants' military expertise and leadership. Amakusa Shiro (also known as Masuda Shiro Tokisada), the young Christian leader of the rebels, entered Hara Castle and had soon attracted a following of 35,000. The force massed

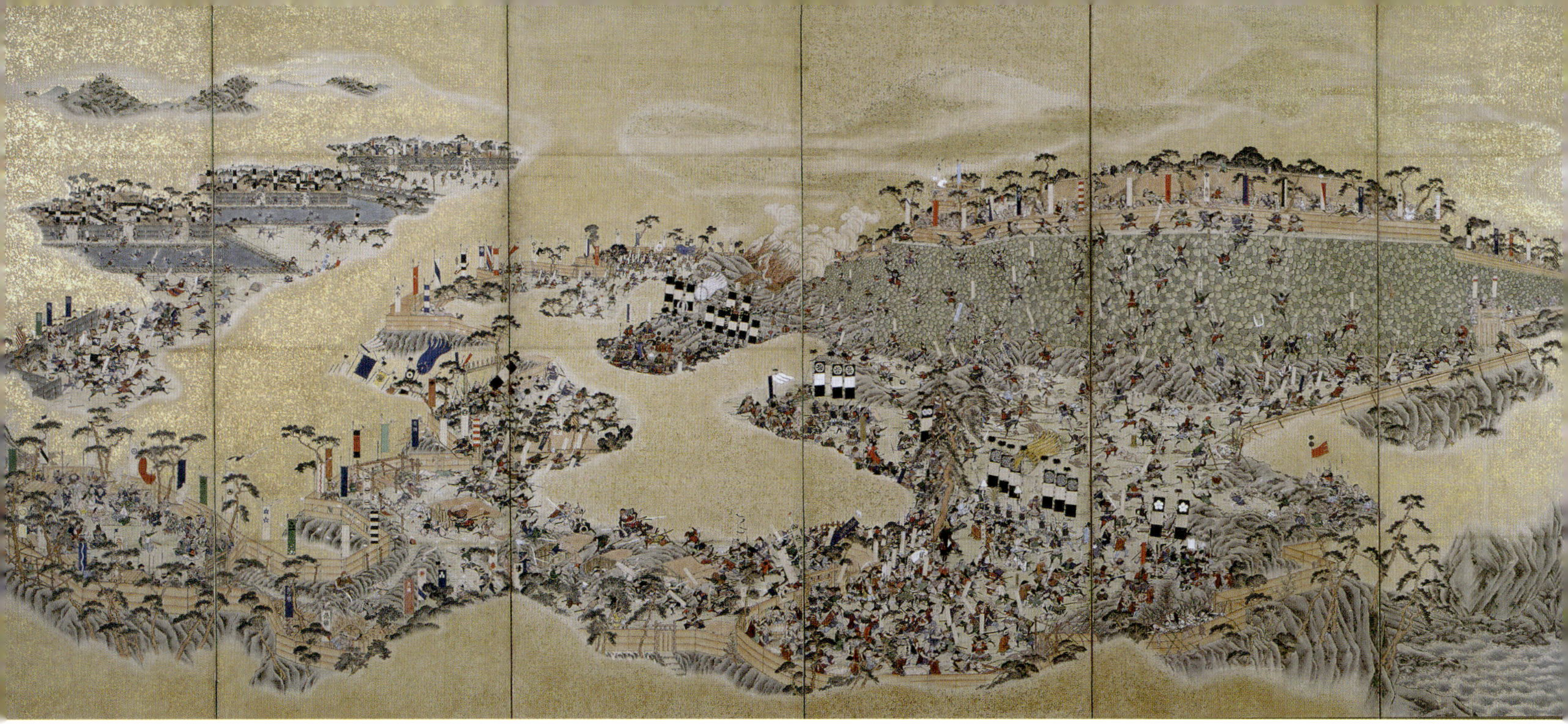

Above: Screen of the Shimabara Rebellion at Hara Castle.

against them, however, numbered 120,000, recruited from daimyō across Kyūshū and on the mainland, as well as from Edo itself. They besieged Amakusa Shiro's makeshift fort for three months, finally making a full-scale attack on 15 April 1638 when they knew the defenders' food and ammunition supplies were running out. After two days of continuous fighting, the rebels' fortress fell. Amakusa Shiro was killed and every man, woman and child was massacred in one of the bloodiest days of slaughter in Japan's entire history. The few rebels who managed to escape the fort were hunted down and decapitated.

As a sequel, the fort was razed to the ground in order that it might never become a rallying point or a place of pilgrimage for future troublemakers. Terazawa Hiroyaka of Amakusa, whose tyranny was the spark that ignited the rebellion, was deposed and committed suicide. The bakufu confiscated the Matsukura Domain, and tyrant Matsukura Shigeharu of Arima

Below: Dejima Island at Nagasaki.

and Shimabara Castle was beheaded on 28 August 1638, having been found culpable for abusing his power and disgracing the shōgunate. He was the only *daimyō* to be beheaded during the Edo period. This was the last major armed conflict in the Edo period until the Bakumatsu period more than 200 years later.

The Shimabara rebellion finally induced the bakufu to adopt the policy of international seclusion and to eradicate Christianity. These two policies went hand in hand, with Westerners such as the Portuguese, the Spanish, the English and the Dutch being both Christians and traders. The bakufu saw that some daimyōs, such as the Tozama of western Honshu and Kyūshū, were growing so rich and powerful from foreign trade that they could feasibly one day present a threat to the authority of Kyoto. They also saw that the Spanish or the Portuguese, for example, with their Western guns, cannon and other weapons, could prove to be valuable allies to ambitious daimyōs seeking to assert themselves against the bakufu, the shōgunate or the emperor. The only way of preventing such a situation from arising was to prohibit all foreign trade at ports other than Nagasaki, which was under the direct authority of the bakufu.

Portugal in particular was singled out for especially harsh treatement under Japan's new exclusion policy: any Portuguese ship that dared to arrive at a Japanese port was to be burned, along with its cargo, and everyone on board executed. This was in retribution for Portugal and the Jesuits' alleged connection with the Shimabara Rebellion. For the next 250 years, Japan existed in a state of self-isolation with minimal outside contact. Only Chinese, Korean and Dutch merchants were licensed to undertake a limited amount of commercial activity with Japan – with the latter, as the only Westerners allowed contact with the country, confined to operating through a single trading station on Dejima Island at Nagasaki. To all intents and purposes, Japan had turned its back on the world.

Armour of the Edo Period

The Momoyama period witnessed a surge in demand for weapons and armour due to prolonged military campaigns.

The limitations of scale armour, such as its weight, discomfort and poor hygiene in field conditions, became increasingly apparent. As a result, the 16th century marked a transition from traditional armour to a contemporary style known as *tosei-gusoku*. These 'modern' armours offered superior protection against firearms, were quicker to produce and displayed greater variety while reducing the amount of intricate lacing. Despite this shift, the transformation was gradual, with many transitional armour types coexisting. Adherents of older traditions continued to favour the *haramaki* and *do-maru* cuirasses, symbolizing their samurai lineage and status.

The Edo period, marking the dawn of Japan's early modern era, ushered in a period of relative peace punctuated by sporadic uprisings like the Shimabara Revolt (see below). The military use of armour ended with the Ōsaka summer battle of 1615. While large-scale warfare diminished, the need for personal protection persisted due to civil unrest, assassinations and peasant rebellions. This led to the adaptation of coverings such as the chain mail armour jacket as well as other types of armour which could be worn under ordinary clothing. Although the samurai class eventually relinquished its military role, armour continued to be produced and worn, with the Satsuma Rebellion in 1877 marking its final battlefield use.

Provincial daimyō were obligated to attend the shōgun's court and wore armour on ceremonial occasions to show off their rank and wealth. The prolonged peace following centuries of conflict afforded samurai the opportunity to cultivate artistic pursuits, including the refinement of their armour. This led to a flourishing of intricate metalwork, embroidery and weaving, transforming armour into exquisite showcases of craftsmanship.

enhanced and embellished with wrinkles and whiskers. Without the test of war to prove whether a piece of armour was serviceable or not, 17th-century armourers proved their skill by making elaborate masks of one piece that were simply works of art which would have proved useless in combat.

Throughout the Edo Period the trend was always for poorer samurai to buy simple armours of Momoyama style while the wealthy commissioned elaborate pieces often modelled after ancient styles. Indeed, by the middle of the 19th century some of these copies were quite accurate reproductions. Unfortunately, the majority of armour preserved in today's museums and collections date from this later, often more ornate period.

Above: Although constructed in the traditional 16th-century *gusoku* (complete set) fashion, this is actually an example of the revival of earlier armour styles during the Edo period.

Left: An example of the *menpo*, an armour mask, from the 18th century.

Left: This helmet is in the form of a *sumi-zukin*, a square hat commonly worn by old men, physicians, and priests. The top of the helmet is lacquered gold to emulate the fabric texture of a *sumi-zukin*. The front crest (*maedate*) represents the protective Buddhist deity Acana engulfed in flames.

Initially, the revival of this armour focused on incorporating decorative elements from the Momoyama period, with styles like the *do-maru* experiencing a resurgence in popularity. As peace endured, armourers, seeking to maintain their livelihoods, began crafting impractical yet visually striking pieces to cater for the growing demand for unique and ornate armour. To display their skill, they ventured into elaborate helmet decorations known as *maedate*, creating lifelike insect and bird crests from copper and other materials.

The armour mask, or *menpo*, that gave the samurai warrior his fierce and frightening countenance was

枚方
淀の城
伏見

CHAPTER 10

The Opening of Japan

Although the Edo period would be remembered as a time of peace, it was also an era that saw the nation go into economic decline. Japan's leaders shut the borders in an attempt to preserve their traditional way of life, but in doing so they sealed the country in a time capsule. While other nations moved on, Japan stayed the same. Its leaders were unable to offer solutions when farms began to fail and when the samurai – idle, now that the wars of the past had ended – struggled to provide for their families, pay for their staff, and maintain their rank in society. Unrest would grow as Japan began to stagnate. When the shōgunate showed signs it was struggling to cope, the West forced the country to reopen for business. This in turn inspired the growth of a fiercely nationalistic movement that opposed the foreigners, criticized the shōgunate and supported a restoration of imperial power. The time of the shōguns was coming to an end.

The decline of the shōgunate began as soon as Tokugawa Ieyasu died. There were occasionally very competent rulers, most notably the eighth shōgun, Tokugawa Yoshimune, who came to power in 1716 and who died 35 years later. He was an excellent politician and managed to introduce some changes within the structure of government and the standing army which slowed down the deterioration for a while. In the meantime, cash-strapped daimyō had to scale back the numbers of samurai they could afford to retain, while those they kept on had to accept a cut to their stipend. In 1732, this slimmed down army had to deal with rebellions across the country caused by a crop failure, famine and inflated rice prices – a cycle that continued across the following years. With death and discontent spreading, the government was eventually forced to order the daimyō to hold strategic stocks of rice reserves. This helped, but only until the rule of Shōgun Ienari (ruled 1787–1841), who proved to be a squandering and reckless leader, and whose extravagances severely depleted the reserves.

The samurai economy revolved around rice and cotton cloth, with rice being the dominant commodity. The *koku*, a unit equivalent to about 150kg (330lb) of rice, enough to sustain an adult for a year, served as the standard measure of value. This meant that wealth, salaries, and land income were all expressed in terms of *koku*. For samurai, this had a significant impact: they were not paid with money but with rice, and they also saved their wealth in the form of stored rice. This system made rice not only a staple food but also the primary form of currency and savings.

Despite the introduction of coinage through increased trade with China in the 10th century, its adoption was slow and restricted. For an extended period, only the upper classes and those living near the capital, Kyoto, commonly used coins. Rice, as a staple, maintained its inherent value, a bale of rice was always worth a bale of rice. However, for trade purposes, fixed prices for staple goods were established using coin. In 996, for example, a *koku* of rice was valued at 1,000 *mon*, a *koku* of barley at 2,500 *mon*, and a *hiki* of silk (approximately 23m/75ft) at 2,000 *mon*. The *mon* was a standard copper coin, circular in shape with a square hole in the centre.

The economic imbalance within samurai society is evident in their salaries. Ashigaru, the foot soldiers, received a modest 4 *koku* of rice annually, while samurai earned significantly more, starting at 100 *koku*. If granted land instead of rice, they paid 50 per cent of the harvest as tax, although 50 *koku* was still a substantial income. By 1711, a *hatamoto*,

Right: A daimyō residence in Edo, 17th century. The direct result of the policy of Sankin-kōtai was that elaborate residences of palaces, barracks and stables grew up in the area around Edo. With more than 100 of these large dwellings, the growing population added to the difficulties of the area.

Above: A typical small rice farm around 1890. Little had changed from times gone by.

Above: Transporting bales of rice to the warehouse. Ieyasu instigated a project to upgrade the main five highways of Japan and so increase ease of transportation.

the daimyō's chief retainers, received a base salary of around 500 *koku*, which could reach as high as 10,000 *koku* depending on their estate and rank. This higher income reflected their greater responsibilities, including maintaining men-at-arms, horses, and appropriate equipment. The cost of living is illustrated by the fact that a samurai's basic streetwear cost 1 *koku*, a set of ashigaru armour cost 4–6 *koku*, a labourer's annual wage was 6 *koku*, and hiring a maid cost 3–4 *koku* annually. Those with land yielding 10,000 or more *koku* were classified as daimyō, while those exceeding 100,000 *koku* were generally referred to as 'castle lords'.

The Tokugawa shōgunate actively encouraged agricultural development and land reclamation, resulting in an increase in rice yields. However, this increase in rice production had unforeseen economic repercussions. The increased supply of rice on the market, combined with the dynamics of the newly introduced coinage currency system, led to a depreciation of rice prices. Where a *koku* of rice had once commanded a price of at least 1,000 *mon* (or its equivalent, one gold Ryō, an oval-shaped coin), producers later found themselves fortunate to receive half that amount. This dramatic price decrease created significant financial strain for both samurai, who received their stipends in rice, and small-scale farmers. A man with an income of six *koku*, for instance, would find that after allocating three to four *koku* for his family's sustenance, very little remained to cover essential expenses such as salt, fuel, clothing, and other necessities. To mitigate the economic hardship caused by fluctuating rice prices, the bakufu, in 1735, implemented a system of officially fixed prices. This system established a set exchange rate in Edo, stipulating that 1.4 *koku* of rice would be exchanged for one gold Ryō.

During this period of peace, the samurai class, while still permitted to carry weapons, found their traditional role significantly diminished. The absence of warfare meant that lower-ranking samurai had few opportunities to gain promotion and increase their income through battlefield achievements. Furthermore, there were limited openings for advancement within daimyō households. As a result, economic and political power gradually shifted towards the merchant and moneylending classes. Some samurai sought to supplement their dwindling incomes through alternative means. While some had traditionally engaged in farming, this practice became less prevalent as they increasingly turned to other trades, often leveraging their military skills to become armourers or pursue other crafts.

The bakufu's 1635 implementation of the *Sankin-kōtai* (alternate attendance) system had a significant impact on the economy. While its stated goals were to prevent daimyō uprisings by keeping them under closer supervision in Edo and to stimulate the capital's economy through their spending, the policy placed a heavy financial burden on the daimyō. The cost of travelling to Edo with extensive retinues, sometimes numbering in the thousands, and supporting them for six months each year, was potentially devastating to their finances. A lower daimyō on an income of 12,000 *koku* heading to Edo, for example, would have an entourage of 12 mounted samurai, 20 foot

Above: A daimyō's procession to central Edo, from a handscroll *c.* 1700.

samurai, 12 horse-holders and 240 *ashigaru* then with bearers and household members it would amount to around 250 people, all of whom had to be paid and fulfil his obligations to the shōgun and the bakufu from his own pocket.

To understand the cost of living during the Edo period, it's helpful to consider some common expenses. For lodging, travellers could choose between bakufu-run hostels, which offered an overnight stay with board for 200 *mon*, and private inns. A simple stay in a medium-quality private inn cost between 70 and 100 *mon*. Other daily necessities and services had varying prices: a litre of sake could be purchased for about 20 *mon*, a new pair of *waraji* (straw sandals) cost 25 *mon*, and a massage cost 50 *mon*. Notably, the cost of female entertainment services within the aforementioned inns was considerably higher, ranging from 500 to 600 *mon*!

High-ranking hatamoto, those with incomes between 1,000 and 3,000 *koku*, faced the greatest financial difficulties. Wealthier *hatamoto* possessed reserves to draw upon, while those lower in rank could sometimes avoid certain duties. Nagasawa Motochika, Master of Court in 1711, exemplifies this struggle. After paying taxes to the bakufu from his 1,960 *koku* income and converting the remaining rice to cash, he was left with 483 Ryō. This sum proved insufficient to cover his mandatory expenses, forcing him to borrow an additional 373 Ryō to make ends meet.

Hatamoto were bound by numerous mandatory expenses that significantly impacted their basic incomes. A primary symbol of their status and profession was the sword. A top-quality blade, such as one ordered from Hizen Tadayoshi in 1619, could cost as much as 400 *koku*, though lower premier blades were less expensive. When facing severe financial hardship, some samurai were known to sell their swords, the very tools of their trade, and replace them with bamboo substitutes for practice and to maintain outward appearances.

The declining military capacity of daimyō estates is clearly illustrated by the changing expectations for troop numbers. In the time of Tokugawa Iemitsu (1604–1651), a daimyō with a 50,000-*koku* domain was required to maintain a force of 1,000 fighting men. However, by 1861, this requirement had plummeted to just 163 samurai, demonstrating a significant weakening of their military power.

The overabundance of samurai in many domains stemmed from the Battle of Sekigahara in 1600. The losing Western daimyō were stripped of substantial portions of their lands, creating a situation where they had far more retainers than their remaining territories could adequately support. Despite their reduced landholdings, they retained a significantly larger proportion of their retainers than their diminished resources could sustain. The Shimazu family's decision to retain a large number of retainers despite losing most of their land after Sekigahara created a severe economic crisis for Satsuma's samurai. Deprived of adequate resources, these warriors faced extreme poverty, with many struggling to obtain basic necessities and forced to rely on growing their own sweet potatoes for food. The sheer number of samurai in Satsuma, one in four people, compared to the national average of one in ten, worsened the problem. While Satsuma represented the worst case of this overpopulation of samurai, the resulting poverty was a common problem across southwestern Japan.

Commodore Perry and the End of Isolation

Above: The Mission of Commodore Perry to Japan in 1854 by Hibata Ōsuke, 1854–1858.

During the 16th and 17th centuries, Japan engaged in regular trade with European powers such as Portugal, Spain, and the Netherlands. However, growing concerns over European missionary efforts to spread Catholicism and their involvement in unfair trade practices led Japan to adopt a policy of isolation in 1639, expelling most foreign traders. For the following two centuries, trade was limited to specially chartered Dutch and Chinese ships. This period of isolation ended in 1853 with the arrival of American Commodore Matthew Perry and his 'Black Ships' in Tokyo Bay, seeking to re-establish trade relations with the Western world.

In the period leading up to Commodore Matthew Perry's mission to Japan, a number of American sailors experienced the misfortune of being shipwrecked and finding themselves stranded on Japanese shores. The stories of their experiences, often involving mistreatment at the hands of the Japanese, spread rapidly through the American merchant community and across the United States. These accounts painted a picture of Japan as an inhospitable and unwelcoming nation, further fuelling the desire among Americans, particularly within the trading community, to establish formal relations and open trade with Japan.

Commodore Perry's arrival was marked by a diplomatic misstep: his letter from President Millard Fillmore was addressed to the Emperor of Japan, demonstrating a lack of understanding of the country's political structure. The letter formally requested the repatriation of shipwrecked American sailors and the opening of Japanese ports for provisioning, refuelling, and trade. In an attempt to impress the Japanese with

Right: Samurai from some 40 domains were mobilized to guard the coasts and gather information. This illustration shows two mounted samurai racing to deliver messages, their sense of panic contrasting with the relaxed attitude of commoners above toward the foreign incursion.

Above: Commodore Matthew Perry (centre) and his officers.

Western advancements, Perry also presented a range of gifts, including a working model of a steam locomotive, a telescope, a telegraph, and various Western wines and liquors.

Commodore Perry's audacious approach, sailing his 'Black Ships' into the previously forbidden waters of Tokyo Bay, served as a clear demonstration of American military power and willingness to use it. This display of force effectively convinced the Japanese authorities to accept President Fillmore's letter. Faced with this show of strength, the Japanese grudgingly agreed to Perry's demands, leading to the signing of the Treaty of Kanagawa on 31 March 1854. This treaty marked a significant turning point, opening Japan to future Western contact and trade after centuries of self-imposed isolation.

The process by which the United States and other Western powers compelled Japan to engage in modern commercial interactions, combined with various internal factors already present within Japanese society, contributed significantly to the weakening of the Tokugawa Shogunate's position.

Similar treaties soon followed with Britain, France, the Netherlands and Russia. In response, the shōgunate accelerated its rearmament efforts, primarily through arms purchases from the Dutch. For several years from 1854, a fierce debate had raged among the shōgunate and powerful daimyō over the merits of increased foreign interaction. Extreme nationalists vehemently opposed opening Japan, deeming it a sacred and unique nation that would be defiled by foreign 'barbarians'. To end the impasse, the shōgun appointed Ii Naosuke, the daimyō of Hikone, as Chief Counsellor in 1858. Without imperial sanction,

Opposite: The assassination of Ii Naosuke, the Chief Minister, outside the Sakuradamon Gate at Edo Castle. Just after 9 am, when the palanquin of the procession approached, a gunshot was the signal and the Rōnin all attacked with their swords. After about 15 minutes of sword fighting, they took the head of the Chief Minister Ii Naosuke.

Opposite: A Foreign trading house at Yokohama, 1861.

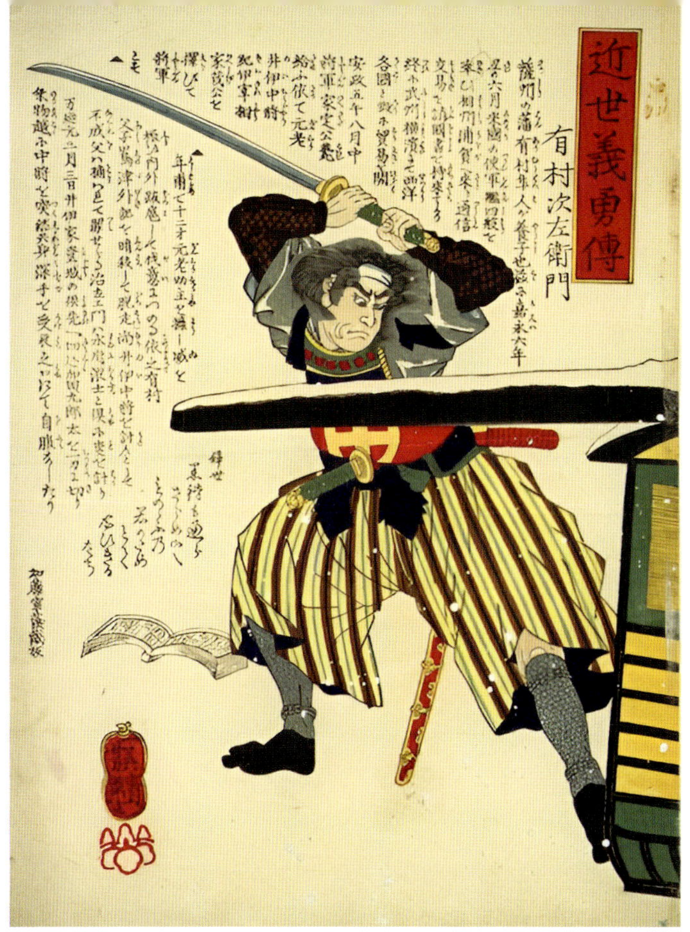

Right: Arimura Jisaemon, The Satsuma Samurai (Rōnin) assassin, one of 18 Rōnin who decapitated Ii Naosuke, March 1860. The other samurai were from the Mito Domain.

Naosuke swiftly concluded commercial treaties with the US and brutally suppressed internal opposition. His high-handed tactics inflamed conservative samurai, who assassinated him at the gates of Edo Castle in early 1860.

Further violence followed as Japan's treaties with the US and other foreign nations ignited fierce domestic debate. The 1862 murder of British merchant Charles Richardson, stemming from a perceived insult to a Shimazu daimyō, further inflamed tensions. The following year, the Chōshū Domain, influenced by extreme nationalists, fired on foreign ships, provoking a joint military response from Western powers. The shōgunate's policy of opening Japan and suppressing dissent fuelled the formation of the anti-bakufu *Sonnō jōi* ('Revere the Emperor, expel the barbarians') movement. This group instigated samurai-led acts of terrorism against bakufu officials, intensifying opposition to the shōgunate. The movement's core consisted of lower-ranking samurai from Satsuma, Chōshū and Tosa, united by the shared goal of overthrowing the shōgunate and restoring imperial authority.

Expel the Barbarians

In early 1863, and against the Tokugawa Shōgunate's policy of welcoming foreigners and trade, Japan's Emperor Komei in a dramatic departure from imperial precedent issued an anti-foreign edict known as the 'Order to Expel the Barbarians'.

This encouraged the Chōshū clan, led by Mōri Takachika, to seize control of the strategically vital but perilous Shimonoseki Strait, through which much of the West's trade with Japan passed. Armed with a combination of outdated and modern cannon, they enforced the emperor's policy of expelling all foreigners, openly defying the shōgunate. This narrow waterway, connecting the Inland Sea to the Sea of Japan and constricted to a mere 100m (328ft) at its narrowest point, was a critical maritime passage. Despite diplomatic efforts by foreign powers, Takachika ordered his forces to open fire without warning on any foreign ship attempting to navigate the strait.

Following a number of attacks on Western shipping and retaliatory actions throughout 1863, an International Naval Squadron was formed the following year, comprising British, French, Dutch and American warships plus around 2,000 troops. Things came to a head on 5 September 1864, when the international squadron ships bombarded Chōshū positions onshore. After initially returning fire, the Chōshū artillerymen realized their weapons were no match for those of the ironclad ships facing them and beat a retreat, along with around 2,000 civilians. According to Ernest Satow, a British diplomat with the fleet, 'the Japanese fought well and with great persistence ... At first many of our shot fell short, but when the range was found, they struck the batteries every moment, as we could see by the clouds of dust that were knocked up. The entire casualties on our side this first day were six men wounded in the *Tartar*, which bore the brunt of the fire'.

Below: The Second Battle of Shimonoseki, 5 September 1864 by Jean Baptiste Henri Durand Brager. The Chōshū Domain, which repeatedly bombarded foreign ships under the name of 'Expel the Barbarians', was bombarded by the four great powers of Britain, France, the Netherlands, and the United States.

Left: Shimonoseki Defenders of the Chōshū Clan. Note the men wearing the samurai *daisho* – a term for a matched pair of swords.

The following day, boats put ashore carrying about 1,900 men, 1,400 of whom were British. The first battery the British entered was already in the possession of the French landing party and some of the Royal Marines who had marched along the beach, capturing and destroying the guns. The Japanese, meanwhile, harassed them in isolated skirmishers. Toward evening, the marines were making ready to embark in their boats when they were attacked by a few hundred samurai led by Yamagata Kansuke. These Japanese troops were in poor shape and, with many wounded, soon retreated to an artillery defended stockade. An assault by two Marine battalions on the right and centre and the Naval Brigade 'bluejackets' on the left saw the Japanese abandon their position after 90 minutes of fierce fighting. After setting fire to the stockade, samurai in black armour and white surcoats were witnessed retreating along the road.

Unable to match the firepower of the international fleet, and amid mounting casualties, the Chōshū forces surrendered two days later, on 8 September 1864. Seventy-two men of the International Naval Squadron had been killed or wounded, with two ships severely damaged; the Chōshū recorded 18 fatalities and 29 injured.

Three Victoria Crosses were awarded as a result of this action. Midshipman Duncan Gordon Boyes, aged 17, carried the Queen's Colour into action with the leading company attacking the enemy's stockade; this is believed to be the last time the Queen's Colours were carried into battle. He kept the colours flying despite the direct fire which killed one of his colour sergeants. It was discovered afterwards that the Colours he carried had been pierced six times by musket balls.

Thomas Pride, as Captain of the After Guard on HMS *Euryalus*, was one of the two colour sergeants with Boyes and was badly wounded. The third VC recipient was Ordinary Seaman William Henry Seeley. He was a US citizen enlisted in the Royal Navy and was the first American to receive the medal.

Right: British sailors capture the Chōshū batteries at Shimonoseki.

The Restoration of Imperial Rule

The Battle of Shimonoseki on 5 September 1864 proved to be a pivotal point in the Meiji Restoration and the modernization of Japan. Although the Chōshū clan lost the battle, its leaders later went on to dominate the governments of the Meiji period. Mōri Takachika saw the futility of opposing the Westerners and the advantages to be gained in using them to his own ends.

Led by samurai Takechi Zuisan and Kusaka Genzui in Tosa and Chōshū respectively, the *Sonnō jōi* exclusionists launched a violent campaign against the bakufu's Kyoto supporters. A cycle of assassinations and reprisals erupted, plunging the city into bloodshed. In response to this escalating turmoil, the Tosa Domain, under the stern rule of Yamanouchi Yōdō harshly punished its own exclusionist *Sonnō jōi* faction, ordering the leaders to commit seppuku.

Sakamoto Ryōma, a low-ranking samurai of the Tosa clan was entrusted in delivering a confidential letter from his cousin, Takechi Zuisan to Genzui Kusaka. During their meeting, Kusaka expressed that under the prevailing circumstances, feudal daimyō and aristocrats would be unreliable guardians of Japan's future. Ryōma, following this ideology, left the Tosa domain without permission to embrace the life of a *rōnin,* a masterless samurai. He journeyed to Satsuma where the leaders harboured aspirations of national unity, envisioning an alliance between the shōgunate and the dominant feudal lords. Ryōma then travelled to Edo. There, he met with Katsu Kaishū, a high-ranking shōgunate official, who had become the commissioner of the Tokugawa navy in 1860, and a key figure in Japan's transition from the old to the new. He helped modernize the navy but could not stop the growing conflict between the shōgun and the emperor. He considered the bakufu 'a decrepit, moribund institution', and declared that, 'A new government must be forged by the most powerful domains'. Ryōma emerged from the meeting persuaded of the necessity for Japan to learn from the West, not simply oppose it. The *rōnin* Ryōma became Kaishū's protégé with a philosophy which was soon to provide him with a key role. When Kaishū was assigned to patrol the sea around Ōsaka, Ryōma accompanied him. Although sympathetic to the anti-Tokugawa cause, Katsu remained loyal to the shōgunate.

In August 1864, in response to the *Sonnō jōi ronin* and Chōshū's role in the attack on the Kyoto Imperial Palace, Emperor Komei declared the Chōshū daimyō rebels and ordered the bakufu to chastise them for their insolence to attack the sacred city of Kyoto. The

Left: An 1861 satirical print expressing the anti-foreign sentiment of the *Sonnō jōi* movement.

Left: Katsu Kaishū. Founder of the Japanese Navy and who would become the most powerful man in the Tokugawa Shōgunate.

Right: Saigō Takamori by Taiso. One of the most influential samurai in Japanese history, known as 'the Last Samurai'.

shōgun then ordered a punitive military expedition by the shogūnate against the Chōshū Domain. In November 1864, a Shōgunal army marched on Chōshū led by Tokugawa Yoshikatsu.

Saigō Takamori, having been appointed commander of the Satsuma Army in February 1864, was instrumental in the defence of the emperor's Kyoto residence under the attack of the *Sonnō jōi.* Saigo's Satsuma army under bakufu orders and along with troops from Aizu domain, marched on Choshu. The expedition ended in a nominal victory for the shōgunate after a peaceful settlement negotiated by Saigō Takamori allowed Chōshū to hand over the ringleaders of the Kyoto incident.

Dissatisfied with the outcome of the first punitive expedition against Chōshū, the bakufu sought a more decisive response. Saigō Takamori of Satsuma had counselled leniency, but Shōgun Iemochi and his advisors believed a harsher lesson was necessary. To prepare for this second, more stringent punishment, Shogun Iemochi relocated to Ōsaka Castle in 1865. At the same time, the western foreign powers, frustrated by the bakufu's failure to implement the commercial treaty, dispatched warships to Ōsaka Bay. The US, the Netherlands, France and Britain issued a stark ultimatum '...if the shōgunate did not open the country to trade, they would bypass it and negotiate directly with the emperor'.

The government was faced with bankruptcy and near collapse and so influenced by counsel and the threat of the foreign force, Emperor Komei reversed his stance on expelling the barbarians and refusing trade endorsing opening the country. This resolved the bakufu's predicament, allowing it to reconcile its conflicting policies.

In May 1865, Saigō Takamori visited Sakamoto Ryōma on behalf of the shōgun and told him of the bakufu's impending second punitive expedition against Chōshū. He tasked Ryōma with the impossible mission of reconciling Satsuma and Chōshū. This was a formidable challenge, as the two domains represented

Left: Emperor Komei.

Right: Sakamoto Ryōma. An imperial loyalist whose effort to forge the Satsuma-Chōshū Alliance (1866) was critical in setting the stage for the Meiji Restoration and the overthrow of the Tokugawa Shōgunate.

opposing ideological poles. Satsuma advocated for moderate bakufu reform, while Chōshū's stance was far more radical and uncompromising. Chōshū's radical faction had forged alliances with ambitious Kyoto aristocrats who ardently championed the restoration of imperial rule.

The *Sonnō jōi* faction, staunchly opposed to foreign interaction, found itself in a perilous position. The year 1866 marked a significant turning point for the faction, culminating in the complete failure of their objectives. Katsura Kogoro, a pro-Imperial loyalist from Chōshū and a key figure of this period, served as a liaison between Chōshū's leadership and the radical young samurai of the *Sonnō jōi* movement at the clan's Edo residence.

Following the expedition, foreign powers were barred from selling weapons to the Chōshū Domain. However, alongside his political activities, Sakamoto Ryōma continued his naval work and tried his hand at trade. In 1865, he founded pioneering company Kameyama Shachū in Nagasaki, a commercial endeavour that also supported the Satsuma-Chōshū alliance by purchasing weapons and ships in Satsuma's name from the British merchant Thomas Glover and supplied them to the Chōshū.

The Chōshū aims were to overthrow the shōgunate and create a new government headed by the emperor. Militia units were organized that utilized Western training methods and arms, and many included non-samurai troops. Chōshū became the centre for discontented samurai from other domains who were impatient with their leaders' caution.

Strengthened by the successful arms acquisition, the pro-alliance faction within Chōshū gained influence, persuading Katsura Kogoro to visit Saigō Takamori at the Satsuma residence in Kyoto in January 1866. It is possible that Takamori deliberately avoided proposing an alliance, hoping to induce Kogoro to plead for Chōshū assistance.

wealthy daimyō. The premature death of Emperor Komei from smallpox in December 1867 proved fortuitous for Chōshū's radical elements. Known for his disdain for both the violent Chōshū samurai and ambitious young aristocrats, the emperor's passing fuelled rumours of assassination orchestrated by extremist nobles in Kyoto. The new young emperor, Meiji, just 14, was a powerless figure in this tumultuous period. His inexperience made him a vulnerable pawn for any faction that could gain control, providing a powerful symbol for their ambitions.

One month after the restoration of imperial power, on 10 December 1867, Sakamoto Ryōma, was

In 1866, the shōgunate sent its second expedition to Chōshū. Members of the Kameyama company were on board the warship *Union*, procured for Chōshū from Thomas Glover & Co., and took part in a Shogunate-Chōshū battle off Shimonoseki. This was Ryōma's only experience of military combat.

Government forces were significantly outmatched by the Chōshū in terms of both morale and weaponry. Moreover, a British naval squadron arrogantly imposed a blockade on Shimonoseki Strait, hindering the shōgunate's naval operations under the guise of protecting international shipping. The defeat of the shōgunate troops by Chōshū forces led to further loss of power and prestige for the bakufu. Meanwhile, the death of the Shogun Iemochi in 1866 brought to power the last shōgun.

Tokugawa Yoshinobu was subsequently chosen as the 15th Tokugawa Shōgun in 1866. Yoshinobu realized the pressing need for national unity and presented a document to the imperial court outlining the transfer of power to the emperor, which was then approved.

The transfer of sovereignty relieved Yoshinobu of the immense pressure exerted by both the anti-foreign *Sonnō jōi* faction and foreign powers. However, it did not diminish his status as Japan's most powerful and

Above: Map of the second Chōshū expedition by Sakamoto Ryōma.

Below: Emperor Meiji in 1873.

Left: Attack on Sir Harry Parkes' delegation, 1868. Illustration of the 'ambush' published in the *Illustrated London News*. The British Diplomatic team were on route from their accommodation in the Chionin Temple to a meeting with the Emperor in the Kyoto Palace. This was not just a group of westerners meandering through the narrow streets but a full, large and well defended official parade.

assassinated at an inn in Kyoto where he often stayed. There are many theories about who ordered and perpetrated the deed, but a police force still loyal to the shōgunate, is considered most likely to have conducted the killing.

With Ryōma's assassination, the final restraint on the unchecked ambitions of Chōshū and Satsuma was removed. In the early days of 'the Coming of the Barbarians', it had been these anti-shōgunate forces that were opposed to the influence of the Westerners and the modernization of the shōgunate forces. These were the samurai who promoted conflict with the Westerners.

In January 1868, to provoke a war with the Tokugawa Shōgunate and overthrow it, the Satsuma clan orchestrated acts of terror by *rōnin* in Edo. Then, on 4 January 1868, the Satsuma and Chōshū forces seized the imperial palace in Kyoto. However, changing allegiance to the anti-shōgunate side did not imply that all these forces became pro-Western. The rise of anti-foreign sentiment led to several attacks on foreigners in 1868, one of which was on the British ambassador Sir Harry Parkes by a group of samurai in Kyoto.

The Emperor Meiji with the consent of the imperial assembly declared his own restoration to full power, the abolition of the title of shōgun and the confiscation of the shōgun's lands. The teenage emperor was now in control. This had the desired effect, and Shōgun Yoshinobu had no choice but to resort to arms. With a force of approximately 15,000, the bakufu army marched on Kyoto from Ōsaka Castle. On 27 January 1868, shōgunate forces attacked those of the Chōshū and Satsuma at the southern entrance of Kyoto. The shōgunate forces outnumbered the 'imperial' army

Right: The Battle at Ueno. A battle of the Boshin War, which occurred on 4 July 1868 between the troops of the Shōgitai under Shibusawa Seiichirō and Amano Hachirō, and Imperial troops.

of Chōshū and Satsuma by three to one, consisting mostly of samurai from the Kuwana and Aizu domains. However, the imperial troops, being fully modernized with Western armaments, were able to repulse the attack and pursue the conflict for four days in what was known as the Battle of Toba-Fushimi. This marked the opening battle of the Boshin War (also known as the War of the Year of the Dragon) the civil conflict that led to the overthrow of the Tokugawa Shōgunate and the restoration of imperial rule in Japan.

The Battle of Toba-Fushimi began near Koeda Bridge in Toba, with Satsuma forces opening fire on the advancing shōgunate troops. Overconfident in his numerical superiority, the shōgunate commander anticipated a swift surrender from the Satsuma. Despite sustained enemy fire, the shōgunate forces, unprepared for battle, opted not to engage. Next, the Satsuma-Chōshū alliance and shōgunate forces clashed near Fushimi. Leveraging superior artillery from higher ground, the Satsuma-Chōshū forces decisively overwhelmed the shōgunate's troops. The shōgunate's Shinsengumi, a specialized police force, launched a reckless charge against the heavily fortified Satsuma position, suffering catastrophic losses from the devastating fire of a Gatlin gun. The battle exposed the shōgunate's ineffective leadership and forced its forces into retreat.

Above: The Battle of Toba–Fushimi. The 'Imperial' troops on the right side with a mix of Samurai armour and new troops.

The fighting at Toba and Fushimi raged on. A turning point came when the Emperor Meiji appointed Prince Yoshiaki as commander of the imperial forces and presented him with the imperial flag. This symbolic act transformed the Satsuma forces into the Imperial Army. Faced with the prospect of fighting the emperor's army, and so committing treason against the emperor, many shōgunate troops deserted, handing the imperial forces a significant advantage. With the desertion and defection of many western clans, the defeated and demoralized bakufu forces retreated to Ōsaka, from where Yoshinobu had already fled.

Defeated at Toba-Fushimi, Yoshinobu retreated to Edo, where he surrendered two months later. With this, the imperial government was restored, its reins seized by the Chōshū and Satsuma clans – the same clans that had once been defeated at Sekigahara.

From Samurai to Soldier

In retrospect, the arrival of Commodore Perry and his 'Black Ships' in 1853 initiated a social, political and military revolution, one of whose consequences was the abolition of the entire class of samurai in the 1870s. Modern rifles and artillery were imported, infantry received new training and soon there was little room for old samurai grandeur with its edged weapons and formal codes of conduct.

The shōgun had surrendered, but the resistance continued. Domains in northern Honshu formed a league, the Northern Alliance, under the leadership of the Aizu. The Aizu Domain was a powerful force in the late Edo period. Renowned for the discipline and bravery of their samurai, the Aizu were staunch supporters of the shōgunate. Under the leadership of Matsudaira Katamori, the Aizu clan played a significant role in maintaining order in Kyoto. Among those supporting the Aizu were members of the Shinsengumi. While most of the Shinsengumi were not from samurai families, they were known for their sword skills and fierce loyalty to the shōgunate. Many daughters of Aizu samurai were trained in the martial arts of *naginata* and spear, reflecting the domain's fierce warrior spirit. Notable figures such as Niijima Yae and Nakano Takeko emerged during the Boshin War, displaying exceptional bravery. Despite the valiant resistance of the Aizu women, the Northern Alliance surrendered in November 1868 following the gruelling Battle of Aizu, which raged throughout the autumn.

After the defeat of the Aizu, many samurai escaped to Hokkaido in Northern Japan with Admiral Enomoto Takeaki, a former shōgunate official, who fled there with several ships of the Shōgunate Navy and supporters to establish a short-lived republic. The final stand of the shōgunate forces occurred when a force led by Enomoto

Left: Satsuma Samurai and Shōgunate Samurai. In these photos from 1867 it can be noted a mix of dress and weapons – samurai dress and *katana* to uniform and musket.

Above: Battle of Aizu, fought between forces loyal to the shōgunate and those who supported a return to imperial rule. The Aizu war became a battle for the entirety of the Aizu clan, with approximately 2,400 casualties on the Aizu side.

attacked imperial troops sent to establish the new government in Matsumae on Hokkaido. His troops were equipped with efficient modern rifles and trained according to French doctrine. However, the new imperial government soon defeated Enomoto's forces, marking the end of the Boshin War and the beginning of the Meiji era.

In 1871, the Meiji Restoration brought sweeping changes to Japanese society. To centralize power, the government abolished the feudal system, replacing domains with prefectures. This dismantled the power of the daimyō and their samurai armies. The rigid class structure of the Tokugawa period – the samurai, the farmer, the artisan and the merchant – were dismantled, replaced by a society divided into nobility, gentry and commoners. The age of castles and private armies ended definitively. Henceforth, the military would be a national conscript force drawn from all social classes. These reforms marked a dramatic shift from a feudal to a modern, centralized nation.

Some die-hard samurai clung to the old ideas, and their discontent with this policy prompted several attempted revolts against the new government. The new imperial army quelled them all.

The Satsuma Rebellion

The Satsuma clan was a significant force in the lead-up to the Meiji Restoration. Their foresight in investing heavily in armaments is evident in the construction of a shipyard, weapons factories and ammunition depots across their domain. This strategic move transformed Satsuma into a military powerhouse.

However, the establishment of the Meiji government brought about a complex change in the power dynamic. While the central government nominally controlled these facilities, the Satsuma maintained a strong degree of influence, if not outright control. This discrepancy in power would contribute to the tensions that erupted into the Satsuma Rebellion.

On 30 January 1877, the central government made a surprise raid on the Satsuma-operated arms and ammunition storage depots in Kagoshima. This bold move was a clear attempt to assert central authority and weaken the Satsuma clan's military power. However, the operation backfired spectacularly. The Satsuma samurai, long steeped in the warrior ethos, responded with force, demonstrating their capability and willingness to defend their interests. By seizing control of weapons and parading them through Kagoshima, the samurai sent a strong message: they were not prepared to relinquish their power without a fight.

This incident ignited the fuse that led to the Satsuma Rebellion. Saigō Takamori, a central figure in the Meiji Restoration, found himself thrust into a position of leadership against his will. Initially, he was displeased with the rash actions of the younger samurai who attacked the government forces. However, the revelation of a government plot to assassinate him drastically altered his stance.

Faced with a choice between exile or armed resistance, Saigō decided to support the rebellion. This decision was influenced by his deep-rooted sense of loyalty to the samurai class and a belief that the government had betrayed the ideals of the restoration. A well-armed advance guard of 4,000 left to march

north on 15 February, followed two days later by a 9,000-strong rear guard and artillery force.

Outsmarting the imperial government, which anticipated him either adopting a defensive position in Satsuma or attacking the capital by sea, Saigō instead boldly marched his samurai army through the heart of Kyūshū, aiming to cross to Honshu and challenge Kyoto directly. His strategy involved rallying support from other samurai domains along the way. Saigō was held up at Kumamoto Castle, east of Nagasaki, which was garrisoned by government forces. Despite being outnumbered, the castle's defenders held firm against repeated assaults. After a gruelling two-month siege, with additional samurai from adjacent domains joining Saigō, the imperial government managed to reinforce Kumamoto with a force of 45,000, forcing Saigō's army into retreat. This significant setback marked a turning point, pushing Saigō and his remaining forces onto the defensive.

Saigō's forces retreated southward to Hisayoshi, where they established a defensive position. After a period of preparation, the imperial army launched an attack. Although it put up fierce resistance, the Satsuma army was compelled to withdraw, employing guerrilla tactics to harass the pursuing enemy. In July, the imperial forces managed to encircle Saigō's dwindling band, but the determined samurai fought their way out, suffering significant losses in the process.

With their numbers reduced to about 3,000, the Satsuma forces made a final stand on Mount Enodake. Overwhelmed by the imperial army's force of 21,000, most of the remaining samurai chose to end their

Below: Siege of Kumamoto Castle (1877) by Yoshitora. Kumamoto Castle experienced its first taste of modern warfare, when a 50-day siege was staged. Inside the castle, a garrison of 3,500 soldiers commanded by Major General Tani Tateki fought against the Satsuma Army of 13,000. Kumamoto Castle demonstrated, in name and reality, that it was an impregnable fortress.

Right: The Battle of Shiroyama, 1877. Saigō Takamōri made a desperate last stand, as a few lightly armed Satsuma samurai engaged the Imperial Army armed with Gatling Guns and ranks of musket fire.

lives through *seppuku*. Those who survived the initial onslaught were forced to rely on their swords as their ammunition ran out. A small contingent of around 500, including Saigō Takamori, managed to escape and retreated to Mount Shiroyama, the site of the rebellion's origin.

The final confrontation, the Battle of Shiroyama, pitted Saigō and his remaining samurai against a formidable Imperial force of 30,000 soldiers. Despite its overwhelming numerical supremacy, the imperial army opted for a cautious approach, spending more than two weeks in meticulous preparation before launching its attack. On 24 September, a devastating three-hour artillery barrage preceded a massive infantry assault that marked the beginning of the end for the samurai.

The last moments of the Satsuma Rebellion were marked by tragedy. Saigō Takamori's fate remains shrouded in uncertainty, with accounts suggesting he died either in the initial artillery barrage or by *seppuku*. However he met his end, Saigō's retainer ensured his master's honour by beheading him. The remaining samurai made a desperate, suicidal charge against the imperial forces, armed with swords against Gatling guns. By dawn the Satsuma Rebellion had ended, with the complete annihilation of its forces.

The defeat of the Satsuma Rebellion marked the end of the samurai era, and it came at a tremendous human and economic cost. The samurai class, as both a military force and a distinct social entity, was irrevocably shattered. Despite this, former samurai continued to hold prominent positions within the military and upper echelons of society. Saigō Takamori, already a revered figure, was elevated on his death to legendary status. Known thereafter as 'The Last Samurai', his tragic end captured the nation's heart. As a testament to his enduring popularity, Emperor Meiji granted him a posthumous pardon in 1889.

The samurai class dominated Japanese society for seven centuries, its power entrenched since Minamoto Yoritomo established the Kamakura Shōgunate in 1192. The resilience of the samurai was legendary, but their ultimate victory in 1615 marked the beginning of their decline. Japan's subsequent exposure to Western ideas and cultures rapidly eroded the foundations of the samurai institution and led to its collapse a little over two centuries later.

Bibliography and Further Reading

Ann and Gabriel Barbier-Mueller, *Art of Armor: Samurai Armor from the Ann and Gabriel Barbier-Mueller Collection*

Bottomley, Ian, and Anthony Hopson, *Arms and Armour of the Samurai: The History of Weaponry in Ancient Japan*. New York: Gramercy Publishing Company.

Brinkley, Capt. F., *A History of the Japanese People*. 1915

Bryant, Anthony J., Angus McBride, *Early Samurai: 200–1500*. Osprey Publishing, 1991

Bryant, Anthony J., Angus McBride, *Samurai 1550–1600*. Osprey Publishing, 1994

Clive Sinclaire, *Samurai: The Weapons and Spirit of the Japanese Warrior*. Globe Pequot, 2004

Hall, John W., and James L. McClain, eds., *The Cambridge History of Japan, vol.4: Early Modern Japan*. Cambridge University Press, 1991.

Hatiro Yamagami, *Japan's ancient armour, Japan*. Board of Tourist Industry, Japanese Government Railways, 1940

Ian Bottomley, Anthony Hopson, *Arms and armour of the samurai: the history of weaponry in ancient Japan*. Crescent Books, 1993

Inazo Nitobe, *Bushidō - The Spirit of the Samurai*

Kōzan Sakakibara, *The Manufacture of Armour and Helmets in Sixteenth Century Japan*

Mitchelhill, Jennifer; photos by David Green, *Castles of the Samurai: Power and Beauty*. Kodansha International, 2003

Mitford, A. B., *Tales of Old Japan*. Rutland, VT: Charles E. Tuttle Co., 1966

Murdoch and Yamagata, *History of Japan*

Murdoch, *History of Japan II to 1656 and History of Japan III 1650+*

Ogawa M., *Art of the Samurai - Japanese Arms and Armor 1156–1868*

Oscar Ratti, Adele Westbrook, *Secrets of the Samurai: a survey of the martial arts of feudal Japan*. Tuttle Publishing, 1991

Papinot, *Dictionary of Japan*

Sadler, A. L., *The Maker of Modern Japan*. Tokyo and Rutland, VT: Tuttle Books

Sansom, George, *A History of Japan, 1334–1615*. Stanford, CA: Stanford University Press, 1996

Totman, Conrad, *A History of Japan*. Wiley-Blackwell; second edition, 2005

Turnbull, Stephen R., *Samurai: a military history*. Psychology Press, 1996

Turnbull, Stephen R., *The Samurai Sourcebook*. Cassell, 2002

Varley, H. Paul, *Japanese Culture: A Short History*. Faber and Faber, 1993

Varley, H. Paul, *The Ōnin War: History of Its Origins and Background*. Columbia University Press, 1967.

William E. Deal, *Handbook to Life in Medieval and Early Modern Japan*. Oxford University Press, 2007

William Wayne Farris, *Heavenly Warriors Evolution of Japan's Military, 500-1300*, 1995

Index

Picture Credits

t = top, b = bottom, l = left, r = right, m = middle

Alamy: 138t, 168, 170

Bridgeman: 49

ColBase: Integrated Collections Database of the National Institutes for Cultural Heritage, Japan: 15t, 33t, 66, 71t, 154, 155b

David Woodroffe: 12b, 14t, 27b, 64t, 75, 78, 96, 121, 131t, 133, 137l, 146b, 147b, 148, 163t

Getty Images: 17t, 54, 116b, 125t, 128, 155t, 157b

Historiographical Institute, University of Tokyo: 47

Matsura Historical Museum: 52

Meiji University Museum: 127b

Metropolitan Museum of Art, New York: 20t, 33b, 68, 70l, 70r, 83, 93t, 141, 146t, 167t, 167b, 172, 174tr,

Osaka Castle Museum: 153

Public Domain: 6t, 7, 23, 31, 37b, 57b, 59, 74, 89, 98, 104, 110, 111, 115, 122, 123t, 123b, 126, 132b, 134b, 136, 137r, 140b, 144t, 149t, 160, 163b, 164b, 165b, 173t, 173b, 175t, 179, 180b

Rijksmuseum: 92

Rod Johnson: 15b, 16, 17b, 18, 21b, 22t, 22b, 27t, 28, 29, 30, 36, 37t, 39, 40t, 40b, 41, 42, 53b, 56, 57t, 58t, 58b, 62, 63, 64b, 65, 67b (Till Weber Photo), 71b, 77t, 80, 82t, 82b, 84, 88, 93m, 93b, 100, 103t, 106, 107t (Hirose Kazumi), 107b, 113l, 117, 118t, 130, 134tl, 134tm, 134tr, 135t, 147t, 150, 151, 156, 157t, 158, 161, 171l, 171r, 177t, 182b, 183, 184t, 184b, 186

Sendai City Museum: 105b

Shutterstock: 60, 85b, 86t, 86b, 103b, 105t, 121 (x12), 131b, 139b, 145t

Wikimedia Commons: 6b, 10, 12t, 13b, 13t, 14bl, 19, 20b, 24, 26, 34, 38, 44, 45, 46, 48t, 48b, 50, 51, 53t, 61, 67t, 69, 72, 76, 77b, 79, 81, 85t, 87, 90, 94, 95, 97, 99, 101, 102, 108, 112, 113r, 114t, 114b, 116t, 118b, 119, 120, 125b, 127t, 132t, 135b, 138b, 139t, 140t, 142, 144b (x5), 145b, 149b, 152, 162t, 162b, 164t, 165t, 167m, 174tl, 175b, 176, 177b, 178, 180t, 181t, 181b, 182t, 187

Yokohama Museum: 14br